WITHDRAWN

ISLAM AGAINST THE WEST

Modern Middle East Series, No. 10
Sponsored by the Center for Middle Eastern Studies
The University of Texas at Austin

ISLAM

Shakib Arslan and the Campaign

AGAINST

for Islamic Nationalism

THE

By William L. Cleveland

WEST

University of Texas Press <✧> Austin

To G.H.K.C.: B.A., M.A., a.b.d., LL.B.

Copyright © 1985 by the University of Texas Press
All rights reserved
Printed in the United States of America

First Edition, 1985

Requests for permission to reproduce material from this work
should be sent to Permissions, University of Texas Press, Box 7819,
Austin, Texas 78713.

Library of Congress Cataloging in Publication Data
Cleveland, William L.
  Islam against the West.

  (Modern Middle East series; no. 10)
  Bibliography: p.
  Includes index.
    1. Arslān, Shakīb, Amīr, 1869–1946. 2. Statesmen—
Lebanon—Biography. 3. Arab countries—Biography.
4. Islam and politics—Arab countries. 5. Arab countries
—Politics and government. 6. Muslims—Arab countries—
Biography. I. Title. II. Series: Modern Middle East
series (Austin, Tex.); no. 10.
DS86.A82C57 1985   909'.0974927   84-29124
ISBN 0-292-77594-6

CONTENTS

85-5615

A NOTE ON SOURCES

Abbreviations

AFS   Archives Fédérales Suisses, Bern, E 4320, Arslan

ASMAE   Archivio Storico del Ministero degli Affari Esteri, Rome

FO   Foreign Office Records, Public Record Office, London

LNA   *La Nation Arabe*

MAE   Archives du Ministère des Affaires Etrangères, Paris

NA   Microfilm Records of the German Foreign Office Received by the U.S. Department of State, National Archives, Washington, D.C.

RR   Shakib Arslan, *al-Sayyid Rashid Rida aw ikha' arba'in sanah*

Transliteration

French and English scholars have adopted distinct systems of Arabic transliteration. This particularly affects a study which focuses on the life of an Eastern Arab active in French North Africa. Julien's l'Emir Chekib is Hourani's Amir Shakib. I have not tried to reconcile them. Names of well-known Maghribi figures are spelled according to the French method as adopted by John P. Halstead in *Rebirth of a Nation*. In other instances, diacritical marks have been reserved for 'ayn and for medial and terminal *hamza*.

The titles of articles written in Arabic are cited in translation in the notes. The specialist who wishes to consult the article will be able to find it; the nonspecialist will have a sharper sense of the topic. Book titles are noted in transliteration. The entry in the bibliography includes a translated title.

The most public of men, Arslan has bequeathed to the biographer an abundance of sources. A prolific and often repetitive writer, his oeuvre included twenty books, two collections of poetry, and some two thousand articles. Although only one of the books is an autobiography (covering the years to 1923), he was never averse to self-advertisement, and large sections of his other works are devoted to his own activities. They are, however, only the activities he wanted known—Arslan remained circumspect about his personal life, his financial arrangements, and his controversial Axis associations.

This gap is partially filled by archival sources. Arslan's activities in Europe and his perceived manipulation of Middle Eastern politics attracted the attention of various European governments, whose files contain revealing comments on his career. They must, however, be used with caution. Not all of them are based on first-hand information, and they occasionally exaggerate his influence and his physical abilities. Their sensationalism says as much about European concerns as it does about Arslan's aspirations. In this context, one exceptional collection of materials should be mentioned. For most of the interwar period, Arslan's base of operations was in Switzerland. His various entanglements discomfited the Swiss authorities, and they elected to keep a close watch on him. He was placed under efficient surveillance, called in for occasional interrogations, and reported on with general accuracy. I regard the prudent Swiss files as dependable sources of information on Arslan's European activities and have used them to resolve some of the controversies surrounding his personal affairs.

In addition to his array of published works, Arslan kept up a prodigious correspondence. The original collection is not in the public domain,[1] but his letters were intercepted with such frequency by various British, French, Swiss, and Italian agencies as to make a small volume in themselves. His communications with official and semiofficial members of the German diplomatic service are contained in the documents captured by the Allies. Letters from Rashid Rida to Arslan are included in Arslan's biography of Rida, and fifty-five of Arslan's letters to Rida, covering the years 1922 to 1935, are reproduced in Ahmad al-Sharabasi's *Amir al-bayan.*

The contributions of a figure of such prominence have not gone unrecorded. Two Arab biographers, Ahmad al-Sharabasi of Egypt and

Sami al-Dahhan of Syria, have created a small publishing industry based on Arslan.[2] In some cases, my interpretations are identical with theirs; often we differ. In exercising the selectivity imposed on all biographers, they have chosen to gloss over the most controversial aspects of the Amir's career—his relations with Jamal Pasha during World War I and his ties to Italy and Germany during the late 1930s. I have seen these controversies as crucial to the development of his reputation and have tried to ascertain their significance. While I have no less respect for Arslan than they do, my assessment of his place in Islamic reformism accords him less originality than does theirs. They have emphasized his commitment to political Arabism while I have downplayed it. They have quite rightly explored his contribution to modern Arabic literature, a subject I have not treated at all. Finally, both of them, in their concern to emphasize Arslan's role in the Eastern Arab world, slight his activities in North Africa. Despite our occasionally divergent emphases, the scholarly debt is mine, and I gratefully acknowledge it.

Some of the sources cited frequently in this study employ the Gregorian and Hijrah years intermittently. For example, in 1930/31 the journal al-Fath discontinued its practice of listing the Gregorian date and began using the Hijrah year exclusively. Similarly, Arslan's published correspondence sometimes uses the Gregorian year, sometimes the Hijrah one. Rather than convert each Hijrah reference, I have cited the dates as they appear in the original source. The table which follows permits a general conversion from the Muslim to the Christian year for the period relevant to the citations in this book.[3]

1344	22 July 1925 to 11 July 1926
1345	12 July 1926 to 30 June 1927
1346	1 July 1927 to 19 July 1928
1347	20 July 1928 to 8 July 1929
1348	9 July 1929 to 28 May 1930
1349	29 May 1930 to 18 May 1931
1350	19 May 1931 to 6 May 1932
1351	7 May 1932 to 25 April 1933
1352	26 April 1933 to 15 April 1934
1353	16 April 1934 to 4 April 1935
1354	5 April 1935 to 23 March 1936

1355   24 March 1936 to 13 March 1937

1356   14 March 1937 to 2 March 1938

1357   3 March 1938 to 20 February 1939

1358   21 February 1939 to 9 February 1940

ACKNOWLEDGMENTS

WHATEVER ERRORS or omissions are contained in this book are the responsibility of the author. Much of any merit it may have is due to the generous assistance I have received from numerous individuals in various research settings. While I cannot mention each of them, it is a pleasure to acknowledge the contributions of those who have most directly given of their time and energy to help create this book.

My colleague John Spagnolo was a sure guide through the labyrinth of nineteenth century Lebanon and a prodigal provider of documents. Donald Reid and James Jankowski entertained my questions and loaned me books from their personal libraries or acquired them in Cairo on my behalf. Rudolph Peters saved me from several errors with his careful read, and Edward Ingram, though his greatest regret is the passing of the British Empire, showed he could review, without undue apoplexy, a manuscript on an individual who encouraged that event. The book owes much to his editorial ruthlessness. It also owes much to the comments, questions, and above all the sustained encouragement of L. Carl Brown and Edmund Burke III. To them I express my gratitude.

Others have helped in various ways. Francis Nicosia introduced me to the research materials on German-Arab relations, David Partington of the Harvard College Library answered my annual inquiries promptly, and the Simon Fraser Interlibrary Loan Division unearthed my strange requests with remarkable efficiency. Thanks are also due to Iris Albina, my excellent research assistant, to Jennifer

Alexander, who typed part of the manuscript, and to Bernice Ferrier, who typed it all, more than once, with more patience than I deserved.

One of the most memorable personalities I have known, Madame Mayy Junbalat, graciously accorded me several interviews during which she helped me understand her father. I thank her for her thoughtfulness and wish her release from the tragedies of war.

I am indebted to the directors and personnel of each of the archives to which I was granted admission, but I should like to give special thanks to the Swiss Federal Archives in Bern and to the courteously efficient assistant director, Mr. Daniel Bourgeois.

Historians may not normally require expensive equipment, but we do need to get to our sources. My research travel was made possible by grants from the Social Sciences and Humanities Research Council of Canada, the Social Science Research Council of New York, and Simon Fraser University. I gratefully acknowledge the assistance provided by these organizations.

Portions of chapter 6 have previously appeared in the *International Journal of Turkish Studies*. I am grateful to the editors of that journal for permission to include them here.

My wife, Gretchen, in the midst of a demanding career change, still managed to endure my endless conversations about the Amir, to correct my stylistic blunders, and to demonstrate that she remains, at heart, an Arabist.

WILLIAM L. CLEVELAND
Eagle Harbor, British Columbia

INTRODUCTION

THIS BOOK is about the last generation of Ottoman-Arabs to grow up before 1914. Born roughly between 1870 and 1890, its members were trained, built careers, and planned futures in the world of the late Ottoman Empire. After 1919, they were forced to rebuild their lives in a world not of their own choosing. While they faced their mature years with a diversity of personal experiences, needs, and outlooks, they tended to view political organization and cultural affiliation in terms of their formation as Ottomans and to regard the post–World War I settlement in the Arab Middle East as neither permanent nor fitting.

This trend is exemplified in the life and writings of the Lebanese Druze Amir Shakib Arslan (1869–1946). This book is principally about him. It studies him as a man of the Ottoman era who brought to the age of emerging national states the organizing principles of universal Islamic empire. Rather than making him a forgotten relic, his message made him, in the seventh and eighth decades of his life, a formidable force in Middle Eastern and North African politics, in Arab-Islamic thought, and in international diplomacy. This book examines these developments and seeks to explain why they occurred.

To the extent that Arslan was representative of his generation of Ottoman-trained Arabs, a study of his life reveals something about the adjustments required and the positions taken by those who had fully developed careers within the Ottoman system but who were forced to come to terms with the postwar world of separate and occupied Arab states. But Arslan extends beyond the typology of representative. He was not only of his times, but sought, with all the means at his disposal, to shape them. In so doing, he became both a symbol and a force, and his importance to the modern history of the Middle East and North Africa rests with what he was perceived to be as well as with what he actually wrote and did. He, and others, cultivated his image, but they were building from solid material, for the reality of Arslan's life was remarkable in itself.

From the time he was seventeen, when he published his first volume of poetry, until shortly before his death, he was constantly in the public eye. The breadth of his career spanned space as well as time. He received his first administrative appointment in Lebanon in 1888 and was chosen president of the Arab Academy of Damascus in 1938; he was elected to the Ottoman parliament in 1913 and was acknowledged as the tactician of the Moroccan independence movement during the 1930s; he became a correspondent for *al-Ahram* in the 1890s and published the final issue of his French-language journal, *La Nation Arabe*, in Geneva in 1938; he was the personal guest of Khedive 'Abbas Hilmi II in Cairo in 1912 and of Mussolini in Rome in 1934. In whatever he did, Arslan attracted attention, generated controversy, and exerted influence.

Western-language scholarship has captured only isolated facets of Arslan's complex life and his network of associations. Hisham Sharabi has portrayed him as an example of a particular style of prewar Muslim activist; Albert Hourani, Majid Khadduri, and Wilfred Cantwell Smith have brought out his contribution to Islamic reformist thought; several French scholars, among them Charles-André Julien and Roger Le Tourneau, have shown his importance as the inspirational and organizational force behind the North African, and especially Moroccan, agitation in the 1930s; and Lukasz Hirszowicz and Rosaria Quartararo have examined his role as a principal liaison between the Axis and the Arabs.[1] A man of diverse achievements and unquestioned impact, Arslan merits a study which brings together the strands of his life and the purpose of his writings, relates them to his times, and explains how he came to exercise such a wide influence. This book is a step in that direction.

Although Arslan's international impact was most pronounced in the years between the two world wars, he was already a well-known personality by 1914, and the ideas which made him famous had been shaped in an Ottoman milieu. This book concentrates on his interwar career, but argues that to appreciate him fully, it is necessary to understand his place within the Ottoman system and his view of the Ottoman Empire as it was constituted during the years he was allowed to serve it. By studying Arslan in this context, it is also possible to see the vitality of the final Ottoman decades for those who lived them as committed Ottomans.

Arslan was raised in circumstances which appeared to confirm the superiority of Western European military techniques, political organization, and social cohesion. Throughout the first forty years of his life, European expansion into Islamic territories was nearly continuous. His own homeland had been reorganized by European diplomacy in 1861; Britain occupied Egypt in 1882; France, ruler of Algeria since 1830, established protectorates in Tunisia in 1881 and Morocco in 1912; Italy launched a direct attack on Tripoli in 1911; and Russia posed a constant threat at the Straits and along the eastern Ottoman border. In addition, new Balkan states were created out of Ottoman territory and, in alliance with one European power or another, proceeded further to carve up the Ottoman domains.

These demonstrations of European material strength stimulated a variety of responses from the Ottoman state and its subjects. At the center, an emerging group of reform-minded civil servants pressed for the adoption of European-style forms of government. The promulgation of an Ottoman constitution in 1876 marked the culmination of their efforts to strengthen the Empire in this manner. However, within thirteen months of the constitution's proclamation, Sultan Abdulhamid II suspended it and ruled for thirty years as an autocratic, self-consciously Islamic sultan-caliph.

Within the Arab provinces of the Empire, different local conditions and great confessional diversity assured that Abdulhamid's efforts to restrict the flow of ideas and to stress the Islamic features of his office would not be uniformly received. Although schematic classifications run the risk of oversimplification, it is generally acknowledged that the dominant political trends among the Arabs during the reign of Abdulhamid and his Young Turk successors were Islamism, Ottomanism, and a growing sense of Arab cultural distinctness.

The latter, while it was shared by Arabs of all faiths, was most pronounced among the Christian community of Greater Syria.[2] Beginning in the late 1840s, a sustained educational effort by American and European missionaries encouraged the formation of a small but active Christian intelligentsia and professional class. Its members pioneered the rediscovery of the classical Arabic literary heritage, began experimenting with new literary forms, especially journalism, and, through their enthusiastic and practical intellectualism, helped shape an era which has been termed *al-nahdah*, or the awakening.

In combination with their aesthetic pursuits, some members of the Syrian Christian community proposed a political association with France as a means to achieve their liberation from perpetual minority status in an ever more oppressive Islamic society. These hopes led some Christian writers to disparage Islamic institutions and to formulate a doctrine of Arab secularism which regarded Islam merely as one of several components of the Arab cultural heritage. Increasingly active after the Young Turk revolt of 1908, exponents of this view organized political societies, debated the possible advantages of political separation from the Ottoman Empire, and, in conjunction with Muslim Arabs, presented demands for greater cultural autonomy from Istanbul.

If certain figures within the Syrian Christian community could contemplate Europe, not as a threat, but as a model and potential ally, their Muslim counterparts did not always reach similar conclusions.[3] By the turn of the twentieth century, an active Islamic reformist movement was well under way in the Middle East. Its center was Cairo, but it had proponents in the major Arab cities of the Ottoman Empire as well. In a broad sense, the movement aimed at stimulating a political and intellectual revitalization of Islam. It has been termed the defense of an injured self-view in that it was a response to the political and cultural threat posed by Christian Europe. It was, however, more than that; it was also an affirmation of the validity of the entire Islamic historical experience, an effort to assert the worthiness of a way of life and cultural tradition.[4]

In the Syrian provinces of the Empire, Islamic reformism worked in combination with Ottomanism to produce a vision of the Ottoman caliphate as a vital symbol of the independence of Islam from Europe. Ottomanism is a difficult concept to define, but it was basically an attempt to generate feelings of Ottoman patriotism which could be embraced by all the subject peoples of the multinational Empire. However, repeated revolts in the Balkan provinces showed that such sentiment could, at best, attract only the predominantly Muslim peoples of the Empire, Arabs and Turks. It most assuredly attracted Shakib Arslan, who found in it a doctrine which served his principles and his material comforts.

In the course of his rise to become a prominent imperial politician, Arslan managed to exploit both his hereditary aristocratic position and the currents of the *nahdah*. It is sometimes overlooked that Christian Arabs were not the only beneficiaries of the awakening. As the example of the Arslan house shows, established Muslim families could also take advantage of the new educational institutions and professional opportunities of the period.[5]

The Arslans were hereditary Druze princes with roots in the Shuf region of Lebanon.[6] Shakib and his brothers may have been secure in their standing as traditional notables, but the politically astute family made sure they attended Maronite Christian secondary schools. As a result, they were able to retain their ascribed prestige while acquiring the qualifications which gave them mobility in a changing society.

Blessed with talent and eager for recognition, Arslan, in the best tradition of the literary awakening, became one of the most celebrated Arab poets of the turn of the century. But other means of expression had become available for those who wished to present their ideas more directly, and Arslan, in another example of his ability to seize new opportunities, took up the profession of journalism and wrote for the great Cairo dailies *al-Ahram* and *al-Mu'ayyad* as well as for a variety of Syrian journals. At the same time, his public offices reflected his careful balancing of the customary and the transitional; he served as governor of the Shuf, but he was also a parliamentary deputy, as were two of his brothers.

In short, during the first fifty years of his life, Arslan established himself as a loyal member of a religiously based imperial state in the process of reform. A feudal prince by birth, he made the modest adjustments required to sustain his prestige during a period of intellectual renaissance and political experimentation. He knew how to make other adjustments as well. Although he had personally benefited from Abdulhamid's lengthy rule, he accepted the Young Turks and was admitted to their inner circles in 1913. In all ways, he seemed favored by his times, and his devotion to the Ottoman system followed naturally from the advantages it accorded him.

However, Arslan was more than an accommodating politician or an accomplished poet. He was above all an activist Muslim, and one adjustment he would not make was to a nationalist organization of society. This view shaped his behavior for the full half-century of his public life, both enhancing and constraining his reputation. While still in his teens, Arslan began a sustained personal relationship with the Egyptian reformer Muhammad 'Abduh; he also met Jamal al-Din al-Afghani, the most noted Islamic activist of the day. 'Abduh's tutelage, al-Afghani's example, and Arslan's own response to his surroundings made him a dedicated exponent of Islamic solidarity and an uncompromising Ottoman loyalist.

By the turn of the century, these beliefs were under attack, and Arslan, a man of position in an established order, saw his way of life threatened by external aggression and internal dissidence. In his view, the former was to be met, not with imitation, but by resistance founded on the moral values, communal bonds, and courageous leadership which had inspired the achievements of the great Islamic empires of the past. As for Arab separatism, it was not so much a political alternative as an invitation for the suicide of the Islamic community. Arslan's world was not one to be sacrificed at the altar of Christian separatism and its unsavory association with France.

When wartime choices had to be made, Arslan committed himself to the existing Ottoman order and did all that a man can do to serve his cause. He participated in the Ottoman campaign to capture the Suez Canal in 1914; he assisted, in ways that are still controversial, the notorious governor of Syria, Jamal Pasha, from 1914 to 1916; and he served as the Ottoman government's special emissary to Berlin in 1917 and again in 1918.

The defeat and dismemberment of the Ottoman Empire in World War I was a terrible blow to Arslan. Perfectly suited to the age in which he matured, he became caught in the crosscurrents of change which swept away the state to which he had given his loyalty, the society in which he had found status, the means of existence from which he had derived comfort—in effect, the whole order which had given him a secure sense of who he was. He was left adrift, and, from one perspective, the final quarter-century of his life is the story of a career cut short, of a lonely and embittered exile. It is also the story of resilience, tenacity, and ambition. From his base in exile, Arslan, driven by his refusal to be relegated to obscurity, launched a new career. The prince became a debtor, the parliamentarian a conspirator, and the poet a polemicist. If he faced the postwar world with the doctrines of a pan-Islamic Ottomanist, he more than held his own.

His postwar rehabilitation was difficult. For a time, he attached himself to the movement for an Ottoman restoration, an endeavor which this book treats as having more substance than is usually recognized. Gradually, however, Arslan came to realize that the division of the Ottoman imperium, the occupation of its Arab provinces by Britain and France, and the abolition of the caliphate were conditions to which he would have to adjust. He did so, not by accepting them, but by throwing all his energies into efforts to reverse them.

With the help of Rashid Rida, Arslan maneuvered himself into the position of head of the Syro-Palestinian delegation to the League of Nations in 1925. From this fragile base, he built a new career as international political agitator and inserted himself so centrally into the major political issues and intellectual currents of the twenties and thirties that to study him is to bring into focus all the controversy of those two decades.

The widespread influence he came to exercise is explained, in part, by his enforced exile. The major regional Arab figures of the period— Zaghlul of Egypt, for example—were primarily concerned with gaining independence for their particular states and with preserving their own positions within the new political structures. But Arslan, deprived of a regional base by British and French restrictions on his entry to their mandates and protectorates, could pose as a universal spokesman whose counsel transcended local concerns and embraced the entire Arab-Islamic cause. His presence did as well; despite the difficulties with which Britain and France presented him, he managed, in the manner of al-Afghani, to roam the Islamic world from Tangiers to San'a, from Belgrade to Jerusalem, and to capitalize on the attention which he invariably attracted.

Some individuals have a knack for generating publicity, for placing themselves at the center of a particularly crucial issue and compelling others to respond to their position. Arslan was such a man. Even though he never lived permanently in any Arab country after 1917, his views and his person commanded such attention that he became an integral part of the Syro-Lebanese conflict with France, an actor in the Palestinian drama, and a leading commentator on the Islamic reformist current emanating from Egypt. In addition, as this book stresses, Arslan played the major role in establishing a common ground between the North African and Eastern Arab struggles for independence. He became the mentor of a group of young Moroccan nationalists, and his orchestration of the international Islamic protest against the Berber *dahir* of 1930 marked him as a desirable associate to Arab Muslims in all regions and, not incidentally, as a dangerous enemy to European imperial administrators. Soon, he was involved with leading Algerian and Tunisian personalities and, in taking up their causes, brought them into the arena of the total Arab-Islamic struggle against the forces of European imperialism. His residence in Geneva became the testing ground for strategies of resistance and, whether he was entertaining King Faysal of Iraq, counseling Messali Hajj of Algeria, disputing with David Ben-Gurion, or receiving various Syrian delegations, he made that residence a center of the international Islamic movement.

Although Arslan's call for the independence of the occupied Arab lands was scarcely unique, the tone of his protest gave it a particular significance. He, perhaps more than any other figure of the period, exemplified the continuation of Jamal al-Din al-Afghani's message of Islamic-oriented resistance to the outsider. For Arslan, Islamic solidarity was the only legitimate means for the attainment of independence; he eschewed Syrian and even Arab nationalism for the more all-embracing doctrine of Islamic nationalism. He did not disavow the usefulness of local resistance movements, nor was he so naive as to call for a single Islamic state. But he did insist that the mutual cooperation which was required to oust the imperial powers could only come through a shared sense of Islamic duty, with all the cultural, political, and moral connotations that the term *duty* contained. His interwar hero was Ibn Sa'ud; his greatest enemies were Sharif Husayn for leading the Arab revolt against the duly constituted Ottoman Islamic Empire and Mustafa Kemal Atatürk for secularizing Turkey. Arslan was particularly hostile to Atatürk, feeling that political independence was not to be used to imitate the West, but to preserve cultural integrity. Order and justice were to be secured by a return to the Islamic concepts of state and society which had assured them in the first place.

Arslan gained popularity espousing these ideas because they were widely held. A major theme of this book is the exploration of Arslan's influence through his manipulation of Islamic symbols. The dangers which al-Afghani had identified in the latter decades of the nineteenth century were not ended with the Great War, but were in fact exacerbated by it. Without the Ottoman Empire, the Arab-Islamic order was made more vulnerable to European control than ever before; without the office of the caliphate, Muslims had no unifying symbol around which to rally. Although secular pan-Arabism and regional independence revolts were adopted to counter this vulnerability, militant Islam was a more familiar and more widely accepted doctrine, and Arslan a long-established proponent of it. He was able to politicize the vital bonds of this Islamic sentiment and to use it with noted success in both North Africa and the Arab East.

The extent to which Islam was employed as a political ideology during the interwar period has sometimes been overlooked because of the way in which modern Arabic thought has been presented in English-language scholarship. Influential historians writing in the 1960s regarded secular nationalism as the doctrine which, in either its liberal or totalitarian form, would emerge as the dominant Middle Eastern ideology. They therefore focused their interpretations of the past on figures who embodied that doctrine.[7] The secular, if not the liberal, strains of this historical focus seemed fulfilled in the Nasserist and Ba'athist experiments in radical reformism and were reinforced by social scientists who found in those experiments confirmation of modernization theory's assertions that national development would only occur in conjunction with increased secularism.[8] Those who had tenaciously borne, and continued to bear, the responsibility of the Islamic tradition came to be regarded by the new political elite of Arab society, as by some Western observers, as reactionary enemies of progress. Such a conjunction of historical interpretation and contemporary developments obscured the appeal which religiously based political action had enjoyed in the past and which it continued to enjoy.[9] Arslan, with his living link to al-Afghani, his affinity with the Muslim Brotherhood, and his preference for strong Islamic leadership, may have been a more representative figure of his era than Taha Husayn, Muhammad Husayn Haykal, or even the secular pan-Arab ideologue Sati' al-Husri. Had the Islamic resurgence of the 1970s and 1980s not occurred, Arslan would still deserve to be studied for his own role in his own times. However, the renewed public emphasis on the Islamic features of Arab society heightens the importance of understanding the views, and the responses to them, of the most prominent Islamic nationalist of his day.

Arslan and some of his associates may also have been slighted by Western scholars because they did not break new ground. Intellectual historians quite correctly seek to identify the seminal thinkers of an era. But the pamphleteers and propagandists also require investigation. They, after all, are the immediate shapers of public opinion, neither too far ahead nor too far behind their contemporaries. Some, like Thomas Paine, try to nudge people toward something new; others seek to garner support for the preservation of what they deem most suitable from the past. Arslan was one of the latter. His constancy may, in the end, have been inadaptability, but for a time his voluminous writings and his direct personal confrontations with the European imperial system reflected the longings of a large segment of educated Arab-Muslims and enabled him to become their spokesman in a final struggle to marshal the forces of the old order against alien values and external control.

It should be stressed, however, that Arslan was more than an agitator and propagandist; he was also an established author in the Salafiyyah or reformist tradition. As a biographer of his friends, Rashid Rida and Ahmad Shawqi, he appealed to the remembrance of the times which had shaped him and produced like-minded men; as a chronicler of the Arab conquests in Europe, he recalled the greatness of the past; and as a reformist commentator, he told Muslims how they could change their present circumstances and remain true Muslims. His unsparing critique, *Why Are the Muslims Backward?*, went through three editions in his lifetime and was published again in 1981; and his four-volume commentary on the Arabic translation of Lothrop Stoddard's *The New World of Islam* continues to be reissued. With these books, his French-language journal *La Nation Arabe*, and his hundred or so articles each year in the Arab press, Arslan was arguably the most widely read Arab writer of the interwar period.

As he tried to manage Muslim affairs, he also sought to manipulate European-Arab alliances. In this, he may have tried too much; his role as an intermediary between the Axis and the Arabs and as the principal apologist for Mussolini's Arab policies caused some to question his integrity and clouded his final reputation. Yet these activities were an integral part of his full career and further illustrate his centrality to the issues of his day.

Although this book is more about Arslan's life in the context of his times than it is a purely personal biography, I have tried to understand the man as well as the trends he represented. An ambitious individual who thrived on publicity, Arslan cultivated his image as a courageous anti-imperialist even as he fulfilled it. This prompted his political opponents to see him as a self-serving opportunist and his supporters to idolize him as the greatest *mujahid* of his age.[10] Even though I have concentrated on Arslan's public career, I have attempted to explain his motives and to see his ideological orientation as consistent with other features of his life.

The approach taken by this book is one which overlaps in time and space. To avoid merely following in Arslan's busy footsteps, I have organized the material in a manner designed to give some perspective to his all-embracing concerns. The first three chapters examine Arslan's life until 1925. Chapters 4 and 5 treat their subject through what may be described as geographical themes: chapter 4 explores Arslan's role in and writings about the Arab East during the 1930s, and chapter 5 treats North Africa during the same period. Chapter 6 constitutes an examination of Arslan's contribution to interwar thought, and chapter 7 reviews the whole interwar period through the organizing principle of Arslan's relationship to Italy and Germany.

I began this study with the impression that Shakib Arslan was a seminal intellectual figure. During the course of my research, I have modified that position slightly, concluding that while Arslan was clearly an influential writer, he was less significant as a thinker than as a phenomenon. Like all such, he was both more and less than he seemed. His ideas were an amalgam of those of his mentors, al-Afghani and Muhammad ʿAbduh, and his power to direct events was more limited than his European adversaries feared. Yet he was a figure of more international influence than he has been credited with, more integrity than his detractors grant, and more finesse than his supporters perceive. He defined a period of transition by holding fast to the Islamic concepts of state and society on which he felt the proper order rested. His inclination toward resistance, propaganda, and agitation made him popular and enabled him, as the self-appointed heir of al-Afghani, to continue the tradition of Islamic activism. It is a tradition which is far from ended.

ISLAM AGAINST THE WEST

CHAPTER ONE.
THE FORMATION OF AN ARAB-OTTOMAN GENTLEMAN

Amir Shakib appeared to want to be more Ottoman than the sons of 'Uthman.　　　　　　　　　　*—al-Sharabasi*[1]

If we cannot defend the deserts of Tripoli, then we will be unable to protect the gardens of Damascus.　　　*—Arslan*[2]

THE FORCES which shape an individual's outlook on society cannot be identified with precision. This is particularly true when dealing with a cultural tradition which discourages introspective autobiographical statements in favor of restrained political memoirs. Nonetheless, the historian who seeks to understand how and why an individual can be said to have had an impact on his times must attempt to explain the social environment in which he was formed.

In the case of Shakib Arslan, the potential limitations of environment are suggested by the following: he was born in the Lebanese village of Shuwayfat in 1869; he was a member of the Druze religious community; and his father was a minor local official. Rural, parochial, and sectarian, this appears to be a setting likely to restrict the horizons of young men by limiting their education and their choice of career. Instead, it produced in Arslan an internationally recognized spokesman for orthodox Islam and an Arab man of letters known from Fez to Baghdad as "the prince of eloquence." By the time he reached his early sixties, his salon in Geneva was frequented by distinguished and aspiring visitors, and his opinions on questions of resistance strategy and Qur'anic theology were solicited from Morocco to Sumatra. His passage from the Shuf to Geneva occurred in stages and was, of course, determined in part by accident and external circumstances. But it was not entirely hindered by the environment in which he was born. Rural Druzes, like their Maronite Christian counterparts, discovered a new mobility in the politically stable and economically prosperous Lebanese-Ottoman world of the late nineteenth century. Arslan successfully blended the substantial advantages of his inherited aristocratic status with the opportunities provided by the changing world around him to become, by the eve of World War I, a reputable poet and journalist and one of Ottoman Syria's most formidable, if not necessarily most respected, politicians. This Ottoman career made possible, and makes historically comprehensible, the later European career by which he is chiefly known. The two are linked, and while they developed in very different settings, they should not be regarded as isolated portions of his adult life. There was a wholeness to Arslan's prewar existence which must be appreciated in its own right; yet it must also be recognized that his full public career before 1914 established the foundations for his postwar eminence. This chapter is concerned with Arslan's formation as an Ottoman. In order to understand his rise to prominence, a consideration of the general characteristics of late nineteenth century Lebanese political society is required.

Until the intrusion of external forces in the nineteenth century, the rivalries among the various confessional groups of Mount Lebanon had been managed without serious disruption for several centuries.[3] Powerful Druze (a form of Islamic *shi'ism*) feudal chieftains coexisted with the Maronite Christian community on the basis of a shared style of life and a common dislike for strong central government. With the conquest of Syria and Mount Lebanon by the Egyptian army of Muhammad 'Ali and the energetic governorship of his son Ibrahim from 1832 to 1840, the customary patterns of communal relations were disturbed. Although the new sectarian antagonisms were temporarily submerged in a joint insurrection against Egyptian control in 1840, the Druze leaders remained bitter over what they saw as the steady erosion of their influence in the Mountain. To recover it, in 1860 they initiated a violent civil war which inflamed the villages of the Mountain and the quarters of Damascus, where Christians were killed in large numbers. At this point, the Lebanese question became fully internationalized, as European and Ottoman authorities intervened with an externally imposed solution. It was a solution which brought a measure of both stability and prosperity to the troubled region from 1861 until World War I.

The new regulations, called in European diplomatic parlance the *Règlement et protocole relatifs à la réorganisation du Mont Liban*, had as their main objectives the protection of the Maronites from the Druzes and the restoration of tranquillity to the Mountain.[4] In effect, the partition of the Ottoman Empire was continued by the creation of an autonomous administrative status for Mount Lebanon.

Because of the new legacy of distrust among the religious communities, it was deemed essential to remove the administration of this new polity from sectarian pressures. This was done with sectarian clauses—the *Règlement* stipulated that all of Mount Lebanon would be governed by a non-Lebanese Ottoman Christian subject. This official was called a *mutasarrif* and was appointed by the Ottoman government with the approval of the six European signatories to the statute. He was to maintain order through an autonomous Lebanese security force and to receive advice in governing by an administrative council of twelve members representing the religious communities in the *mutasarrifiyyah*. Maronite and Druze dominance was reflected in their holding four and three seats, respectively, on this council. Although the *mutasarrif's* powers were prescribed, he did have some independence of action through his ability to appoint the governors (*qaʾimaqam*s) of the seven subdistricts (*qada*s) of the Mountain. The personality and prejudices of the *mutasarrif* could therefore make a difference in the way he interacted with the local power structure. That most of the *mutasarrif*s were of a high caliber did not mean that a great Druze family like the Arslans would get along with them all equally well.

If the new *Règlement* contained the possibility for continued Druze influence, their religion itself seemed to constrict the community. Its complex and closely guarded doctrines are intertwined with early Ismaili concepts, and its appearance dates from the reign of the Fatimid caliph al-Hakim (996–1021). Although named after one of the principal missionaries of the new faith, al-Darazi, the religion centers on the divinity of al-Hakim, the uncompromising unity and unknowability of God, and the messianic belief in the ultimate return of the divine ruler who is merely in a state of "temporary occultation."[5] When opposition to these ideas became too strong in Egypt, the small community moved to Syria and attracted converts in the mountainous regions that are now part of south-central Lebanon and southwestern Syria. In 1031, the community closed its doors to new converts and initiated the process of clandestine ritual and inbred solidarity that has marked it to the present day.

External observers have often found the Druze a clannish and unfriendly community, and "dour Druze" has become a stock phrase of historians.[6] In defense of their faith and their communal lands, the Druze warriors acquired a well-deserved reputation as fierce and determined fighters. They could also be supple politicians and, in the case of the Arslans, could acquire positions of nobility, making the broad categorization of Druzes as mountain peasants inaccurate. In the development of the feudal system peculiar to Mount Lebanon, the Arslans were recognized by the late eighteenth century as the most prestigious of the Druze houses. They became one of only three Lebanese families whose males had the right to use the title *amir*, roughly equivalent to prince, on a hereditary basis. Their power base was located in the Shuf, a region of Druze concentration about ten miles south of Beirut where, throughout the nineteenth century, they engaged in a ceaseless contest for supremacy with the Junbalats, another ambitious Druze family.

For the leaders of the Arslan family, Druze communal solidarity did not mean political isolation. The *Règlement* did more than protect Maronites; it also recognized the Druze position within the *mutasarrifiyyah* and so provided the opportunity for an ambitious family to expand its political power. The Arslan amirs were active in the aftermath of the civil war, cementing their relations with the *mutasarrif*s and establishing important contacts at the center of Ottoman power in Istanbul. During the final decades of the nineteenth century, the dominant member of the family was Amir Mustafa, Shakib's paternal uncle, who became well connected in the court of Sultan Abdulhamid II. In addition, from the early years of the *mutasarrifiyyah* until his resignation in 1902, Mustafa was *qa'imaqam* of the Shuf. It was he who cultivated, or intimidated, a succession of *mutasarrif*s and ensured the Arslans' power base until his death in 1910. Even that inevitable occurrence was used to promote the family's position, as Mustafa's funeral rites were conducted according to Sunni, not Druze, practice.[7] Mustafa's relatives profited from his efforts and served as local officials, foreign envoys, imperial deputies, and prominent men of letters in the final years of the Ottoman Empire. It was a highly visible, broadly talented, and profoundly ambitious aristocratic family. Its position assured its young men a certain prominence at birth; its ambition assured them every opportunity to enhance that prominence.

Thus, the political climate in which Shakib Arslan was raised, and in which he exercised his first adult responsibilities, possessed a threefold pull on a leader's loyalty and sense of duty: first, to the family; second, to the protection of the interests of the Druze community (often synonymous with family interests) in the wider sphere of the politics of the *mutasarrifiyyah*; and third, to. the Ottoman Empire with its imperial policies and its universal Islamic aspirations. The first two of these worlds would hold Shakib for a time, but it was the wider context of imperial-Islamic politics which would finally claim him and determine his loyalties.

His rise from the Shuf to the inner circles of the Ottoman establishment was not his achievement alone; two of his three brothers also broke from their rural background and their Druze identity to make names for themselves in Arab-Ottoman society. Although the dynamics of family relationships cannot be known for certain, the move of the Arslan brothers away from Druze exclusivity may have been encouraged by their father, Amir Hamud, an agreeably ecumenical man who appeared more interested in literature than in his post as director of an administrative subdivision (nahiyah) in the qada of the Shuf.[8] Amir Hamud broke with Druze custom by marrying a Circassian woman (as Shakib was to do), who bore him four sons. Shakib, the second-born, held a pronounced and very public affection for his mother which exercised an active influence on him throughout his adult life. If her strength of character corresponded to her physical nature, she was a remarkable woman: when Shakib was sixty, she traveled from the Shuf to Suez to spend a few hours with him; when he returned to Lebanon as an ailing seventy-six-year-old, she was on hand to receive him.

Shakib's father left the guidance of the family's political fortunes to his powerful brother, Amir Mustafa, a man unlikely to allow four nephews to languish in the Shuf. Mustafa may have planned their education; he definitely ensured their favorable placement in the political system of the mutasarrifiyyah.

Mustafa's success is reflected in the careers of two of Shakib's brothers whose activities show the mobility afforded the Arslans by the prestige of their name and the circumstances of the mutasarrifiyyah. Nasib (1867–1927), the eldest and the closest personally to Shakib, spent much of his adult life in Beirut, where he was involved in a variety of literary circles and participated as a journalist in the Arab protest movement against the policies of the Committee of Union and Progress (CUP) before World War I. 'Adil (1883–1954), the youngest, attended Istanbul University and showed great promise as a poet. However, he became better known for his political activism in a long line of official and unofficial roles spanning service to the Ottoman state as qa'imaqam of the Shuf (1914–1916) and deputy to the Ottoman parliament (1916–1918), to the cause of Syrian independence as a combatant in the Druze-led Syrian national uprising against the French Mandate in 1925–1926, and finally as a minister (1946–1949) in the first government of independent Syria.[9]

The breadth of 'Adil's early career was, in part, made possible by the experiences of his two eldest brothers. From their earliest training, Shakib and Nasib received an education which went beyond the parochially Druze and seemed designed to open up broader horizons for them. Their schooling coincided with the early years of the Arab nahdah, or awakening, and their position in one of the great families enabled them to reap the benefits of the educational changes which were then percolating into Syria and the *mutasarrifiyyah*. Missionary activity, by both American Protestant and European Catholic organizations, led to the establishment of new schools among the Christians of Mount Lebanon. The appearance of these foreign missionary schools prompted the local religious communities to expand the educational opportunities for their sons, and at times daughters as well, in order to prevent them from having to obtain an education at the hands of French Lazarists, American Presbyterians, or Russian Orthodox priests. The Maronites revitalized their seminary at Ayn Waraqa in 1834; the Muslims founded a university in Beirut in 1874 to compete with the Syrian Protestant College (1866) and the Jesuit Université de Saint Joseph; and the Ottoman government provided increasing subsidies for Islamic schools in the Syrian provinces.[10]

By the time Shakib began his education, he was able to benefit from these expanded opportunities and to participate in the intellectual currents of the Arab *nahdah*. On the basis of institutions attended, his education was eclectic and multisectarian. When Shakib was six, he and Nasib were enrolled in an American school in the Shuf. This was not as unusual as it might seem. Beginning in the mid-1830s, the American Protestant mission concluded that the Druzes, squeezed as they were between the Sunni Ottoman authorities and the powerful Maronites, were the most likely non-Christian sect for conversion. Several plans, none of which ever reached fulfillment, for gaining control of Druze education and evangelizing among them were drawn up over the years.[11] Although these schools usually tried to teach only in the local idiom, Shakib remembered English, and the Psalms, as part of his curriculum.[12] Such rural schools often lasted no more than a semester, and Shakib left his after only one year.

In 1879, in what appears to have been a concerted move to prepare the young men of the family for leadership in a changing Lebanon, Shakib and Nasib enrolled in Madrasah al-Hikmah, the leading Maronite school of Beirut. Founded in 1874 by the Maronite bishop of Beirut, Yusuf al-Dibs, the institution was to make its mark as an important preparatory school, numbering among its graduates several of the leading literary and political figures of modern Lebanon. The seven years which Shakib spent at Madrasah al-Hikmah had a special importance for him. Socially, he moved from his rural origins to an urban environment. Although he returned to the Shuf in 1887 as family politics dictated, he was formed in the cosmopolitan atmosphere of Beirut and remained an urban man for the rest of his life. He also acquired a taste for the literary atmosphere which only an urban environment could provide. As a child of the Arab awakening,

Arslan was caught up in the excitement of cultural renaissance and later wrote of his school years in Beirut: "We became infatuated during that time with news of writers, poets, and men of letters; it was our sole concern and we viewed the entire world as poetry and prose."[13] His reading was voracious, his interests eclectic. The teachers at Madrasah al-Hikmah recognized his enthusiasm and his intellectual gifts, and he responded precociously to their encouragement. By the time he was fourteen, some of his compositions had appeared in the local periodical press, and when he was seventeen he published his first volume of poetry, al-Bakurah. Even in his teens, he sought a public forum and began to project the image of self-confidence, bordering on arrogance, that marked him as an adult.

In addition to developing his talents in Arabic literature, the curriculum at Madrasah al-Hikmah included intensive training in French, a language Arslan used extensively and comfortably for the rest of his life.

After assuring that the Arslan brothers acquired a suitable Arabic and French background at their Christian preparatory school, the family sent them to an Ottoman government institution, Madrasah al-Sultaniyyah, in order that they might concentrate on the Islamic sciences and gain a firmer grounding in Ottoman Turkish. After one year at this latter institution, Arslan's formal education was completed. He was eighteen. In all respects, he had been given the best that the nahdah had to offer. His seven years at the Maronite school gave him entree to the literary circles of Beirut and Damascus and marked him as a man of the new era; and his credentials from the state-sponsored Madrasah al-Sultaniyyah, including a full command of Ottoman Turkish, qualified him for official and unofficial assignments in a state which was changing but which remained Ottoman.

One thing he did not have was a university education. He was deprived of it by the political demands of the mutasarrifiyyah. Thus, while he was well-educated for the era, he may have been dissatisfied that he was not given a chance to achieve the full academic recognition for which he was so clearly qualified. An intellectually competitive individual, Arslan regarded himself as the equal of any graduate of the Syrian Protestant College or the Mektebi Mülkiye (civil service college). A compulsive lifelong program of self-education, an occasionally forced erudition, and a habit of ostentatious citation in his later writings may have been his way of compensating for his lack of more extensive formal education.

However, patrons were still more helpful than university degrees in securing personal advancement. Arslan was fortunate in attaching himself to one who was inspiring and who would soon become important. In the final year of his studies in Beirut, he became a student and protégé of Muhammad ʿAbduh, the Egyptian reformer. This constituted the determinative intellectual influence of Arslan's life. His commitment to ʿAbduh's ideals would lead him, four years later, to ʿAbduh's circle in Cairo and, in 1892, to Jamal al-Din al-Afghani's residence in Istanbul. For all the vicissitudes of his career in the decades that followed, Arslan was firm in his belief that he was a faithful heir to the message of Islamic reformism and political activism which he had received directly from two of the major figures of the age.

For students of the modern Middle East, the names Jamal al-Din al-Afghani and Muhammad ʿAbduh have become almost synonymous with the redirection of Islamic thought. Extensive scholarship has seen in them a watershed, and if they are now regarded as more conservative than originally believed, their influence is still perceived as widespread. Al-Afghani (1838–1897) was more political activist than systematic theologian.[14] Rejecting the premise of some reformers that the Western threat could be countered only by thorough Westernization, he called instead for the internal regeneration of Islam which would create Islamic political power grounded within the Islamic tradition. Self-conscious reassertion, not blind imitation, would provide the strength required to repel the intruder in both the material and cultural worlds. Part teacher, part agitator, al-Afghani conspired alike with rulers and those who wished to overthrow them. His populist Islamic radicalism and his willingness to court controversy inspired both devotion and mistrust, and he was expelled at various stages of his life from Afghanistan, Egypt, the Ottoman Empire, and Iran. Although, as Professor Keddie has shown, there was a certain ambiguity to al-Afghani's doctrines and character, there was none in his personality. Forceful, eloquent, and charismatic, he inspired young Muslims in the different lands where he resided to carry on his program of activism. His memory became even more inspirational than his presence; his posthumous reputation took on legendary proportions, and he became, as he remains, a revered figure in the pantheon of Muslim heroes who contested the encroachment of the West.

Among his disciples, the Egyptian Muhammad ʿAbduh (1849–1905) is usually recognized as the most significant.[15] After an early phase of political activism which found him temporarily banished from Egypt, ʿAbduh joined forces with al-Afghani in Paris, where they edited al-ʿUrwah al-Wuthqa, a journal with considerable circulation and impact in the Arab world. ʿAbduh later adopted a more restrained approach to Islamic reform than had his mentor. Working within the established system, he sought a practical reform of the educational institutions of Islam and a spiritual purification which would lead to a reconciliation of independent reasoning and divine revelation and so make the social principles of the religion compatible with contemporary demands for change. At the same time, ʿAbduh employed the utmost care not to sacrifice the essential core of religious experience which permitted Islam to remain meaningful to its adherents.

Both al-Afghani and ʿAbduh acknowledged the weakness of the Islamic world in the face of Western European material dominance and cultural confidence; neither man accepted the innate superiority of Western civilization. They had about them a sense of possibility, of redress, that attracted young Muslims of the most diverse backgrounds. Their influence on Shakib Arslan, the Druze from the Shuf, was personal, intellectual, and continuous.

Arslan was under their spell before he knew them personally. With his talent for cultivating the powerful and the influential, he contrived a meeting with each of them. ʿAbduh, still in exile from Egypt, lived in Beirut from 1886 to 1888. Arslan met him at the Syrian Protestant College toward the end of 1886. His version of their first encounter served to enhance his own legend; he asserted that ʿAbduh told him that he knew his name through reading his *qasidah*s in the press. He then said to the seventeen-year-old so immersed in literature: "You will be one of our best poets."[16] Arslan was an instant disciple.

When ʿAbduh began teaching at Madrasah al-Sultaniyyah, Shakib and his brother studied under him. However, it was their interaction outside the classroom that inspired Arslan's dedication to ʿAbduh's mission. Arslan's account, written years after the events, still conveys the intellectual excitement which ʿAbduh brought to his circle of students. Night after night a group of them gathered at the residence of the president of the Beirut municipality (ʿAbduh's dwelling, which Arslan described as "always submerged with visitors," was not large enough) and listened enthralled to the discussions of the learned Egyptian on a variety of topics relating to Islam and Arabic.[17] Arslan adopted ʿAbduh as his intellectual guide; his ability to establish a close relationship with an Egyptian graduate of al-Azhar showed, as did his entire educational experience, the special openness of the Arslans' Druze household. According to Shakib, "My father became acquainted with the famous *ustadh* and a strong friendship formed between them. We visited his house socially, and he visited us in our home in Shuwayfat."[18]

For Arslan, ʿAbduh served both as an intellectual mentor who expanded his appreciation for the political potential of reformed Islam and as a social patron who introduced him to people who mattered outside Mount Lebanon. Although he may have portrayed ʿAbduh as a greater intellect than he actually was, the uplifting impact of his presence in Beirut was undeniable: "We saw in him an ʿalim unlike the ulema with whom we were acquainted, an ʿalim who combined both the rational and traditional sciences to the utmost degree and who examined all things with the perception of a philosopher whose insight towered above the usual views. . . . We had never experienced a vision like his before."[19] Profoundly affected by his contact with the Egyptian, Arslan dedicated the first poem of al-Bakurah to "Muhammad ʿAbduh, the ʿalim of action, the complete philosopher," who "left behind the sweetest spring for the intellect."[20]

In 1888, ʿAbduh was allowed to return to Egypt and Arslan was called to assume the political role expected of a son of a princely family. His father had died in 1887, and, although Shakib was only eighteen, he was appointed by the mutasarrif to fill his father's post as director of the nahiyah of Shuwayfat. He held this office for just over two years and then resigned. His memoirs give the impression that he was not ready to settle into the predictable role of Druze chieftain and that he felt constrained by Shuwayfat: "I yearned for what was higher and further."[21] For the next two and a half years, from early 1890 to 1892, he satisfied these longings in a series of journeys which broadened his view of the world, launched him in the society of Cairo and Istanbul, and persuaded him that the traditional Arslan role in the Shuf was incompatible with the horizons which had been opened to him.

He began his journey in Cairo, where he was honored as Muhammad ʿAbduh's guest for two months and was introduced to, and apparently accepted by, ʿAbduh's circle. It was a heady experience to debut among the cultural elite of Egypt. Arslan was aware of the opportunity ʿAbduh was offering him, and he made the most of it. By the time he left Cairo in late 1890, he had met Saʿd Zaghlul on a number of occasions, made friends with Ahmad Zaki, and accepted commissions to write for al-Ahram and al-Muʾayyad. In addition, he had an audience with Khedive Tawfiq, to whom he presented a flattering poem.[22] This began a pattern which characterized Arslan's behavior for the rest of his life. If he was somewhat on trial during this first Egyptian visit, he was nonetheless a cultured prince, and access to the powerful and influential was his by right. He became accustomed to receptions in his honor and to requesting meetings with monarchs and presidents, never indicating that he expected anything less than to be received. More often than not, he was.

He followed his successes in Cairo with a stay of nearly two years in Istanbul, where he sought to ensure that his family's relationship with the Ottoman authorities remained on an amicable footing and that his own ambition stood a chance of being rewarded. What little information exists on this sojourn confirms Arslan's ability to move with ease among well-placed politicians and intellectuals.[23] He especially cultivated Hasan Fehmi, the minister of finance, and the aging but still influential Münif Pasha (1828–1910), minister of education and an outstanding patron of Ottoman scholarship and learning throughout his long career. These two years may also have provided the occasion for at least one meeting between Arslan and Sultan Abdulhamid.

In 1892, Arslan left the Ottoman capital for Europe on the trip which had become nearly obligatory for the educated young men who aspired to lead Ottoman-Arab society. He was neither intrigued nor awed. He had been raised to distrust the West, and his exposure to the centers of Western culture—Paris and London were his principal destinations—evoked no commentaries on European political systems, no descriptions of cities or their architecture, no comparative discussion of morals, manners, or behavior. To Arslan, Europe represented an imperial threat, not an admirable culture. He held to this view for the next fifty years.

The few remarks he made about this trip concerned his meeting with the Egyptian poet Ahmad Shawqi, with whom he was to have one of the deepest of all his friendships among the cultural elite.[24] Arslan had admired Shawqi's work and was delighted to meet the poet in a Paris hotel. They were enchanted with one another and became, in Arslan's phrase, "like brothers." Among the two promising young talents at the start of their careers, there developed, as Shawqi wrote, "a friendship without affectation."[25] It was one of those rare relationships that could be sustained through correspondence and that deepened despite infrequent meetings; it stands out among Arslan's many friendships as intensely personal and vivid.

Arslan's return to Istanbul from Europe in 1892 coincided with the arrival of Jamal al-Din al-Afghani in the Ottoman capital. He had been invited by Sultan Abdulhamid, who admired al-Afghani's pan-Islamic doctrines and hoped to use them to reinforce his claim to the caliphate. Al-Afghani's reputation as a dangerous agitator was also well known, but Abdulhamid felt his extensive police network could neutralize this unwelcome aspect of the famous man. Although the relationship soon soured, especially after al-Afghani's alleged complicity in the assassination of the Persian ruler Nasr al-Din Shah in 1896, his first months in Istanbul were favored ones.[26]

It was during this period that Arslan succeeded in gaining an audience with the distinguished visitor. As he recounted the episode, al-Afghani asked him to describe what he had seen in Europe, and Arslan related his experiences with such eloquence that al-Afghani was moved to grasp his hand and exclaim: "I congratulate the land of Islam which has produced the likes of you."[27] Arslan never let the episode be forgotten and did all he could to ensure that it remained a part of his public image. His instincts for self-promotion were sound, and he gained nearly as much from his brief personal association with al-Afghani as he did from his lifelong espousal of the man's ideals. He was also genuinely moved by al-Afghani's approval, and it is remarkable how his later life paralleled that of the man he called "the greatest force for the awakening of the East."[28]

These experiences and personalities exerted a considerable pull on Arslan. His two Arab biographers regard them as decisive. Although their statements tend to read too much of subsequent events into the world view of a young man in the decade of the 1890s, it is plausible to argue that Arslan's travels convinced him to work for the reform of Islam and the preservation of the Ottoman Empire. They may also have shown him that he belonged in the society of Cairo and Istanbul and made him determined not to let his return to the *mutasarrifiyyah* relegate him to the role of isolated feudal politician. He had been given a cause and a masterful Arabic style which he enjoyed displaying. He found a way to combine them, and to keep his name before the public, through political journalism. According to one account, Arslan was persuaded to become a journalist by Muhammad ʿAbduh, who convinced him that he could exercise more influence as a prose writer than as a poet.[29] Whatever the source of his inspiration, there is no question that Arslan's polemical essays reached a far wider audience than did his poetry, and that he was, from the 1890s to the early 1940s, one of the Arab world's most prolific journalists.

When Arslan entered journalism, it was a relatively new profession in the Arab-Ottoman world. It was also in flux, as the censorship imposed by Abdulhamid drove many of the early Arab journalists out of the Ottoman provinces to Egypt, where both the periodical and daily presses expanded rapidly in the relatively permissive journalistic climate established by Lord Cromer. In its early years, the Egyptian press was largely a Syrian Christian enterprise. Of the three major Egyptian Arabic dailies in the period before World War I, two—*al-Muqattam* (founded in the late 1880s) and *al-Ahram* (founded in 1876)—were edited by Syrian Christians and served as mouthpieces for British and French interests in Egypt. The third paper—*al-Muʾayyad* (founded in 1889)—was controlled by Shaykh ʿAli Yusuf, a native Egyptian and a graduate of al-Azhar, who took a strong nationalist and Islamic stance in his publications.[30] Although Arslan wrote for *al-Ahram* and other Christian-edited journals, he was drawn to the views of ʿAli Yusuf and established his own literary reputation mainly in the pages of *al-Muʾayyad*.

Arslan's literary output was not confined to political journalism. At the same time that he practiced as a vocational intellectual engaged in the events of his age, he continued to publish poetry and to engage in the activities associated with a learned aristocrat dabbling in scholarly pursuits.[31] He was an inveterate seeker and editor of old manuscripts and published two such works while in his twenties: *al-Durrah al-Yatimah* of Ibn al-Muqaffaʿ and the collected letters of al-Sabi.[32] He also became interested in Chateaubriand and translated his novella *Les Aventures du dernier Abencerage.*[33] Even in these amateur endeavors, Arslan's sense of purpose shows through—Chateaubriand's story was important because of its portrayal of the Islamic presence in al-Andalus, and the two manuscripts, with their superb classical Arabic, supported Arslan's contention that "it is necessary to search the works of our ancestors, to preserve their style, and to imitate their example."[34] Arslan's journalism reflected similar concerns. Thus, although he had no qualms about contributing to a journal, *al-Muqtataf*, edited by Christian secularists, his own articles treated more conventional Islamic subjects.[35]

Through his diverse publications, Arslan had established a sound literary reputation by the early years of the twentieth century. If he was a lesser figure than Shawqi, Hafiz Ibrahim, or Khalil Mutran, he was nevertheless regarded as a major writer. Mutran himself admired Arslan's early poetry and called him a master of the Arabic language.[36] Another well-known Lebanese critic and man of letters, Marun ʿAbbud, wrote that during his student days in the early years of the century, he felt Arslan's poetry was superior to Shawqi's. He was sure that if Arslan had not turned his energies to politics he, and not Shawqi, would have been honored in the Arab world as "the prince of poets."[37] As it was, Arslan came to be known as *amir al-bayan* (the prince of eloquence), an epithet which reflected his rigorous adherence to the stylistic norms of classical Arabic as it redeveloped in the nineteenth century. This was an integral part of his prewar status. In the age of the *nahdah*, literary talent alone could help secure fame and recognition. Arslan, assured of social and political standing by birth, elevated his reputation considerably through his literary achievements.

His style and his perspective marked him as traditional rather than innovative. As was to be the case in the postwar years, he occupied an uneasy position between old and new. With his impeccable European attire and his articles in the new scientific journals, he appeared to be the epitome of the Westernized intellectual. But he was neither a secularist nor a Westernizer. He was a Druze chieftain who had matured at a time of exceptional mobility in the *mutasarrifiyyah* of Mount Lebanon, who had been given a special opportunity to associate with some of the leading intellectual personalities of his age, and who had inherited the means to travel widely. He concluded that there was nothing amiss in the world as it was ordered. To be sure, he accepted the need for reforms if they could strengthen the society already in place. He adopted the pan-Islamic concepts of al-Afghani and the reformist commitment conveyed to him by ʿAbduh; these were deeply held beliefs, and he courageously acted on them. Yet he was also aware of his princely position and the prestige it accorded him. He was more than a Druze feudal chieftain, but he was that as well.

During the twenty-five years that Arslan made Lebanon his principal residence after 1892, he kept his ties to the old feudal relationships from which his power and influence originated. His role as Druze prince needs to be kept in mind in order to understand his political behavior and social attitudes. Arslan was not without local ambition and proved reasonably adept at surviving the infighting which characterized the political life of the *mutasarrifiyyah*. Although he held no official positions for a decade after 1892, passing references in his memoirs indicate that he combined his writing activities with a commitment to the family's political well-being. When the reign of Muzzafir Pasha as *mutasarrif* (1902–1907) produced a brief crisis for the Arslan clan, Shakib did not retreat into worldly aloofness. The struggle was his, and he participated fully in it.

The crisis was caused by the reemergence of a long-standing rivalry between the Arslans and the Junbalats for dominance in the Shuf. Wary of Amir Mustafa's power and intrigues, the new *mutasarrif* appointed a member of the Junbalat family as *qaʾimaqam* of the Shuf. In a brief holding action, Shakib succeeded his uncle in the office for a few months in 1902. However, the *mutasarrif* was not to be deterred from his objective of ousting Mustafa's family from power, and Shakib was forced to resign. When the Junbalat faction took over, the Arslans felt that the political survival of their house was threatened, and they devoted their energies to recapturing the position of *qaʾimaqam*. Their opportunity to do so occurred in the circumstances created by the Young Turk revolt. By the autumn of 1908, the new holder of the office which had come to symbolize

Poet, journalist, Druze leader: Arslan at age twenty-five.

Arslan dominance in the Shuf was Shakib himself. The incident which gained him the appointment is discussed below; his instigation of it showed him to be a worthy associate of his uncle Mustafa. While the cosmopolitan Amir of later years seemed far removed from the arena of feudal power struggles, Shakib's views of politics were formed in the environment of the *mutasarrifiyyah*. He brought to his numerous future confrontations two discrete qualities—abrasiveness and survival—which may have been acquired in the political battles of the Shuf.

As Arslan conspired with his relatives in Mount Lebanon, he also maintained his interest in the wider world of Ottoman affairs and laid the groundwork which would bring him to the center of imperial power.

When Sultan Abdulhamid invited Jamal al-Din al-Afghani to reside in Istanbul in 1892, his gesture was more calculating than a simple offer of royal hospitality to a distinguished servant of Islam. Abdulhamid's keen appreciation of his weakened international position led him to adopt a policy of pan-Islam. A central ingredient in his strategy was to link the office of the sultanate with the caliphate and so strengthen the Ottoman Empire internally by uniting its diverse Muslim peoples, especially Arabs and Turks, into a solid Islamic bloc.[38] In addition, Abdulhamid hoped that by posing as the caliph of all Muslims, he would gain a certain measure of moral authority over the Muslims of India and North Africa. By playing on British and French fears of his ability to use his Islamic authority to rouse the Muslims in their imperial possessions, he intended to make pan-Islam a factor in international diplomacy. If pan-Islamic unity seems in retrospect a fantasy, it served such a felt need at the time that it attracted support from a wide circle of Muslims both within and outside the sultan's political territories.

In Egypt, patriotism and reformism coalesced into a vision of the independent Ottoman caliphate as an indispensable ally through which to end the British occupation. Men like Mustafa Kamil and Shaykh ʿAli Yusuf of *al-Muʾayyad*, however much they are associated with demands for Egyptian independence, also viewed their society in Islamic terms and publicly supported Egypt's ties to the Ottoman caliphate. Arslan's friend Ahmad Shawqi expressed the longings of a major segment of Egyptian society when he claimed of the Ottoman caliph, "And Egypt has need of thee."[39]

Syrian intellectuals and politicians, whether from doctrinal concerns for Islamic reformism or from more concrete considerations of political solidarity, also favored the strengthening of the Islamic bonds represented by the revived caliphate. Typical of such individuals were Muhammad Kurd ʿAli, ʿAbd al-Qadir al-Maghribi, and their mentor, Tahir al-Jazaʾiri.[40] But even among the strongest exponents of pan-Islamic Ottomanism, few turn-of-the-century public figures in the Arab provinces wished to be known as friends of the Turks. Shakib Arslan was an exception.

The crystallization of Arslan's political and social views occurred during the latter part of Abdulhamid's reign. He adjusted but did not modify them during half a century of public prominence. He was in perfect accord with his sultan-caliph and forever regretted the passing of his office and the dismantling of his empire. Like Abdulhamid, Arslan saw that the Islamic territories over which the Ottoman Empire exercised political authority were in danger of being isolated and occupied by the Western imperial powers just as Algeria, Tunisia, and Egypt had been. To prevent this occurrence, the Ottoman state needed to be strengthened. This did not imply the wholesale adoption of European concepts of state and society. On the contrary, it meant a regeneration of Islam, a reassertion of Islamic solidarity, and a reinforcement of the office of caliph. Arslan joined his poetic voice to Shawqi's and asserted that "thankful praise is the right of the caliph who is an adornment to religion and to the world."[41] Arslan had been educated during the *nahdah*, but remained untouched by the sentiments of Arab separatism it sparked in others; he had visited the Paris of the Third Republic and the London of Gladstone, but found no attraction in the doctrines of European liberalism; he knew prestige as a Druze, but committed his political future to the survival of the Ottoman caliphate. In the complex process by which an individual acquires beliefs and the urge to express them, Arslan discarded everything that could not be regarded as part of his authentic Islamic cultural heritage. He combined his unyielding commitment to this heritage with an equally tenacious ambition to play a political role in preserving it.

During the tumultuous final decade of the Ottoman Empire, from the Young Turk revolution of 1908 to the armistice of Mudros in 1918, Arslan was given his chance to serve his cause. The army officers who led the revolt made modest demands on the sultan in 1908, but they set in motion a chain of events which led to Abdulhamid's overthrow in 1909, to the consolidation of political power around the triumvirate of Jamal, Talaat, and Enver in 1913, and to the fatal alliance with Germany in 1914. After an enthusiastic reception, the restoration of the 1876 constitution in 1908 did not reconcile the peoples of the Empire to rule from Istanbul, and it became necessary for the government to make choices about the nature of the Ottoman state and the symbols by which it should seek to strengthen the loyalty of its subjects. Simultaneously, from without, ambitious states, great and small, sought to gain territory and prestige at the expense of the weakening Porte. For Ottoman patriots like Arslan, these conditions necessitated meeting a continuous series of crises. He thrived on the challenge and emerged during the final convulsion of Empire as a man of immense physical vitality and passionate loyalty. He participated in nearly every confrontation—military, ideological, and political—the Ottoman Empire faced in its last years. In tracing his activities during this period, it is possible to gain a fuller appreciation of his Ottoman loyalties and his Islamic political orientation.

His first public embroilment in the immediate aftermath of the Young Turk revolt concerned the status of the restored constitution in Mount Lebanon and the related issue of his family's position in the Shuf. Although he was a committed monarchist, Arslan approved of the Young Turks' success in forcing Abdulhamid to restore the constitution. What he found most favorable in this action was the support it gave to his belief that reform was possible under the traditional system. He also hoped to become a deputy to the parliament which would convene in Istanbul. However, neither Arslan's ambition nor his vision of reform received encouragement from the new *mutasarrif* of Mount Lebanon, Yusuf Franku Pasha (1907–1912), whose administrative methods and political outlook were conservative and authoritarian.[42] Although the Arslan family actually benefited from Franku Pasha's appointment, they joined with other leaders of the *mutasarrifiyyah* to express their resentment at his style of rule. Their instrument of protest was the restored constitution. In September 1908, a delegation of Lebanese notables gathered at Bayt al-Din and pressured Yusuf into proclaiming the application of the constitution to the *mutasarrifiyyah* and dismissing some of his unpopular appointees. According to Arslan's account of the incident, when a shaken Yusuf Pasha appeared before the delegation to swear his loyalty to the constitution, it was Arslan who stood at the *mutasarrif*'s side and held his trembling hand.[43]

In the wake of his decisive action in this event, Arslan was immediately appointed *qaʾimaqam* of the Shuf. In his memoirs he states, probably truthfully, that he did not really want the position and that his real goal was to represent Mount Lebanon in Istanbul.[44] However, his uncle insisted that he accept the office, and he obeyed the wishes of the family patriarch. He held the post for just over two years and then resigned in a dispute with the *mutasarrif*, who quite understandably never found Arslan acceptable. Arslan did not comment about the performance of his official functions, and one is left with the impression that he was not particularly interested in day-to-day administrative duties and, further, that he was still searching for a broader arena than that afforded him by the traditional Arslan role in the Shuf. The Young Turk revolution had created circumstances which gave him that arena and propelled him from local chieftain to imperial politician and public figure.

When Abdulhamid was finally deposed in April 1909, Arslan gave his support to the new regime and to its efforts to repel foreign invasion. He may have regretted the departure of a strong monarch, but he was shrewd enough to see that power rested with the military establishment and patriotic enough to recognize that Ottoman survival depended upon successful military performance. If he made certain political accommodations, he also made an intense personal commitment to the Ottoman cause as defended by the Young Turk regime. His commitment was most evident in his reaction to the Italian invasion of Libya in October 1911, when he went to the battlefield himself. This response, although more direct than most, was not unrepresentative of the reverberations which the Italian invasion produced throughout Arab Islam. In Tunisia, there were open anti-Italian riots; in Egypt, a strong wave of pro-Ottoman sentiment swept across all levels of society. Fear of a systematic European campaign against Islam was heightened by the fact that French forces had occupied Fez in the spring of 1911, initiating the final stages in the process that added Morocco to the international system of protectorates.

Arslan acted as though the Italian invasion was directed at him personally. Driven by a compelling sense of urgency, he rushed out of Mount Lebanon to spend a frenzied year as soldier, relief-worker, and propagandist. In as farfetched a plan as any amateur military tactician ever devised, Arslan persuaded the Ottoman commander in Damascus to release a number of troops and officers for service to the Libyan front. With Arslan accompanying them, they were to cross British-controlled Egypt disguised as a Bedouin contingent. The originator of this questionable campaign got no further than al-ʿArish before he was detained and eventually sent by boat to Jaffa.[45] Undeterred, Arslan boarded another ship and sailed for Alexandria. He spent the first months of 1912 in Cairo working for the newly formed Egyptian Red Crescent Society. As always, he found time to cultivate the politically powerful, starting what was to become a lifelong friendship, punctuated by lengthy periods of personal animosity, with Khedive ʿAbbas Hilmi II.

When he finally reached the Ottoman forces in Tripolitania in April 1912, the war was at a stalemate. He remained in the region for over two months, and the contacts he made with the Ottoman officers there were to serve him well when the triumvirate took power in 1913. He became a particularly close friend of Enver Pasha at this time and, although thirteen years his senior, developed an attitude of almost worshipful fascination for the mercurial Young Turk leader, in whom he saw an authentic Islamic hero.

Arslan made no military contribution to the defense of Tripoli, but his presence at the battlefront added considerably to his reputation, as did his widely circulated publications on the Libyan affair. From November 1911 to June 1912, he wrote a series of rousing articles for *al-Mu'ayyad* in which he revealed the depth of his commitment to the Ottoman Empire and the bitterness of his attitude toward European imperialism. The articles became famous and helped extend Arslan's audience, and his range of personal contacts, into North Africa. This was made possible through the efforts of *al-Mu'ayyad*'s editor, Shaykh 'Ali Yusuf, who acted as one of the leaders of a pan-Islamic organization called al-Ittihad al-Maghribi. 'Ali Yusuf recruited North African students in Cairo to the organization and, in 1911 and 1912, managed to increase the distribution of his newspaper in Morocco.[46] Arslan was surely involved with the work of al-Ittihad al-Maghribi, and his enduring links to North Africa were probably established by his essays in *al-Mu'ayyad*. They contained a call to duty, to unity, and to resistance.

In them, he defined for the first time his version of Ottoman patriotism, claiming that "the Ottoman Muslim, like his Christian and Jewish brothers, is active in the defense of the territory of his fatherland. . . ."[47] Tripoli represented for the Empire as a whole, and for Arslan individually, a chance for decisive action against European encroachment. The Italian invasion was a challenge to the essence of the Ottoman-Islamic system, and it required an active response "to preserve for ourselves what remains of our dignity."[48] This meant a willingness to make the ultimate sacrifice: "Rather than preserving our lives in the cause of honor, we prefer to die with honor."[49]

Participation in the struggle went beyond the need for action for its own sake. The struggle was in the name of the Ottoman state and the seamless fabric of Islam over which it governed as the only Islamic political authority left on earth. The symbols by which Arslan identified the cause were unequivocal: "Call upon God, O Ottomans of the protected kingdom, for your continued existence in the world and for the removal of the yoke from your necks. . . . Call upon God, O Easterners, for the preservation of this one state which must not perish. . . . Call upon God, O Muslims in all regions of the caliphate, for the preservation of the spark of life of Islam. There will remain only sacrifice until eternity."[50] His own role was expressed with equal directness: "We love the Ottoman Empire and will loyally support it as long as there is land. We will defend our fatherland, hoping that our efforts will increase the self-confidence of Islam and attract martyrs to its cause."[51] Islam was Arslan's basis of justification for Ottoman political authority: not good government, not dynastic principles, and certainly not democratic ones, but the conviction that the caliph of Islam should have authority in those regions where Muslims lived.

Arslan further argued that Istanbul's failure to respond wholeheartedly to the Italian invasion would weaken the loyalty of other regions under Ottoman authority and would encourage an already arrogant Europe to further acts of aggression. Arslan's vitriolic anti-imperialism, first expressed in the al-Mu'ayyad articles, would echo in his writings for the rest of his life. He began his unceasing campaign against what he saw as a European conspiracy which condoned the piecemeal dismantling of the Ottoman state and which would later establish the Mandate system. There was a rage to his rhetoric. One senses it is not just genuine patriotic fervor, but personal frustration on the part of one who was assured of his own talents and found it intolerable to be part of a declining power whose ruling elite was regarded as inferior by Europeans. Yet all his bitterness could not make up for the lack of troops in Tripolitania.

Threats from other fronts forced the Ottoman government to abandon Tripoli and to conclude an unfavorable peace with Italy. When Arslan heard of the probable evacuation of Ottoman forces from Libya, he traveled to Istanbul to see if he could persuade the government to keep fighting in North Africa. He was engaged in these futile discussions when the First Balkan War began in October 1912. Once again, Arslan plunged into the cause, this time coordinating the activities of the Red Crescent and the Egyptian Benevolent Society on behalf of Muslim refugees from the Balkans.

In January 1913, the coup d'état which solidified the hold of Enver and the Unionists on the Ottoman government occurred in Istanbul. Arslan gave his full support to this regime. He felt that political infighting had contributed to the loss of Tripoli, and he welcomed a strong government. He also concluded that in order to remain strong, the government required a program of cooperation and unification. Only in this way would the Empire as a whole be preserved against piecemeal European occupation. In effect, he became a virtual spokesman for the new regime; he found in the CUP leaders a group of individuals who appeared committed to the political program he had long espoused and who were prepared to give him a central role in persuading others of its usefulness. They, in turn, discovered in Arslan a well-

An Arab-Ottoman gentleman: the deputy from Hawran, circa 1915.

placed Arab notable, an unquestioned patriot, who was willing to endorse their policies in the most forceful public manner. The chance to acquire an ally of his standing was not to be missed, and they charged him with explaining their goals to the Arab community.

During most of 1913, Arslan became a roving emissary for Ottomanism, traveling to Beirut, Damascus, and Jerusalem and undertaking a mission to Medina in the company of another well-known pro-Ottoman propagandist, ʿAbd al-ʿAziz Jawish. Arslan's expressed admiration for this individual is an important indicator of his own political perspective and style of action. Jawish (sometimes written Chawish; 1876–1929), gained notoriety as the outspoken editor of al-Liwaʾ, the organ of the Egyptian National party. For his inflammatory pro-Islamic articles during a period of Muslim-Coptic tension, he was exiled to Istanbul in 1911. It was an active exile, and his residence became a virtual political club for advocates of Ottoman-Islamic solidarity. Like Arslan, he was to find himself in Berlin in 1919, where, in close association with the Amir, he drifted through an uncertain existence as a proponent of continued Islamic militancy.[52]

Arslan used his travels through the Arab provinces to sound out Arab opinion and, when necessary, to attempt to change it. He argued with Arab separatists and with even the most moderate decentralizers, emphasizing the dangers of divisiveness and the importance to the Arabs of the protective shelter of the Ottoman state.

Also active in a pan-Islamic propaganda campaign among the Arabs at this time were the special agents of Enver Pasha's personal security force, the Teşkilat-i Mahsusa. Although no evidence has been found linking Arslan directly to these activities, his close association with Enver and his commitment to a pan-Islamic ideology strongly suggest that his travels during these months were part of a government-coordinated program.[53] In this way, Arslan became closely identified with the CUP, and, while his ties to the regime enabled him to become one of the most prominent Arab figures of the time, they also caused him to be regarded with a certain suspicion.

Arslan's singlemindedness and his clear sense of purpose and direction were unusual in a period filled with intellectual confusion and political equivocation. For many Arabs, the liberalism promised by the constitutional reforms of the Young Turks was vanishing in the harshness of tightening centralization and increasing Turkification. To combat these policies, several Arab societies were formed in Istanbul, the Syrian provinces, Cairo, and Paris.[54] A few secret plotters may even have advocated a program of Arab separation from the Ottoman Empire. However, such militants were few, and the major emphasis of the societies was on the need for governmental decentralization and for the restoration of the Arabic cultural, especially linguistic, position in the Arab provinces. Although each sectarian and regional grouping could give a special coloring to the general Arab outlook, there was a broad consensus that some form of continued Arab association within the Ottoman Empire was desirable and possible.

It is important to recognize that the late Ottoman state had internal viability. The decade before World War I cannot be viewed merely as a prelude to Arab nationalism. Political leaders did not plan to separate from Istanbul; Arabs still served as officers in the Ottoman army, still attended the higher academies in Istanbul, and still aspired to appointments in the official hierarchy. To be sure, they hoped for some form of decentralization which would offer greater scope to their ambitions within the Arab provinces themselves. Nevertheless, the majority of the Arab elite sought survival within the framework of a strengthened Ottoman state, not in separation from it.[55]

Shakib Arslan was exceptional in this overall sentiment because of his intransigent support for the policies of the Young Turk regime. Unlike more ideologically attuned spokesmen, he did not write in terms of Ottomanism, Islamism, Turkism, or Arabism. His was a more practical message: a divided Empire would fall to Europe. During his tour of the Arab capitals, he placed against the dangers of divisiveness the need for Ottoman-Islamic solidarity: "I spoke of the inappropriateness of the split between Arabs and Turks and of the necessity to adhere to the Empire. I warned about the policy of foreigners who wanted to suggest there were difficulties between Arabs and Turks in order to exploit them to their own advantage, take over Ottoman territories, and turn them into colonies."[56] He argued that the differences between Arabs and Turks were superficial or were created by imperialist manipulations. He had written during the Tripoli War that "Arabs and Turks" was a new phrase and that it would be suicide for the Ottoman state ever to permit itself to be defined in terms of these two component parts rather than as the whole.[57] Where some saw in local autonomy a release from the heavy-handedness of the Committee of Union and Progress, Arslan saw in it an invitation to be colonized.

In his view, the proposals for provincial autonomy sprang from the ill-considered ambitions of certain Arab politicians. He pressed this point most forcefully in a series of lead articles written for the pro-Unionist newspaper *al-Ra'y al-'Amm* during the first months of 1913. Directed primarily at the leadership of the Cairo-based

Ottoman Decentralization Society, the most moderate and broadly supported of the prewar reform societies, the articles revealed the full range of Arslan's political personality; they included intemperate personal attacks on prominent Arab reformers, an insistence on his own patriotism in the face of charges of betrayal, and a defense of Ottoman unity as both a pragmatic and a principled response to the needs of the moment.

From Arslan's perspective, all Arab attempts to reorganize, however peacefully, their relationships with Istanbul were treasonable. Thus, he could write that the Decentralization Society's program of provincial autonomy was tantamount to "dismembering the limbs of Ottoman unity and placing our country under direct foreign rule."[58] Those who sought to undermine a state guided by the shari'ah, who rejoiced in its setbacks, who encouraged the spread of dissension, were guilty of self-deception which would lead to disaster for all: "Decentralization means passing an eternity in hell; the party thinks it is building a palace, but in reality it is digging its own grave."[59]

Arslan was equally disparaging of other attempts to present specifically Arab concerns. Of that cornerstone in the myth of Arabism, the Paris Congress of June 1913, he wrote, "I was displeased at the holding of this Congress."[60] Despite the moderation of the Congress's resolutions, Arslan regarded the gathering as treasonable, and he urged the notables of all sects in Syria to deluge Istanbul with telegrams of protest. His own enthusiasm in this endeavor was such that he was accused by Christian leaders in Damascus of instigating a scheme to forge signatures on telegrams and to alter the texts of pro-Congress telegrams after they had been signed.[61]

For all his involvement, Arslan had no clear platform of reform. To him, the debate was not between constitutionalism and authoritarianism, and he was willing to subordinate considerations of political liberty to considerations of political existence: "I have not been deceived by words of reform and decentralization and other such expressions used by corrupt men to entice the masses and make them heedless of the dangers threatening their state, their homeland, their religion, and their worldly existence."[62] The search by the various communities for equal rights would have to be postponed until the Empire emerged successfully, and with unity, from its current crisis.

As Arslan became more outspoken in his defense of CUP policies, public opposition to him developed. One Beirut reformer regretted the Amir's alienation from "his friends of yesterday," and Arslan himself acknowledged that "many of my friends and brethren became angry with me for my attitude toward this Ottoman policy."[63] One of them was Rashid Rida, a leading force behind the Decentralization

Society and the most prominent religious commentator among Muhammad 'Abduh's disciples. Although Rida's cautious program of an Arab-oriented Islam embraced within the Ottoman state might seem to have much in common with Arslan's platform, Rida could not countenance Arslan's association with the CUP and criticized him in his famous journal al-Manar. His criticism, growing more common among Arab reformers, that Arslan was a simple accomplice of the CUP was not nearly as damaging as his attempts to undermine Arslan's credibility in the area Arslan cherished most. The man for whom Islamic loyalty was the touchstone of identity was denounced by the leading Islamic spokesman of the time as belonging to a sect (the Druze) which was not truly Islamic and as unworthy of posing as a defender of the faith.[64] Rida would later modify his opinions, but for now the Amir was under heavy attack.

However, neither the participation of his friends in the Arab reform societies nor their criticism of his stance dissuaded Arslan from his sense of purpose. He was, after all, defending a position of which al-Afghani would have approved. The bond which would keep the external world at bay was provided by Islam and its caliphate, which could survive only with the unified support of all the Empire's subjects. Arslan could further feel justified in his own role, not as a passive poet, but as a passionate activist in the al-Afghani mold. He was convinced, as he always was, that his cause was just. Others shared his view, but few were as outspoken. In the summer of 1913, the Unionist government initiated a series of conferences in which Arab opinion was to be heard and, if possible, placated. Arslan attended for the express purpose of protesting the Paris Congress, and he stated his views with such force that one of the participants in the proceedings, As'ad Daghir, was moved to comment on Arslan's special place in the spectrum of Arab opinion.[65] What struck Daghir was the vehemence with which Arslan opposed the activities of the Arab societies, the depth of his support for Unionist policies, and his marked concern for the ambitions of Britain and France in the Arab territories. To Daghir, Arslan was unique in his ability to support Arab demands for reform while defending the government's obstinacy in implementing them. Another commentator has simply noted that Arslan was "one of the prominent Arab zu'ama' who continued their friendship with the Turks."[66] In Arslan's opinion, to criticize the state was to undermine it. Coherent central authority was preferable to the anarchy of provincial autonomy. Perhaps Arslan, like other supporters of Ottomanism, felt that Abdulhamid's policies had worked reasonably well and that change had caused only disaffection and defeat.

In April 1914, Arslan was elected a deputy to the Ottoman parliament from the district of Hawran, a predominantly Druze area south of Damascus. When he traveled to Istanbul to assume his parliamentary duties, he was closely identified with the cause of Ottoman-Islamic solidarity. This was in keeping with the world in which he had been raised and in which, as he entered his forty-fifth year, he had become recognized as a man of many and diverse achievements; former *qaʾimaqam* of the Shuf and translator of Chateaubriand; Druze chieftain, admired poet, and widely published journalist; an intimate of Enver Pasha and Ahmad Shawqi; an active servant of the state as a civilian volunteer in wartime and as a representative to the Ottoman parliament. He was, in sum, the perfect embodiment of an Ottoman Arab gentleman in the epoch of the Meşrutiyet. If he had concerns about the Ottoman state, he believed the course of history, with a push from men like himself, would resolve matters in favor of the traditional values. On the basis of his many contributions to state and society, he could contemplate a respected and honored middle age as he embarked upon yet another service to his sovereign. In the coming conflict, he would stake everything on the preservation of the status quo. As a result of this commitment, the war would not only shatter his world, it would tarnish his reputation and make him a wandering exile.

CHAPTER TWO.
WAR AND EXILE

As is well-known, I was one of those opposed to King Husayn
both before and during the war for his revolt against the
Empire of the caliphate and, even more than that, for his
alliance with the British Empire.   —Arslan[1]

Many people claimed that Amir Shakib had no firm political
principles, and that he used the Empire and its influential
men for his own purposes. . . . I was one of those who dis-
approved of his partisanship with the Unionists and his
defense of them, although I understood his political principle
of preferring the Ottoman State over all foreigners.
                                                —Rashid Rida[2]

ON 28 OCTOBER 1914, the Ottoman Empire entered
the Great War, and the Middle East was forever changed. While the
battles which were fought in the Middle Eastern theater were minor
affairs compared to the carnage of the Western front, the political
consequences of the Ottoman defeat had a profound impact on the
lives of those who inhabited its diverse territories. So, too, did the war
itself. It meant not only the mobilization of large numbers of military personnel, but also rigorous measures of internal security.

Although long regarded as militarily moribund, the Ottoman Empire defended itself tenaciously against the uncertain ventures of its
enemies. Ottoman forces held off the spectacular Dardanelles invasion in 1915, captured the major part of an entire British army at Kut
al-Amarna in 1916, and prevented any serious British thrust from
Egypt into the Arab provinces until Allenby's great offensive began
in late 1917. The soldiers and officers who manned this military machine consisted of Arabs as well as Turks, and one of the generals
who commanded the Ottoman forces opposing Faysal's Arab troops
in their rush for Damascus in 1918 was Yasin al-Hashimi, an Arab
from Baghdad. But if, as is now recognized, "the vast majority of
the Arabs remained loyal supporters of the Caliphate and the Sultanate,"[3] the civilian population of Syria and Mount Lebanon had
activists who saw the war as a chance to press for administrative
changes in the Arabs' relationship with Istanbul or, in the case of
certain Christian groups, to replace Ottoman protection with that
of France. To ensure that the attitudes of a few agitators would not

suborn the loyalties of the majority of the Arab subjects, the Committee of Union and Progress sent one of the ruling triumvirate, the
minister of marine, Ahmad Jamal Pasha, to be commander-in-chief
of the Ottoman Fourth Army, headquartered in Damascus, and to
serve as de facto civilian governor of the Syrian provinces. Under
Jamal Pasha's administration, the special status of the *mutasarrifiyyah* of Mount Lebanon was terminated and the region was treated
as a regular Ottoman territory, with the notable exception that its
inhabitants remained exempt from conscription. From the summer
of 1915 until his recall in January 1918, he instigated a reign of terror
in the regions under his control and alienated important sectors of
Arab opinion from the Ottoman government. As a particularly outspoken member of one of the more prominent pro-Ottoman families, Arslan was naturally affected by the policies of Jamal Pasha.

As might be expected from his actions during the Italian invasion
of Tripoli, Arslan favored the Ottoman Empire's alliance with Germany and its entry into the war. Neutrality, advocated by some
members of the Committee of Union and Progress, would not, in
Arslan's opinion, deter the Allies from partitioning the Empire to
serve their own interests.[4] Only through direct engagement could
the Empire be preserved and the dignity of Islam asserted. Arslan
welcomed the conflict and gave his support to the caliphate and the
armies which defended it. Most Arabs initially did the same. Few,
however, plunged into the cause so wholeheartedly, and few were as
closely associated with the Unionist leadership, especially with
Jamal Pasha, as Arslan. It was an association which linked him in
the minds of many Arabs to the harsh regime of that most hated of
Turks.

That Arslan was drawn so centrally into the events of the war
stemmed from the special position of his family and from his own
dynamic personality. The Arslans had long-standing contacts in Istanbul, and their support of the CUP after 1912 did not go unappreci-
ated. By the time Jamal Pasha arrived in Syria in December 1914,
both Shakib and his brother Nasib were deputies to the Ottoman
parliament, while a younger brother, 'Adil, was *qa'imaqam* of the
Shuf and would soon become a parliamentary deputy as well. Patriotism had its political advantages; so did Ottoman rule. Shakib
and his brothers approved of Jamal Pasha's abolition of the special
privileges of the *mutasarrifiyyah*, preferring, as did other Druze
families, the loose umbrella of the Islamic-Ottoman state to the con-
fines of a European-sponsored, Christian-dominated enclave.[5] In this
instance, Arslan's strong pro-Ottoman stance and his role as Druze
chieftain were complementary. It is not surprising to find that few

Druzes were convicted of anti-Ottoman activities during the war. They had every reason to hope for an Ottoman victory.

Because of his excellent connections with Enver Pasha, Arslan was especially favored by Ottoman officials. His status was apparent from the moment Jamal Pasha arrived in Syria. According to Arslan, he was part of the delegation of welcome for the Ottoman commander, and "when I greeted him, he told me that Enver Pasha had often spoken to him about me and that he was very pleased to make my acquaintance."[6] For the time being, Arslan was content with Jamal Pasha's recognition and placed himself at the disposal of the Ottoman commander.

In Jamal Pasha, a man possessed of "a belief in the virtues and future of an Ottoman nationalism based on Moslem solidarity," Arslan saw a commander whose views complemented his own.[7] Although deeply flawed, Ahmad Jamal Pasha (1872–1922) has too often been characterized in one-dimensional terms by those whose sole intention is to reveal him as deserving of the epithet *al-saffah*, the blood shedder. Interestingly enough, one of the fullest portraits of Jamal is drawn by George Antonius, who shows the sincere concern the Ottoman commander had for the Islamic caliphate and explains how his initial policies in the Arab provinces were conciliatory and designed to maintain the allegiance of the Arabs to the Ottoman state. But Jamal's religious beliefs and administrative skills were joined to a driving ambition which led him to rash acts of military bravado. When they failed, he turned in frustration against those whom he saw as having thwarted his grand designs and instituted a reign of terror against them.

Arslan felt that Jamal Pasha's religious orientation was proper for an Ottoman statesman, and he shared the commander's impatience to achieve something, to demonstrate in some forceful manner the vitality of Islamic Ottomanism. He eagerly participated in Jamal's first military venture, a campaign to capture the Suez Canal in a quick strike. Throughout his adult life, Arslan possessed a romantic attraction to heroic, if ill-conceived, combat. His poor military judgment did not temper the impetuosity of his response when faced with the possibility of action. With an enthusiasm reminiscent of the days of the Tripolitanian War, Arslan sought to garner men and supplies for the attack on the Canal. Working among the Druzes, he collected 120 volunteers whom he intended to lead to Suez. But instead of finding glory in Egypt, he spent dreary weeks in the fortress at Ma'an, marching through the desert, waiting at the cold and isolated Sinai outpost of Nakhl, and finally marching back to Syria without ever having seen any action.[8] He was perhaps fortunate.

Jamal's troops were poorly equipped, the campaign was inadequately planned, and the assault was thoroughly repulsed. An angry Ottoman commander sought scapegoats among the civilian population of Syria.

Arslan had quickly established himself as an intermediary between Jamal Pasha and the Arab populace. In sectarian-based Mount Lebanon, a Druze leader might be expected to support the containment of the Christian communities during periods of crisis for the Ottoman Empire. However, Arslan's stance during World War I appeared to favor a conciliatory, if superior, attitude toward the Maronites. While Ottoman authorities often viewed them as a potential fifth column waiting to support a French landing, Arslan, although opposed to the Francophile sentiments of many Christian leaders, preferred to alleviate their fears in order to win their loyalty to the Ottoman cause. Naturally, some of his actions may have been based on personal and family alliances built up over the years. But his main objective was to preserve the unity of the Ottoman state by maintaining internal tranquillity in one of its provinces. He later wrote: "I used to say to the Druzes, 'He who has a Christian friend whom he visits once a month, should, under the present circumstances, visit him once a week. And if you are able to perform any humanitarian deed for the Christian sons of your *watan*, now is the time to do it, for our main pillar is harmony. On the other hand, ignominious deeds will be returned in kind.'"[9] In this instance, his arguments are persuasive and consistent.

Despite his well-intentioned policy of Ottoman patriotism, Arslan discovered that the role of intermediary could be hazardous. By assuming a degree of public responsibility, he became associated with all that was unpleasant during the war years. Because of his strong progovernment stance before the war, his easy access to Jamal, and his relatively unrestrained personal existence, Arslan came to be regarded by some as a collaborationist who aided Jamal Pasha in carrying out his policy of repression. The accusation followed Arslan for the rest of his life, and of all the controversies which constantly swirled about him, none was more difficult to lay to rest. Whenever his opponents wished to strike at him, no matter what the real issue, they raised the question of his actions during World War I. The rumors surfaced in the most diverse quarters: a British Foreign Office report of 1922 referred to Arslan as Jamal Pasha's "right hand man" in the persecutions of 1915; in 1927, a New York Arabic-language newspaper accused him of having sent his compatriots to the gallows.[10]

Forced to defend himself repeatedly against these serious charges, Arslan wrote page after page of detailed explanation and justification, and called, rhetorically, on the several witnesses who knew the truth to exonerate him. Yet for all the evidence he and his supporters brought to his defense over the years, his role from 1914 to 1916 cannot be defined with certainty; he remains for this period of his life what Touma has called him—"the man of equivocal situations."[11] Four such "situations" received particular attention both during and after the war: the treatment of the Maronite patriarch; the deportation of several hundred Arab notables to Jerusalem and Anatolia; the hangings of Arab leaders in Beirut and Damascus in 1915 and 1916; and the failure of the famine-relief effort. They need to be examined, for they formed an enduring part of Arslan's reputation. They also shed light on the nature of the power he had accumulated, the ways in which he chose to use it, and the constraints which even a pro-Ottoman Arab civilian faced in wartime Syria. As a trusted government loyalist, he enjoyed a favored position and worked with Jamal Pasha to ensure that local conditions served the war aims of the state. Yet at the same time, as a responsible local notable, he also sought to mitigate the brutality of the state-appointed governor. It was a difficult situation, and it is doubtful that there was a more controversial Arab public figure in Greater Syria during 1915 and 1916 than Arslan.

When Jamal Pasha first arrived in Damascus, he summoned both Maronite Patriarch Huwayik and the *mutasarrif* to reside in Damascus, where they could be under his immediate supervision. This would have been a humiliation of the patriarch and could have alienated the Maronite community from the Ottoman cause. Arslan used one of his first audiences with Jamal to suggest that Huwayik would best serve the needs of his flock by remaining in Mount Lebanon. Jamal was persuaded by this counsel, and Arslan was praised by the Maronite leaders for preserving the sanctity of their patriarch.[12]

Quite paradoxically, this incident laid the basis for criticism of Arslan's attitude toward the patriarch. In the months that followed, Jamal Pasha hardened his position, and Yusuf Huwayik was forced to present himself several times to the Ottoman commander. When this was contrasted with the courteous treatment Jamal Pasha accorded the leading Druze religious dignitary, including a personal visit to his residence in the company of Arslan, some Maronites felt that Arslan was actually working to degrade the office of the patriarch.[13] The charge cannot be supported, but it is representative of the sectarian tensions which permeated Mount Lebanon and of the sentiments held toward the Druze prince, whose service to the imperial cause unduly enhanced his regional influence. If the leaders of the various interest groups were uneasy with Arslan's growing power in Greater Syria, they nonetheless acknowledged his commitment to internal harmony; he was identified as a moderating influence on Jamal and was called upon with increasing frequency to act as an interlocutor with the Ottoman commander.

Soon after the failure of his Suez expedition, Jamal was required to reduce his troop strength by sending reinforcements for the defense of the Dardanelles. This added to his sense of insecurity, and he began to take sterner measures to ensure the stability and loyalty of the province. Lacking political finesse, Jamal Pasha concluded that a population cowed by force would be quiescent, if not overtly loyal.[14] His most frequently used tactic was deportation, usually to either Jerusalem or Anatolia. Between the inauguration of his reign of terror in 1915 and his recall in January 1918, he condemned perhaps 1,000 individuals to exile in Anatolia; those banished to Jerusalem probably numbered less than 100.[15] Arslan, because of his access to the commander, was expected by the families affected to intervene on their behalf. As in the case of Patriarch Huwayik, Arslan had an initial success which gave the impression that he could persuade Jamal as he wished, and, when the deportations continued, he was accused of ignoring the plight of his compatriots.

The deportation policy was introduced in early 1915. In much the same way that he had hoped to keep an eye on the Maronite patriarch, Jamal Pasha ordered about twenty of Mount Lebanon's notables to establish themselves first in Damascus, then in Jerusalem. These individuals were, in Jamal's opinion, tainted by close association with either the French or British consuls before the war and were therefore potentially disloyal. Among them were Khalil al-Khuri, a prominent Maronite, and Salim Bey al-Maʿushi, the qaʾimaqam of the Jazin district. Arslan came to their defense with all the influence he had, telling Jamal Pasha that these were not just his personal friends, but old and respected associates of the Arslan family, whose members would be upset at their continued exile.[16] There is corroboration for Arslan's account by Khalil's son, Bisharah al-Khuri, the first president of Lebanon, who wrote in his memoirs of "the effort of al-Amir Shakib Arslan in the presence of Jamal Pasha to obtain [my father's] release from his exile during the war."[17] The intercession was successful, and the two men were allowed to return to their homes in Lebanon.

The dilemma of one who could achieve such success with the capricious governor became immediately apparent. If Arslan could get two men released, why not more? His position was made all the more difficult by Jamal Pasha's practice of seeking Arslan's advice on selected individuals whose releases he was considering. This became generally known, and Arslan was praised for his mediation by those who were released and condemned by the families of those who remained in exile. One author suggests that Arslan's claim to have worked equally hard for the release of all the exiles may not be true and points out that it was more than coincidental that the only Druzes who were permanently deported were Shakib's political enemies, Tawfiq Majid Arslan and Fuʾad Arslan.[18] Indeed, at one point in his efforts to arrange the release of additional individuals from among the Jerusalem exiles, Arslan even told Jamal to allow one of his opponents to return so that it would not appear as though he was acting only on behalf of his political or personal friends.[19] Even patriots had to protect their political flanks.

By bringing his influence to bear in this manner, and by using his family's position as a lever to obtain the pardon of certain individuals, Arslan left himself vulnerable to charges of favoritism. But as he has pointed out, he was not a totally free agent. Although his access to Jamal gave him a chance to intercede, he had no power to override the decisions of the commander, and the threat of his family's displeasure had to be used sparingly. There is no evidence to prove that he was responsible for selecting anyone for exile, and there is much which shows his concern for the well-being of the exiles. Nevertheless, the suspicion lingered among many families that perhaps Arslan could have obtained the pardon of the one individual about whom they cared.

The case against Arslan became more substantial as Jamal Pasha's policies turned from exile to execution. By the middle of 1915, Jamal was a harassed governor: his forces were depleted and his province simmered with discontent. Rumors of underground movements constantly reached him, and he decided to intensify his repression. In an early gesture of conciliation toward the Arab leaders, Jamal had chosen to suppress evidence contained in documents seized in the French consulate during the first weeks of the war.[20] Now, with the pressures on him increasing, he produced the documents and pronounced the Arabs mentioned in them guilty of treason. As he wrote, "I decided to take ruthless action against the traitors."[21] This action consisted of arrests, of hearings before a military tribunal set up at Aley, and of the hanging of eleven individuals in Beirut on 21 August 1915 and of twenty-one more in Beirut and Damascus on 6 May 1916.[22]

Because the hangings included the innocent with the guilty, they became a symbol of the martyrdom of Syrian Arabs to the cruelty of Ottoman oppression. By his heavy-handed policies, the Ottoman governor aroused anti-Turkish sentiments of an intensity that his victims would surely not have inspired had they remained alive. With the proclamation of the Arab revolt in June 1916, their deaths took on a patriotic aura and became associated with the cause of Arab separatism.

For some, anger at these acts came to include the individual whose association with Jamal Pasha appeared to place him in a position of having been able to prevent the executions had he so wished. Arslan, the target of this damaging accusation, has gone to great lengths to defend himself from any charges of complicity in the hangings and to clarify his relationship with Jamal Pasha at the time. It is an intriguing portrait of a man close to the center of power but without the ability to influence events.

When the arrests of dignitaries began in 1915, Arslan, like others, thought they were merely temporary incarcerations for the purpose of extracting information. The hangings in August jolted him, and he became concerned for the lives of the several dozen notables who were imprisoned in Aley in late 1915 and early 1916. He claimed to have argued with Jamal Pasha about the sentences of death with such persistence that Jamal finally threatened Arslan's own life; to have attempted to get messages to Talaat in Istanbul about the dangers inherent in Jamal's policies; and to have warned Enver about the deteriorating situation during the latter's tour of inspection in Syria.[23] Arslan stated that his failure to change policy was not due to his lack of effort. He had pushed Jamal as hard as he felt he could, and when the governor ordered the executions, he was powerless to do anything.

Arslan's detractors have pointed out that he was not as helpless as he made himself out to be and that in cases where his own family was involved, he was able to influence Jamal Pasha's decisions. ʿAdil, the youngest of the Arslan brothers, was less circumspect in his associations than Shakib and became active in al-Fatat, one of the more prominent Arab secret societies. Some of the victims of the 1916 hangings were members of this organization, and ʿAdil was reputed to be a suspect. He was not arrested because of Shakib's closeness to Jamal.[24] The man of equivocal situations deplored revolt against the legally constituted authorities as he protected the members of his immediate family who may have countenanced such revolt.

Although he began to lose confidence in Jamal Pasha, Arslan's activities remained bound to the larger cause of Ottomanism, and his loyalties to the Ottoman state were not shaken by events in Syria. It was most likely this continuing pro-Ottoman stance which made him vulnerable to another accusation on the part of some Lebanese after the war, namely, that he did nothing to alleviate the suffering caused in Lebanon by the famine. It was a serious charge in the eyes of the accusers. With the loss of manpower through conscription and deportation and the confiscation of land and crops by the army of occupation, the civilian population of Syria and Lebanon faced terrible hardships during the war. Crops were further depleted by a plague of locusts in 1915 and this, combined with the collaboration of some Syrian merchants and Ottoman officials in withholding produce and the effective coastal blockade by the Allies, caused a famine which ravaged the region in the latter part of the war.[25]

Arslan, who left Syria in late 1916 and spent most of the following year in Istanbul, contended that he worked tirelessly in the Ottoman parliament and in private with Ottoman authorities to arrange for international relief organizations to distribute foodstuffs in Lebanon.[26] Given his earlier experiences with relief organizations, Arslan's defense in this instance appears fully justified. Why he should be singled out as especially responsible for the famine is not clear. As Touma shows, the blockade hurt his friends and family as much as it did the other inhabitants of Lebanon.[27] Yet, however farfetched the charge might be, it was damaging enough to stick with Arslan and become one of the factors establishing him as an accomplice of Jamal Pasha.

Throughout this discussion of Arslan's behavior during the first two years of the war, his position near the center of power has provided the major controversy. How did he let himself become entangled in such circumstances? Why did he not disassociate himself from Jamal Pasha? The answers to these questions can be found in Arslan's character, in his political and social beliefs, and in the special complexities of Mount Lebanon. Arslan was clearly a man of involvement. He could not, in this time of crisis, remain passive. Never, it seemed, did he let pass a chance for action. Not only was he involved in the political controversies outlined above, but he also devoted himself to other ventures, among them the organization of a volunteer force to protect the Lebanese and Syrian coast. His memoirs depict a man always on the move, constantly riding between various cities on some mission or another. The same source further reveals a man who believed deeply that he was engaged in a just cause. Throughout the war, Arslan's loyalty to the Ottoman state and the Islamic caliphate remained unshaken. Until the executions of 1915, he found no fault with Jamal Pasha's stringent security measures: "I was in complete accord with Jamal Pasha until he began this new policy of terror and oppression which I saw as a great danger to the future of the Ottoman state."[28]

This attention to the larger issues of state and religion at the possible expense of local concerns characterized Arslan's wartime outlook. Thus, when he criticized the Ottoman governor by writing that "the policy of Jamal Pasha in Syria was one of the greatest disasters for the Ottoman Empire and the Islamic *ummah*," he did not mention the starving countryside or the exiled notables.[29] His objection to Jamal's policies was not so much their severity as their failure; rather than preventing a split between Arabs and Turks, they caused one. As he complained to the commander in late 1915, "the policy of force is contrary to the interests of the Empire, and I fear its consequences."[30] Again and again, Arslan's arguments took this direction. For example, in his request to Enver Pasha to help arrange for the release of the second group of prisoners, he stated: "Some of those detained in Aley are my friends and some are my enemies, but that is not the issue. The only issue is the interest of the Empire and the community of Islam."[31]

Most often, Arslan explained his position, not as anti-Arab, which it was not, but as pro-Islamic. In this context, his response to the proclamation of the Arab revolt illustrates the consistency of his Ottomanism. He was furious with Sharif Husayn because he could not countenance an Arab revolt against what he considered the legitimate Islamic caliphate. What the Arab nationalist movement came to embrace as a struggle for liberation, Arslan always regarded as a treacherous act of separatism directly responsible for the postwar European occupation of the Arab provinces. Although he later made his peace with Faysal, he continued to regard Husayn as the perpetrator of an unforgivable crime, the splintering of the world of Islam.

Arslan's vision of a politically integrated Islamic community explains in part his relationship with Jamal Pasha. The Ottoman commander had a deep respect for the social observances of Islam: he was committed in the same way that Arslan was to the preservation of the Ottoman state, and he held sentiments on the political role of Islam which were nearly identical. For Jamal, Husayn's proclamation of the Arab revolt, in addition to its purely military and political implications, was "an offense against the unity and majesty of Islam."[32] The beliefs he shared with Jamal enabled Arslan to remain in Syria after the hangings of May 1916 and to permit his name to be associated with Jamal Pasha's propaganda newspaper, *al-Sharq*. The paper attempted to appeal to the Islamic sentiments within the Empire and to create an international Islamic front in support of the Ottoman caliphate.[33] At the local level, it was designed to bolster Jamal's increasingly unpopular policies in Syria. The Ottoman authorities sent German orientalists to Damascus to serve on the staff and to provide information about the benefits of the wartime alliance to Islamic peoples. A locally recruited editorship gave the publication respectability. Arslan was editor-in-chief, Muhammad Kurd ʿAli and ʿAbd al-Qadir al-Maghribi were editorial directors.

Al-Sharq appears to have been little more than propaganda for Jamal Pasha's policies. Arslan admitted that the central authorities destroyed the paper by dictating its content, and he resigned from the staff in late 1916. However, his association with this publication and the policies it defended—the announcements of, and justifications for, the hangings of May 1916 first appeared in a special issue of *al-Sharq*—was one more example of his collaboration with Jamal Pasha.

The year 1916 brought several changes in Arslan's life. For one thing, he made the decision at age forty-seven, relatively late even by the standards of Arab society, to get married. His bride, Salima, was at least twenty years younger.[34] Born in the Caucasus region of Russia, she fled the tsarist persecution of Muslims when she was very young, first going with her family to al-Salt in present-day Jordan, and then settling in Istanbul, where she met Arslan. Although Salima spoke little Arabic at the time, she was married to the future prince of eloquence in Beirut in the summer of 1916. Their son Ghalib was born in Aley the following year. In the convention of Arab autobiographers, Arslan has not revealed his feelings about his wife. However, their marriage was marked by long periods of separation, by financial difficulties, and by a husband possibly more concerned with his public image than his familial duties.

Even their initial time together was short. In late 1916, Arslan went to Istanbul to resume his activities in the Ottoman parliament. He never lived permanently in Syria again. Nevertheless, as suggested at the beginning of this chapter, his reputation among many Arabs was based on their perceptions of his actions during the somewhat less than two years from December 1914 to the autumn of 1916. Mixed with the praise of later years was a sense of unease about Arslan's wartime associations. It was as though those who wished to extol him had to clear their consciences of what they had heard about his activities in Syria, and his supporters took occasion, either in their memoirs or in various responses to particular events, to present detailed statements of Arslan's well-intentioned efforts during the war.[35] Yet in these writings, too, there is a note of caution, a kind of apologia for the period 1914–1916 when, as one of his admirers later wrote, "he was for the Turks and Germans. . . ."[36]

During the final two years of the war, Arslan's activities were markedly different than during the Syrian period. The physical rigors of one existence were exchanged for the more cosmopolitan duties of parliamentary representative and European emissary. For most of 1917, Arslan was in Istanbul tending to his responsibilities in the Ottoman parliament. Later in that year, and again in mid-1918, he undertook special missions to Germany at the request of Enver Pasha.[37] Enver felt that by sending a trusted personal envoy, he could obtain information not normally available through the regular channels of the German-Ottoman alliance. His main concern was with the German attitude toward the eastern territories of the Empire, a region in which he had long been especially interested. Arslan successfully made the transition from the Shuf to Wilhelminian circles. With his refined manners and his political adroitness, he established contacts with the diplomatic and academic community which he cultivated in the years to come. As an inveterate journalist, he also used these missions to propagandize the Ottoman cause among the German public and to argue for the continuation of the German-Ottoman alliance.[38]

At the final triumph of the Arab revolt, the entry of Faysal's troops into Damascus in October 1918, Arslan was in Berlin acting for the Ottoman cause. As the collapse of the Empire appeared imminent, he made a strenuous effort to return to the Middle East and was en route on the Black Sea when the armistice of Mudros was signed in November, signaling the surrender of the Ottoman Empire to the Allies. The direction of Arslan's journey suddenly changed. At the port of Nikolaev he encountered a group of Arabs, including his close friend ʿAbd al-ʿAziz Jawish, fleeing Istanbul after discovering that their wartime loyalty to the CUP government could now land them in prison.[39] Arslan decided that he, too, might be in danger in British-occupied Istanbul, and he joined the political refugees in their difficult journey through Russia to Berlin. He then went on to Switzerland, where he passed uneasily the first of what would become twenty-eight years of exile. In his memoirs, Arslan wrote of how Enver had told him, when he left on his second mission to Germany in the late summer of 1918, that it should only require one month. But, he wistfully noted, "I have been in Europe ever since."[40]

Until 1919, Arslan had flourished as a leading member of the Arab-Ottoman elite. It was an elite to which he belonged by birth, but he had not contented himself with inherited status. His career was characterized by dedicated service, distinguished literary achievement, and a share of political manipulation. If he was more public in his pursuits than most, it was not just because he wished to display his talents, but because he believed that duty required an active personal commitment. His commitment was to the preservation of the Ottoman Empire and the Islamic order for which it stood.

He had belonged to that order and had benefited from it. But now, at age fifty—his devotion to the legally constituted state the cause of his exile—he seemed a marginal figure. He would recover and rise to international prominence, but in 1919 it was not clear how.

In all ways, Arslan was made quite rootless by the Ottoman defeat, and he found adjustment to the changed circumstances particularly difficult. He was slow to recognize the finality of the Ottoman collapse and seemed unable to comprehend the new forces which were claiming the loyalties of former Ottoman subject peoples. Superimposed on the dislocations of personal identity, which found him grasping for an era that had passed, were the physical dislocations of exile. His wife and son remained in Lebanon while he sought a place to settle and a resolution of his dual Ottoman-Arab heritage.

After passing most of 1919 in Switzerland, he returned to Berlin. Although Berlin remained his base until late in 1924, he was never really in one place for very long. Even among the exiles, his postwar odyssey was a tortuous one, and his frequent lack of direction was especially disconcerting to one who had always been so sure of his place. For seven rootless years, he wandered between Western Europe and the East, from Lausanne to Moscow, from Rome to Istanbul, always sure of his anti-imperial, pan-Islamic stance, but caught peculiarly between emergent Arabism and a twilight Ottomanism as represented by the CUP in exile.

This is not to say that he was untouched by the Arab protest movements which were forming at the time. His gradual involvement in political Arabism is examined in the following chapter. Here the concern is with the other and, at the time, more persistent stream of his identity as it was manifested during a period which other biographers have ignored because it reflects Arslan's lingering pro-Ottoman preferences.

After his successful flight from the Black Sea in November 1918, Arslan made no further attempts to return to his family in Lebanon. In part, he was prevented from doing so by Great Power politics and in part by his own predilections. His first eighteen months as an exile corresponded, not to the French Mandate over Syria, but to the brief moment when the political aims of the Arab revolt seemed to be fulfilled in Faysal's Damascus. To the new Arab Kingdom came many of the Arab elite, irrespective of their wartime loyalties. Arslan remained in Europe; in the immediate aftermath of the war, he continued to hope for an Ottoman restoration and was not yet prepared to commit himself to a purely Arab political movement.

He was not alone in his pro-Ottoman orientation. The core of the CUP leadership had fled Istanbul on a German gunboat before the

Allied occupation. Under Talaat's direction, they reassembled in Berlin, where they mounted a determined bid to return to power.[41] Other supporters of the Young Turk regime, scattered from Geneva to Moscow, from Malta to Eastern Anatolia, also dreamed of resurrecting the political, social, and moral foundations of the Ottoman system and of resuming the positions they had enjoyed within it. Unrealistic as these hopes may appear in the light of later developments, the contest between Mustafa Kemal and the old CUP leadership for the control of postwar Turkey was close indeed. None wished more strongly for a reemergence than Arslan. Although a full discussion of the postwar Young Turk movement lies outside the scope of this study, Arslan's special relationship to it requires explanation. His vision of the future was bound to the past through his commitment to the CUP objectives.

A CUP restoration appeared feasible for two reasons: the chaotic circumstances prevailing within Anatolia following the armistice of Mudros; and the desires of Germany and Russia to derail the postwar settlement which was taking shape. The CUP leaders were sheltered in Berlin by the German military establishment and encouraged by the Bolshevik government, which provided them with subventions.[42] The latter relationship was established by Enver Pasha, who believed that the nascent independence movements of the lightly governed Muslim peoples on the southern border of Russia could, if properly channeled, provide direct military assistance to the restoration. Since these movements were, in 1920, directed against the Allied occupation of the Caucasus, the Bolsheviks, their own military capabilities severely strained, could support Enver's schemes. In early 1920, Enver announced from Moscow the formation of a "Union of Islamic Revolutionary Societies" designed to act as a kind of Muslim revolutionary international; and at the Baku Congress of Islamic Peoples, held in September 1920, he presented a statement in the name of Islamic revolutionary movements from Morocco to India.[43]

This calculated use of an aroused Islamic sentiment explains, in part, Arslan's attraction to the CUP restoration. Islamic political resurgence linked to anti-imperialism was a cause he had long made his own. That he should continue to support it and lend his still remarkable energies to it was to have been expected. Equally expected, but nonetheless striking, was his espousal of this cause in association with the discredited CUP. While most politically sensitive Arabs—and Turks—were quick to break their ties with the CUP leaders, Arslan remained an integral part of their circle, and it was with them, not with Arab politicians, that he kept his closest associations in the years immediately following the war.

With support from Talaat, Arslan was elected president of the Berlin Oriental Club, an organization designed to bring together Muslims from all regions of the world. Even in this activity, his identification with the CUP was such that a British Foreign Office report of 1921 described him as "president of the Oriental Club and leader of the Turkish Nationalists in Berlin since the death of Talaat."[44] From the references Arslan made to the club, it appears that the exiles passed much of their time there plotting their return to power. The impression also lingers that their actual accomplishments were negligible. Despite their ambitious schemes, they were a pathetic group, ridden by fears of extradition, living under assumed names, dreaming hopeless dreams of restoration, and hounded by the problems which beset all political refugees—what to do, where to settle, how to survive. Given this oppressive atmosphere, it is not surprising that the flamboyant escapades of Enver Pasha in the Caucasus caught their attention and, among some at least, kindled hopes of a return to power on the crest of a militant Islam again triumphant.

Arslan was one of Enver's most ardent admirers. He had been particularly drawn to the Young Turk leader from their first encounter in Libya and remained committed to his memory long after his death.[45] For a time, their lives were linked in an unusual association of literary aristocrat and military adventurer. What they shared was political naiveté and the belief that an aroused Islamic sentiment could be coherently directed so as to become a major factor in international relations. In a letter written to Mustafa Kemal on 16 July 1921, Enver asserted: "As for me, I shall follow only an ideal. And that is to rally the Moslems and come to grips with the European monsters who are crushing Islam."[46] This was Arslan's lifelong ideal as well. Although he occasionally recognized the recklessness of Enver's schemes, he was hopelessly captivated by Enver's hero-image. He even undertook an arduous journey to Moscow in June 1921 at Enver's urging. Although Arslan said very little about the trip, British Foreign Office documents assert that he met with Chicherin and discussed the politics of the Caucasus region.[47] An unanticipated result of the trip was to give Arslan the reputation of being a Communist sympathizer.

Soon after he returned to Berlin in July 1921, the CUP restoration began to collapse. Enver's hopes for a military demonstration of CUP strength in Anatolia were dashed by the Kemalists' victory over the Greek invaders and the consolidation of their own military position. At the same time, the Bolsheviks lost their enthusiasm for mobilized Islamic armies roaming their southern flanks and sent the Red Army to occupy the area instead. Enver nevertheless remained consistent in his pursuit of desperate Islamic causes; he died leading a cavalry charge against a Red Army force in August 1922. His death grieved Arslan deeply, but also served, in conjunction with other events, to bring home to him the futility of his hopes for a full Ottoman restoration.

In Europe, too, the leadership of the CUP exiles was decimated as the hatred generated by their most notorious wartime policy turned on them; Armenian gunmen found vengeance on the streets of Berlin, where they assassinated Talaat in March 1921 and Dr. Azmi and Dr. Bahaeddin Şakir in 1922. In Rome, the former Unionist grand vezir, Mehmed Said Halim, was killed in 1921, and in distant Tiflis, Jamal Pasha, the ruthless wartime governor of Syria, became yet another victim of Armenian assassins in 1922. These deaths effectively destroyed the refugee movement for the restoration. Moreover, the situation in Anatolia was no longer in flux. Mustafa Kemal abolished the Ottoman sultanate in November 1922 and gained diplomatic recognition for his republic through the Treaty of Lausanne in July 1923.

Arslan responded to these changes by turning his attention more and more to the issue of European occupation of the former Ottoman Arab provinces. He did not immediately discard his hopes for an Islamic-based movement; he merely reoriented them to center around Turkish-Arab cooperation. He made his first postwar visit to Istanbul in late 1923 in an effort to create a common Arab-Turkish front to drive the French from Syria. However, Mustafa Kemal rejected the appeals of those who urged him to reestablish Ottoman boundaries in non-Turkish-speaking lands. Arslan then settled in the Turkish city of Mersin, near the Syrian border, where he spent the first eight months of 1924. There are overtones of intrigue in his choice of location, and French intelligence reported that he was the acknowledged leader of Arab revolutionary committees in Damascus and Aleppo.[48] In this instance, the French information is incorrect. Arslan's behavior in Mersin supports the decidedly apolitical explanation he gave for his presence there: "I hoped to see my family and friends, some of whom I feared might die before I could return, especially my mother and brother. Since my mother could not come to Europe, and I could not enter Syria, Palestine, or even Egypt, I . . . went to Mersin in order to be as close as possible to Syria to facilitate my mother's trip."[49]

The family reunion took place in the spring of 1924, and Arslan wrote of his pleasure at seeing his mother and being reunited with his wife and son after a separation of six years.[50] For one of the few times in his married life, Arslan devoted his full attention to Ghalib, taking care of his upbringing and planning his education. Yet the restless Amir was unsuited for an idyllic family life. Although he had chosen to live in Mersin for its promise of tranquillity as well as its proximity to Syria, he soon found himself chafing at the isolation imposed by residence in southern Turkey. Petulantly, he complained to Rashid Rida about the constraints of small-town living: "If I were to wear a kaftan to the market place, no one would notice. Weeks go by without my having any visitors . . . and in five months I have been to only one banquet."[51]

Uncomfortable with his exclusion from political influence, Arslan left his family and returned to Europe for several months in the late summer of 1924. He established new contacts with the Arab exile community in Switzerland and cemented his relations with German officials in Berlin.[52] By January 1925, he was back in Mersin. Although he remained there for another eight months, he did not intend to adopt a permanent residence so far removed from the centers of political, and social, activity. When the Syrian revolt against the French Mandate broke out in the summer of 1925, exiles in Cairo and Europe proposed a delegation to represent Syria's interests before the League of Nations. Arslan regarded the matter as "a pressing urgency" and decided to return to Europe.[53]

Whatever Arslan's residence in Mersin may have intended, it came to mark a turning point in his break with Ottomanism and his growing identification with political Arabism. After the period in Mersin, he formed new, primarily Arab associations, and took part in a type of political activity which called for an orientation to the future, not the past. He did not abandon his preferences for an Islamic union against imperialism, but he did refocus his political concerns with an emphasis, not on an Ottoman restoration, but on activities more closely associated with the Arab militants whose cause he had once found distasteful. To do this successfully, he had to establish his own credentials as an Arab Muslim and to shed his reputation as an accomplice of Jamal Pasha. It was a formidable task; it was also a very public one and brought Arslan the attention which he needed.

CHAPTER THREE.
ADOPTION OF THE ARAB CAUSE

When the dust cloud was dispersed, when the secrets among
the allies were exposed, and when my former opponents
learned that what I had predicted had actually come to pass,
they returned and placed their hands in mine and relied on
me. —Arslan[1]

It is not the quality of the master which interests the
Syrians, but the question of being their own masters.
—Arslan[2]

THE PRINCIPAL focus of Shakib Arslan's personal commitment in the immediate aftermath of World War I was on the restoration of the Ottoman system, and, as set forth in the preceding
chapter, his associations were mainly with the once-powerful rulers
of that system. There were, however, events within the former Arab
provinces which also demanded Arslan's attention and drew him
into the orbit of Arab as well as Turkish exiles. The establishment of
the Mandate system in Syria and Palestine created major disruptions
in the customary pattern of administrative relationships in the region and caused a realignment in the political associations of the
leading individuals and families. Even while he was in Berlin, Arslan
was touched by the dismantling of the old system in the Arab East.

No sooner had France asserted control over Mandated Syria with
the capture of Damascus and the dissolution of Faysal's kingdom in
July 1920 than it implemented what Stephen H. Longrigg has in-
triguingly termed "a multi-statal structure" and others have called a
policy of divide and rule.[3] Although the reorganization of territories
was a constant feature of the Mandate until independence, the basic
administrative divisions were drawn in 1920. The main beneficiaries
were the Maronites of Lebanon. French policy ensured that they, and
other Christians, would not be dominated by the Sunnites of Damascus. This was done by the creation of an autonomous Greater
Lebanon within which the Maronites formed the largest single
grouping. They did not, however, form a confessional majority of the
population, for the old *mutasarrifiyyah* was joined to the predomi-

nantly Muslim areas of Beirut, Sidon, the Biqa, and other regions which had been at the heart of traditional Syrian political, commercial, and agricultural life. The Syrian core was further truncated by the establishment of the state of the Alawis in the important coastal district of Latakia, the government of the Jabal Druze in the Hawran, and the state of Syria around the cities of Damascus, Aleppo, Homs, and Hama, centers which became isolated from the traditional outlets for their products. Of course, the British Mandate in Palestine represented the separation of yet another region from what many Arabs had regarded as Greater Syria.

These territorial divisions gave rise to diverse responses among the Arab leaders within and outside the Mandated areas. The Maronites were generally satisfied with French protection and saw their interests best served by the preservation of Greater Lebanon. It is probably also true that many Syrian Muslim notables were prepared to work within the Mandate framework so long as their traditional status could be maintained. However, in Damascus, and especially among the officials remaining from Faysal's government, there were strong pan-Arabist sentiments as well as genuine feelings of anger and frustration at the imposition of the Mandate, the loss of political independence, and the arbitrary division of territory.

French Mandate authorities further alienated Syrian nationalists and local notables alike by their heavy-handed officialdom. It was an all-pervasive imperial presence, from the several French *conseillers* to each ministry in each of the four states of Syria to the array of technical advisers and the detested Services Speciaux, a military information unit which acquired a far-reaching influence in the Mandate.[4] As the British gradually relaxed their hold on the Iraqi Mandate to the point where it was granted independence in 1932, French policy in Syria was increasingly resented by the nationalist elite there who felt their state was far more prepared for self-government than was the awkward amalgamation of underdeveloped provinces which formed Iraq.

To individual members of the Syrian political and intellectual classes, French policies were often painfully disruptive. From the start, the Mandatory authorities adopted the practice of banishment and death sentences for nationalists.[5] Most of the members of Faysal's two cabinets, as well as the officers who had fought in the Arab revolt, were, at one time or another, arrested or convicted in absentia. In these conditions, the number of Syrian political refugees swelled, and the organizations in exile increased. As the Syrian elite had fled the oppressiveness of the Hamidian regime for the relative tolerance of Cromer's Egypt in the last two decades of the nineteenth century, so they again congregated in Cairo, where they founded journals as their predecessors had done and organized committees of protest. They were also active in the cities of Europe, especially Paris and Berlin, in Buenos Aires, and in Detroit and New York, "where they ceased not to judge, usually on fragmentary and biased information, the public affairs of their old homes and to send telegrams to Geneva, Paris or Beirut in advocacy of any or all of the possible policies for Syria and Lebanon."[6]

For the student of modern Middle Eastern history, this change of circumstances represents a crucial juncture. From the perspective of an examination of the Ottoman Arab political and social elite, it is a change especially, although by no means solely, germane to that Arab generation born from roughly the mid-1860s to the mid-1880s, men who had had time to establish career patterns and possibly achieve distinction within the Ottoman Empire; men for whom the Empire was a fact of life and the sultan-caliph a focus of loyalty. After 1919, this generation had to adapt to the disappearance of the Empire, to the presence of British and French imperial administrators, to the abolition of the caliphate and the division of the *patrie*, to the elimination, in effect, of the institutions and symbols by which they had defined themselves. Some rebelled, some compromised to await better days, and others became exiles by Mandatory decree or émigrés by personal choice.

Arslan was a prominent member of the latter category. This chapter explores the second and decisive part of his postwar adjustment and his reemergence as an influential spokesman for the Arab-Islamic cause. Through a combination of personal initiative and timely publicity, he became more than just another banished member of the old regime. As organizer of societies, president of congresses, mentor of young nationalists, prolific journalist, and Syrian representative to the League of Nations, he united in his person the movements of Arab, Islamic, and colonial discontent. It was not a status easily attained. For one thing, the role of spokesman for a particularly Arab political and national viewpoint did not come naturally to him. Nor was he at first seen as a welcome recruit to the Arab cause. Before he could become a dominant figure in the Arab exile movement, he had to come to terms with the failure of Ottomanism and recast his pan-Ottoman identity into a more suitable Arab mold.

His pro-Ottoman stance before and during the war was not in itself an insurmountable problem, given the careers of men like Muhammad Kurd 'Ali, Sati' al-Husri, Yasin al-Hashimi, and many others who became closely identified with either pan-Arab or regional nationalisms despite their earlier support for Ottomanism. Arslan's position in this regard was initially made more difficult by his linger-ing attachment to the old form of association. His final shift of alle-giance was facilitated by the collapse of the CUP movement and the simple reality that there was no Ottoman government to restore. And the very policies of the new Turkish state forced him to de-nounce it. There was no room for cooperation between a staunch ad-vocate of the caliphate like Arslan and the vigorous state secularism of Atatürk. He was, therefore, driven to seek an Arab identity, albeit one defined by Islam.

In the early 1920s, he issued an occasional pronouncement on Arab matters, the most notable of which was a proclamation of 1923 calling for the creation of an Arab league to combat the weakness inherent in the existence of several individual states.[7] Further to but-tress his claim as a representative of Arabism, Arslan often exploited a statement allegedly made to him in a letter from King Faysal in which the then monarch of Iraq proclaimed: "I affirm that you were the first of the Arabs to speak to me on the issue of Arab unity."[8] Out of context, Faysal's statement could be interpreted as attributing to Arslan an early program for the political unity of the several Arab states carved out of the Ottoman Empire. More likely, it refers to sentiments similar to those he expressed in an article entitled "The Hour of Unity Approaches, O Arabs," which has a much narrower focus than its title suggests, being confined to the personalities of the Arabian peninsula.[9]

Despite these and other affirmations of his concern for the Arab cause, it was not until Arslan settled permanently in Switzerland and accepted responsibility for representing the Syrian cause at the League of Nations that he made a concerted effort to gain acceptance as a purely Arab spokesman. It is not coincidence that a series of ar-ticles on his own Arabness appeared at this time. They indicate that he saw his Druze origins to be more of an impediment to his accep-tance in his new role than his Ottomanism had been. He thus went to extreme lengths to assert the Arabness of the Druzes and to elimi-nate any suspicions of Druze exclusiveness or religious deviation. His arguments were more assertive than conclusive. He claimed for the Druze an Arabic speech unrivaled in its excellence outside the Arabian peninsula. He also asserted that Druzes and Arabs were identical in appearance, a fact which had been observed by no less a personage than "my teacher, Muhammad ʿAbduh."[10] He was es-pecially careful to link the Druze, as a religious grouping, to the Fatimid Ismailis and so assert the inherently Islamic character of Druze beliefs. He stressed the community's observance of orthodox Islamic practices and its reliance on the Qurʾan. His emphasis was such as to gloss over the significance of the clandestine ritual and the supplementary texts.[11] However forced these arguments may appear, they did reflect Arslan's own preferences. His entire life was a repudiation of Druze exclusivity, and his marriage outside the community was a sharp break with preferred custom. Although his princely title rested with the political prestige of his family as Druze, he was remarkably successful in establishing himself as an orthodox Muslim serving the interests of Sunni Islam. When Arslan returned briefly to the Levant in 1937, the French high commissioner reported that some members of the Lebanese Druze community reproached the Amir "for his apparent conversion to Islam [sic]."[12] His Azharite biographer, Ahmad al-Sharabasi, while sensitive to the sectarian ambivalence of Arslan's position, concludes: "Amir Shakib was a Sunni."[13]

Rashid Rida played the major role in reintegrating Arslan with the Arab leaders who had been alienated by his wartime policies. Rida had known Arslan since 1895. The two men were fond of one another, admired Muhammad 'Abduh's reformist Islam, and believed that his doctrines could be implemented in postwar society. They had a terrible disagreement over Rida's support for the Ottoman Decentralization Society ("the enemies of the Empire," in Arslan's view), but their friendship was restored after the war.[14]

Much as the CUP had hoped to exploit Arslan's status in 1913, so Rida wished to utilize his potential in the postwar climate. He knew Arslan to be a skillful publicist, a bold and forthright personality, and a man who shared his views; such a figure should not be allowed to dissipate his energies in shadowy plots in Berlin and Mersin. Rida brought him into the mainstream of the Arab resistance and, until his death in 1935, watched over him, publishing several of his books, despairing at times over his intransigence, but always protecting him, for Arslan was not only a friend, but an effective spokesman for Arab independence and Islamic revival. As their association deepened, each benefited from it.

Rida made the first gesture of reconciliation. During the period of Faysal's Syrian kingdom, he wrote to Arslan in Berlin, saying: "The past is over. Let us meet and agree on ways of dealing with the present."[15] This process of rehabilitation was carried further by the Syro-Palestinian Congress held in Geneva in the late summer of 1921. The Congress was the first manifestation of organized Arab protest following the imposition of the French Mandate in Syria and was called in order to formulate a coherent stance against the Mandate system and to decide how best to present it to the League of Nations.[16]

The driving force behind the organization and funding of the Congress was Prince Michel Lutfallah, a wealthy Greek Orthodox merchant-landowner from the Syrian community in Egypt. His father, Habib Pasha, was an individual of great entrepreneurial boldness who accumulated a fortune as a merchant and a moneylender. He used his wealth to purchase vast cotton acreages and became one of Egypt's largest and wealthiest landowners.[17] He was made a pasha by the Egyptian government and, in the final year of his long life, was granted the hereditary title *amir* by Sharif Husayn Ibn ʿAli on the basis of that dignitary's shaky authority as king of the Arabs. Thus, in addition to leaving his three sons vast wealth, he also left them useful titles. This combination gave one French journalist the impression that the Lutfallahs "are reproached for their fortune, which is considerable, their rise to noble status, which is *trop récent*, and their ambition, which has been called overweening."[18] Michel (b. circa 1880), the eldest son and the one with whom Arslan had the most sustained contact, was an active leader of the Syrian community in Cairo and, after the war, a vigorous organizer for the cause of Syrian independence.

The Congress proved to be of the utmost importance for Arslan. He was elected its secretary and used that office to emerge as a prominent figure in exile circles. Lutfallah was elected president, Rashid Rida vice-president. The latter two, along with a shifting bloc of other exiles including Asʿad Daghir, formed the standing Executive Committee of the Congress and worked in Cairo. The Congress also decided to establish a permanent European delegation which could represent the Syrian and Palestinian people before the League of Nations. Arslan, Ihsan al-Jabiri, and Sulayman Bey Kinʿan, a Lebanese Maronite, were chosen for this task.[19] The remainder of Arslan's life became closely interwoven with al-Jabiri's, and service to the Syro-Palestinian Delegation defined their careers for much of the interwar period.

From a distinguished Aleppine family, al-Jabiri (1882–1980) was as established as the Lutfallahs were nouveau and as imbued with the ideal of service to the Ottoman state as they were with personal political ambition. After a legal education in Istanbul and Paris, al-Jabiri presided over the municipality of Aleppo and later served in the sultan's palace as secretary to the two successors of Abdulhamid. His sophisticated ways led Faysal to appoint him chamberlain in the Syrian kingdom. When the French took Damascus in July 1920, al-Jabiri accompanied Faysal in his escape to Europe and then joined the exile groups there. Not considered as personally forceful as

The Syro-Palestinian Congress, Geneva, 1921. Seated, from left: Sulayman Kin'an, Rashid Rida, Michel Lutfallah, Tu'an 'Imad, Tawfiq Hamad, Arslan; standing, from left: Ihsan al-Jabiri, Shibli Jumal, Najib Shaqir, Amin al-Tamimi.

Arslan, he nevertheless served the Syro-Palestinian cause with dedication and was, in Arslan's words, "my companion in arms in the patriotic struggle which we undertook together."[20]

Arslan himself engaged in a variety of protest activities which brought him an increasingly high level of recognition from both his compatriots and his European adversaries. In May 1922, he addressed the Congress of the League of Oppressed Peoples in Genoa on the need for closer ties with disinterested powers such as Italy; in July he was in London to protest the League of Nations decision to endorse the dual Mandate for Syria and Palestine; and in August he appeared in Rome seeking Italian support at the League of Nations.[21] An Arab activist who maintained a residence in Berlin could not avoid the scrutiny of British and French representatives. The British ambassador in Rome reported the presence of the Syro-Palestinian delegation at the Islamic Union Congress, and Lord d'Abernon in Berlin kept a close watch on the movements of the Syrian refugees in that city, identifying Arslan as their leader and expressing the opinion that they were funded from Switzerland.[22] Arslan was still seen as a Turcophile by British officials, and the Foreign Office's interest in him had as much to do with his perceived influence on events in Eastern Anatolia and the Caucasus as it did with Arab Asia.

However, his stance during the Syrian revolt of 1925–1926 placed Arslan decisively at the forefront of the Arab cause in the minds of his own compatriots and of European leaders. The revolt was a major event in the postwar Arab world. Combined as it was with the simultaneous success of ʿAbd al-Krim's movement in Morocco, it threw briefly into question the strength of the French imperial edifice. Although Syrian publicists successfully portrayed the different uprisings within Syria as a unified nationalist crusade, the motives and objectives of the Syrian participants exhibited considerable diversity. The partisans of Sultan Atrash, the Druze chieftain who initiated the revolt in the Jabal Druze in July 1925, sought Druze autonomy and the preservation of the feudal nobility against the modernizing trends of the Mandate administration; the urban notables of Aleppo, Homs, and Hama saw French policies as a threat to their traditional bases of power and prestige; and nationalist intellectuals centered in Damascus called for outright independence and the creation of a Syrian Arab nation.[23] Yet even if the revolt was prompted by different grievances from different segments of the population, it achieved some notable successes in its early stages. The French garrison was forced to withdraw from the Jabal Druze, and by the autumn of 1925 there was sporadic insurgence on the outskirts of Damascus.

Frustrated by their inability to contain the uprising, French forces engaged in one of the most ill-conceived displays of force in all of their imperial wars. For two days beginning on the evening of 18 October 1925, Damascus was subjected to an intense air and artillery bombardment which severely damaged the old city and killed many of its civilian inhabitants. The ensuing outcry over the desecration of a revered Arab Islamic city spread beyond the borders of Syria and reinforced the anti-European protests of other Muslim peoples. The Cairo weekly *al-Shura* headlined, "France Destroys Damascus as the Mongols Did Baghdad."[24] Nor did it escape the notice of the committed militants that the rebellion of ʿAbd al-Krim in the Rif Mountains of Morocco had achieved stunning successes against the Spanish forces and was, by the late summer of 1925, spilling over the protectorate boundaries into the French zone and threatening Fez itself.

In response to the Syrian revolt, the European delegation of the Syro-Palestinian Congress was reactivated in August 1925. Arslan was asked to resume his leadership of the delegation and was encouraged by Rashid Rida to return from Mersin to Switzerland. He realized that if he wished to play an important role in the Arab cause, this was his opportunity.[25] For all his desire to restore his reputation, he knew how disruptive the change would be. He was always an outsider in Europe, an individual for whom neither the intellectual achievements nor the material delights of Western civilization held any noticeable attraction. But Mersin provided no scope for his energy, his ambition, or his vanity. In September 1925, he returned to Switzerland, and in the following year he brought his wife and son from Mersin, rented a small house in Lausanne, and began that phase of his career which bestowed on him the title *mujahid al-sharq fi al-gharb*, the warrior of the East in the West.[26]

As the policies of the Mandatory power came under close international scrutiny, Arslan, as an official spokesman of one of the few organized Syrian groups in Europe, reaped a publicity windfall that brought him into public prominence in Europe and the Middle East. His association with the Syrian question at the League of Nations also presented him with the opportunity to demonstrate his patriotism and to win final reinstatement in Arab circles. His return to prominence was not due to good timing alone. Once he committed his emotions and his reputation to the cause of Syria at the League of Nations, that cause received considerable visibility. In an interview given in 1929, Arslan explained his technique:

> The Syrian case is pending political appeal before the grand jury of the League of Nations. This is so that foreigners will not use the silence of the Syrians as evidence of their satisfaction with the current situation. Customarily, the victim does not content himself with appealing to the court alone; he accompanies his legal defense with propaganda and pamphlets alerting public opinion to his affliction. Praise be to God that the Syrian delegation is doing its duty before the courts and public opinion. The Syrian case is alive and well. Whenever the nations meet in Geneva, France finds herself face to face with the Syrian delegation.[27]

Arslan's interpretation of the rights of a defendant might cause some unease in legal circles, but his description of the breadth of his activities was accurate. Indeed, the observations of the editor of *al-Shura* are not, in this case, exaggerated: "In truth, since arriving in Switzerland, our great man has spared no effort in serving his fatherland. No door exists upon which he has not knocked."[28] No other individual from a Mandated territory is mentioned in the minutes of the Permanent Mandates Commission for the 1920s with such frequency as Arslan. He and al-Jabiri, through the volume of their petitions and their tenacity in obtaining appointments, forced the Commission always to be aware of the Syro-Palestinian delegation. As the vice-chairman remarked, "Each of the members of the Commission had heard them privately."[29] Even though the delegation did not actually have any Palestinian members, it interpreted its mission as embracing the Palestinian as well as the Syrian question. While Syria was given first priority in 1925–1926, the delegation, directed as it was by the Ottoman-era figures of Arslan and al-Jabiri, soon expanded its concern to include "south Syria." Arslan thus placed himself in the position of being one of the first Arabs to present the Palestinian case to the world at large. As long as he was seen to have the support of the exile politicians and of some portion of the population of Syria and Palestine, he was treated seriously in Europe and had an impact on the agenda of the Commission.

His most effective moments were probably at the beginning of his period of representation. Although the Syro-Palestinian delegation had no official international sanction, the Commission was so disturbed by the Syrian revolt and the French policies which may have caused it that Arslan and the petitions of his delegation were given more consideration than was later the case. During its session of October 1925, the Commission decided not to receive the annual French report on Syria until it had been updated to include the background to the revolt and other specific information on the treatment of the Syrian population. The new information would then be discussed at a special session of the Commission, scheduled for Rome in February 1926. By the end of the October meeting, Arslan's petitions had been noted in the minutes and he was seriously regarded as the spokesman for Syria in Europe. Henry de Jouvenal, before departing for Beirut to take up his new appointment as high commissioner in November 1925, asked Arslan, as the leader of the delegation, to come to Paris to discuss the Syrian situation with him. The prestige provided Arslan by de Jouvenal's gesture was immense. *Al-Shura* headlined, somewhat misleadingly, "France Invites al-Amir Shakib Arslan to Paris to Negotiate Syrian Affairs."[30]

Although these particular discussions produced no signed agreements, on the basis of the exposure the delegation had received, Arslan expected to obtain a hearing before the full Commission when it met in an extraordinary session in Rome. He, al-Jabiri, and Najib al-Armajani established themselves there and asked to be heard as "the duly appointed delegates of the Syrian nation."[31] This request sparked a lengthy debate and showed the Commission at its most cautious. Finally, by an inflexible reliance on procedures, the Commission drafted a reply to Arslan which briefly and flatly stated,

"The Commission considers that the circumstances do not permit it to accede to your request."[32] Although the presence of the delegation in Rome kept it in the public eye, its failure to be admitted to the hearings must have been insulting and disappointing to Arslan. The Commission's final report was equally frustrating. After hearing the French presentation, the Commission noted that while certain practices of the French Mandatory authorities could be criticized, the Syrians were not yet ready for "the strenuous conditions" of independence, and all parties should attempt to cooperate for the smooth functioning of the Mandate.[33]

Events in Syria mirrored the decisions taken at Rome. By the summer of 1926, the revolt was effectively over and the French Mandate authority settled firmly on the region for the next twenty years. But the positions taken by various Syrian and Lebanese groups in the course of the uprising had continuing repercussions among the exiles and the political leaders within the region alike. Close connections existed between these two groups, and important decisions were often made in Cairo or Europe because that is where France forced many of the most active politicians to live. Theirs was not an exile against an established independent regime which they wished to overthrow; Arslan was no Lenin. He was an aristocratic politician banished from a society which had not been overturned, but was simply occupied by an alien power. Thus, while he was outside his homeland, he was not external to its politics. This was true of his brother, 'Adil, of al-Jabiri, and of other banished figures as well. For example, two members of the Syro-Palestinian delegation in Europe eventually assumed important local offices, Riyad al-Sulh as prime minister of Lebanon in 1943 and al-Jabiri as governor of Latakia in 1937. In the circumstances peculiar to Syria, Lebanon, and Palestine in the 1920s and 1930s, a figure like Arslan, with entrenched local interests and an established prewar reputation, could represent territories in which he was not permitted to live. Exile politics marked Arslan for the rest of his life, but they were conducted not only in the volatile exile milieu, but for control of Greater Syria.

Because of his assumption that he was the principal Eastern Arab negotiator with the European powers, Arslan was assured of extensive coverage by the Arab press. Such attention also guaranteed that he would be the subject, once again, of extensive criticism. Many of the controversies in which he became embroiled were trivial or personal, but they had to be dealt with if his views on more significant matters were to have credence. During the collapse of the CUP movement in Berlin, Arslan had presumably become aware of the need for an exile to appear to have strong support within his homeland as well as among his fellow expatriates in order to be effective. The struggle for influence was a perpetual feature of the exiles' existence. It began with the Syrian revolt, but had its origins in the fabric of Syro-Lebanese society.

Under the Ottoman system, the geographical and political divisions among the traditional Syrian elite had been absorbed within the larger imperial framework. With the creation of a distinct political entity, those divisions turned inward and fed upon themselves to the detriment of the formation of a cohesive nationalist movement.[34] Strong regional affiliations within the state formed one dimension of intra-elite conflict. But so did the uncertain boundaries of the Syrian state itself. Was it to have a separate, independent existence? Was it to include Lebanon? Or was it to serve as the core for an even larger Arab state within which Syrian nationalism would be subsumed? In the aftermath of the revolt of 1925–1926, these issues remained unresolved, especially the problem of local identification, which was exacerbated by the French policy of divide and rule.

These divisions were mirrored in the politics of the exile organizations and were further intensified by the individual ambitions of the various personalities involved. This was especially evident in the vicious, often pointless, infighting among the executive of the Syro-Palestinian Congress.[35] It is not the intent of this study to investigate each petty quarrel or personal jealousy. Yet it is evident that the atmosphere of mutual suspicion which permeated the organization weakened its ability to act decisively and may have influenced the public positions taken by some of its members.

In the aftermath of the Syrian revolt, the ranks of militant exiles in Cairo increased. From the perspective of Arslan's career, the most significant new personality was Dr. ʿAbd al-Rahman Shahbandar (1882–1940). A native of Damascus and a graduate of the medical school of the American University in Beirut, Shahbandar had opposed the Turkification policies of the CUP and had passed most of the war years in Cairo working for the Hashimite cause. A relentless propagandist and political organizer, in 1919 Shahbandar returned to Damascus, where his annoying criticism of the government prompted Faysal to declare that Syria could best be served if the skills of its specialists were confined to the areas of their expertise: ". . . the *zaʿim* should command troops, the politician should manage affairs . . . and the physician should treat the sick."[36] This admonition was lost on Shahbandar. After participating in the Syrian revolt of 1925–1926, he returned to Cairo, allied himself with Michel Lutfallah's faction within the Syro-Palestinian Executive, and began espousing a pro-Hashimite political position and a doctrine of secular nationalism.[37]

He and Arslan became bitter enemies, their antagonism fueled by the clash of their ambitions and their personalities as much as by their different visions of the future. Arslan called Shahbandar a "malicious man" for the accusations leveled at him and vowed: "I shall not make peace with a man who treats me in this fashion."[38] Unfortunately for the Syrian nationalist movement, Arslan kept this vow.

The Shahbandar-Arslan animosity contributed further to the factionalization of the Syrian exile community. An illustration of how personal disagreements could escalate into a major crisis among the Syrians is provided by the events of late 1925. Arslan started the quarrel in November when he accepted High Commissioner Henry de Jouvenal's invitation to discuss the Syrian question in Paris. Never one to doubt the centrality of his role, Arslan assumed that he was empowered to negotiate on behalf of the entire Syro-Lebanese community. De Jouvenal made a similar assumption, and the two men had a fruitful discussion; the high commissioner later told the Permanent Mandates Commission that they had been close to agreement on some points.[39]

However, Arslan had bargained from a position which others did not agree he held and had offered concessions that were not his to give. First, he had accepted the concept of Greater Lebanon, agreeing that France could create a separate Lebanese state by adding to the old boundaries of the *mutasarrifiyyah* several districts that were traditionally Syrian. Arslan's accommodation on this point may have served to protect the local Arslan power base. In virtually all of the Lebanese administrations formed during the Mandate, a member of the Arslan family served as either a cabinet minister or a leader of the opposition. It is conceivable that in an amalgamation with Syria, the Druze families from the Shuf would not have had as important a "national" role as they did in a Lebanese polity.

Arslan also demanded that Palestine be integrated with Syria and that both Syria and Lebanon be granted independence and membership in the League of Nations. These demands were predictable and, with the notable exception of the acceptance of Greater Lebanon, were consistent with the nationalist goals of most Syrians. Less predictable were the concessions Arslan was prepared to make to France. They included the continued teaching of French in Syrian schools, the restriction of foreign military advisers to French officers, the promise of Syrian troops to help France in case of war, and a thirty-year alliance between the two countries. These concessions seemed extravagant, but Arslan never disavowed them. In this case, at least, he was prepared to compromise in order to achieve independence. And he spoke, not as an individual, but as a representative; what he said became part of the record of Franco-Syrian diplomacy.

The controversy which followed the publication of Arslan's proposals revealed the fragility of the ties between the exiles and the incompatibility of their aspirations. The dispute was especially bitter among the members of the Executive Committee in Cairo. By entering into direct negotiations with a high-ranking official, Arslan had stolen a march on the Cairo Executive and bypassed the Syrian leaders in the field, one of whom was Dr. Shahbandar.[40]

In the years that followed, recrimination piled upon accusation so that the effectiveness of the entire Syro-Palestinian Congress was much reduced. In the autumn of 1927, Lutfallah attempted to arrange Arslan's dismissal from the European delegation for exceeding his authority in dealing with de Jouvenal; Arslan retorted that he was empowered to act without consulting Cairo and refused to relinquish his position.[41] At the same time, Lutfallah and Shahbandar were expelled from the Cairo Executive, and the Syrian exile movement became more divided than ever.

The bitterness created by Arslan's initiative toward France left him in need of strong expressions of support if his position as "duly designated delegate" was to have any credibility in the eyes of the PMC or the Arab public. From the moment he returned from Mersin, he and his supporters undertook a vigorous effort to produce tangible evidence of the existence of a widespread constituency. They could claim a substantial victory when it was announced that the Sixth Palestinian Congress had designated Arslan to defend the interests of Palestine before the League of Nations.[42] Arslan contended in a preamble to one of his petitions that the Syro-Palestinian delegation "is regarded by all oppressed Arabs as the interpreter of their grievances to the League and to the civilized world. . . ."[43] The search for support was extended to North America. In the wake of a visit by Arslan to the United States in 1927 (discussed in chapter 4), a flood of telegrams reached the French foreign minister, of which the following is typical: "Emir Arslan and his companions are the only and sole representatives of Syria before the French government and before the League of Nations."[44] Similar messages arrived from Wisconsin, Ohio, and New York. The contrived nature of these telegrams matters less than the intense struggle for support which they represent. At the personal level the campaign was marked by bitter journalistic exchanges. Arslan was most seriously affected when Dr. Shahbandar raised the issue of his relationship to Jamal Pasha, an accusation necessitating denials and explanations on the part of Arslan and his associates.[45]

This was one dimension of Arslan's existence as an activist exile. It was a world without political responsibility. Positions were taken with one eye on the French and the other on the reactions of one's compatriots. Arslan, like the others, was perpetually susceptible to accusations of exaggerated militancy or treasonable compromise. He showed more boldness than finesse and tended to stake out a position before all the information on a subject was available. This necessitated the expenditure of a great deal of energy defending and refining his original views, which were more often than not attacked by one faction or another. Yet there was a consistency to his overall perspective, an uncompromising opposition to the occupation of Arab lands by Europeans, which created a favorable impression among an Arab audience which came to look on him as their conscience in Europe. During the whole interwar period, his writings expressed his outrage at being viewed as a colonial, at being denied sovereignty, at being termed "a native spokesman" by the Mandates Commission. Instead of having the high civilization of Arab Islam recognized in the postwar world, the Arabs were divided and manipulated by a European colonialism which hypocritically purported to act in the name of humanity, but in reality was motivated "by the oil of Mosul, the cotton of Cilicia, and the silk of Syria."[46] As proof of the advanced level achieved by the inhabitants of Greater Syria, Arslan offered his own form of racism: "The population of these countries is quite evolved and indisputably belongs to the white race. It must be recalled that Syria was the cradle of civilization and from it developed the moral and religious ideas which now rule mankind." Therefore, "the Arab nation, which is aware of its past, of its rights and needs, will not consent to be treated for a long time as *mineure*, the equal of the blacks of Cameroon and Togo."[47] To those who had once been the elite of an independent empire, as well as to a younger generation which had expected something more from the Arab revolt and the British promises, these sentiments contained a certain appeal.

Therefore, despite the split in the Syro-Palestinian Congress and the recriminations which accompanied it, Arslan's prestige remained high. The campaign on his behalf succeeded in portraying him as a distinguished and dedicated figure performing a duty in Geneva which came to be recognized as unique and essential and, by 1928, he had become an authoritative commentator on virtually every major issue which confronted the Eastern Arab world in its relations with Europe. Not that he was alone in his concerns. But he had a special position from which to voice them and to attract others to

In the office of *al-Shura*, Cairo, 1939. Muhammad ʿAli al-Tahir is seated behind the desk.

his person. On the one hand, he could command an audience because of his title as representative to the League of Nations, a claim which gave him the appearance of an official spokesman. Because of this, the Syro-Palestinian delegation became the repository of the hopes of many literate Arabs during the interwar years. If the delegation achieved little in its efforts before the Permanent Mandates Commission, it nevertheless made a substantial impact in the Arab East merely by its existence.

Those who were attracted to Arslan reveal, through their own public positions, something about the Amir's own. Among the numerous journalists and politicians with whom he was associated over the years, two stand out as personal friends as well as major contributors to his *mujahid* legend. Rashid Rida, the most notable, has already been mentioned. Although Arslan met him only infrequently after 1921, he maintained a voluminous and intimate correspondence with the contemporary he most admired and of whom he said: "I was tied to him, and he to me, by spiritual bonds the like of which existed between me and no other Arab."[48]

The second of Arslan's close and durable collaborators was Muhammad ʿAli al-Tahir (1890s–1974). Born in Palestine, al-Tahir was an inveterate polemical journalist and a tireless political activist who expressed his contempt for British Middle Eastern policies in a series of newspapers he edited in Cairo.[49] Counting himself "a son" of Arslan, he always offered the Amir a front page on which to express his views. Unlike some who abandoned Arslan after 1945, al-Tahir remained loyal and did what he could to assist the man he called "a king without a crown."[50]

A third journalist, Muhibb al-Din al-Khatib (1885–1969), may have been more an ideological ally than a close friend. Of Syrian origin, al-Khatib had acted as secretary of the Arab Paris Congress of 1913 and edited Sharif Husayn's official newspaper, *al-Qiblah*. After the war, he emerged as a staunch advocate of Muslim fundamentalism at its most basic, and served as secretary of the Young Men's Muslim Association in Egypt, mingled with the Muslim Brotherhood, and published a weekly newspaper, *al-Fath*, which expressed the opinions of those opposed to the secular liberalism of the time. Arslan was a frequent contributor of lead articles. Al-Khatib also published the weekly *Majallah al-Zahra'* and operated a publishing house, pointedly named Salafiyyah press, which produced several of Arslan's books.[51]

Many of the figures drawn to Arslan were, like al-Tahir and al-Khatib, the pamphleteers and popularizers of the interwar period, the defenders of the old order, the opponents of secular change and foreign domination. His appeal extended across generations; through the efforts of his brother 'Adil and the Syrian activist Shukri al-Quwatli, he retained the respect of younger, more secular activists as well.[52] Partly because of his distance from them, he became their ideal. His resistance was a reflection of their own; his exile a symbol of the punishment they all endured at the hands of Europe; his appearance of indomitability a hope for each of them. The journalists, through their coverage of nearly his every move and their publication of his unending stream of articles, established and sustained his reputation among a wide segment of the literate public.

By the late 1920s, Arslan had gained acceptance as a spokesman for the Eastern Arab cause. His weak point, as Shahbandar had demonstrated during the struggle for control of the Syro-Palestinian Congress, was his vulnerability to charges of collaboration with Jamal Pasha. Even High Commissioner de Jouvenal, in testimony before the PMC, attempted to undermine the credibility of one of Arslan's petitions by noting that such extreme arguments could be explained only by the fact that "the Emir Arslan had been the agent of Jemal Pasha in Syria and that he was at that moment [i.e., had been at that time] the head of the Druze volunteers serving Jemal Pasha."[53] Clearly, the issue would not vanish. Nonetheless, Arslan's patriotic activity in Europe served to rehabilitate him in the eyes of all but the most bitter of his political opponents, and his aggressive polemics assured that new controversies would replace old ones.

The recognition which Arslan received from the Arab public attracted the attention of the Mandate powers whose policies he was protesting. The growing European concern for Arslan's movements was remarkable for its scope and for its often alarmist inaccuracies. The French consuls in Geneva and Lausanne reported on his activities while an observer with the title of *commissaire spécial* kept watch from Annemasse on the Arab students in Switzerland and reported to the director of the Sûreté Générale on whatever he thought might be of interest. Arslan came within the scope of these observations, first as an agitator among the students, then as a more formidable adversary who was reported to have returned to Turkey in 1926 in order to coordinate all the pro-Syrian organizations in that country.[54] While the *commissaire spécial* placed Arslan in Turkey, de Jouvenal placed him in Berlin, where, according to the high commissioner, he was attempting to recruit German officers to lead the rebel bands in Syria.[55] It was also reported that while Arslan was in Rome for the PMC meetings, he had arranged for an agent to purchase German arms for the Turkish government and to divert them to the Druze rebels of Syria through the Syrian Committee in Istanbul.[56] The cumulative effect of these reports on policymakers compelled them to believe they were dealing with a powerful and influential schemer. As these theories of conspiratorial plots continued over the years, they came to play a large part in the myth that grew up around Arslan. To a sensitive French officialdom which had just witnessed two major revolts in its Arab territories and had been subjected to international criticism for its handling of them, Arslan, as "the person who has taken part in all the movements of insurrection directed against us since 1920," touched a raw nerve.[57] When the Palestine question became more inflamed, British foreign service officials also turned their attention to the Amir, abandoning their earlier concern for his potential in Turkey to chart his influence in the Arab world.

Much of the attention which Arslan received was prompted by his close ties to Germany. From the first weeks of his exile in 1918 until shortly before his death, Berlin was a constant factor in Arslan's life. In the difficult postwar years, he was made to feel welcome in the Weimar capital; German officials did him small favors and leading orientalists genuinely admired him as a seminal literary figure.[58] He became involved in a number of Berlin-based organizations which had the potential to serve German interests in the Middle East. In addition to his post as president of the Oriental Club, he was also instrumental in founding the Society for Islamic Worship in 1924, an organization intended to provide a sanctuary for Muslims in Germany.

During the 1920s, his public posture was still that of an aggrieved party seeking an advantage wherever it might be found. At a tea given in his honor in Berlin, he told the guests that "we care for Germany only on the condition that she not demonstrate the same greed for our lands that Britain and France have. If Germany should someday seek our lands, she will become an enemy just like the other two."[59] For the moment, the relationship appeared mutually advantageous and under Arslan's control. It would not always remain that way.

In addition to the adjustment of political loyalties which the end of the Ottoman imperium forced Arslan to make, he was also required to reorient his personal life in ways that were quite demanding. It may be assumed that his style of living in the years before 1918 was comfortable and that he had access to the amenities normally associated with a member of the Lebanese/Ottoman political and social elite. The French occupation of the Levant and his exile in Europe meant that Arslan's income from the Middle East was substantially reduced at a time when his need for cash increased. It was a harsh transition for one accustomed to the comforts of a Lebanese notable: "Here in the land of exile, we have to do everything ourselves as there are no servants."[60] Although he readjusted his manner of living, he was chronically short of funds. If the activities of the Syro-Palestinian delegation were to continue, Arslan had to have additional income. That he managed at times to obtain it has led to much conjecture about the sources of his support and to accusations that his political loyalties reflected those of his patrons. His financial affairs became a part of his public persona and figure prominently in this study. In his constant search for funds, Arslan was drawn into some potentially compromising associations.

Shortly after the war, his banker, Dr. Mikha'il Bayda, persuaded Arslan to purchase a small apartment building in Berlin as an investment.[61] It was an unfortunate decision. The terrible German inflation of the postwar years caused the market value of the building to plummet, and the annual rental income of 7,000 DM was so reduced by taxes and currency restrictions that Arslan received very little of it. Moreover, ownership of the building entangled Arslan in some relationships that were not of a financial nature. In 1925, a Berlin magistrate ordered the ground floor of the building returned to the previous owner unless certain repairs were carried out within a specified time. Dr. Bayda successfully handled the matter in Arslan's absence.

He was "helped greatly" in the matter by a letter he carried from Baron von Richthofen of the Foreign Office.[62] Arslan acknowledged von Richthofen's assistance, and the baron replied: "That which I did for you, chère Excellence, was only my duty and the least that I could do for such an illustrious and sincere friend of my country."[63] Financial matters had a way of becoming political ones.

When the depression struck Europe, Arslan's debts increased, and he was forced to sell land in the Shuf in order to meet the mortgage payments on the Berlin apartment building. His letters to Rashid Rida are filled with details of his economic distress and reveal a man whose finances were made chaotic by a combination of bad luck and bad management. Indebtedness became a persistent feature of Arslan's life and caused him much unease.

In order to finance his extensive travels and carry out the full range of his duties at the League of Nations, Arslan required more than he wished to borrow. That he received subsidies is known; that he could be bought is questionable. Until Arslan's falling out with Michel in the late 1920s, the Syro-Palestinian delegation was funded by the Lutfallahs.[64] In addition, Arslan received a direct personal subsidy from a prewar acquaintance, ʿAbbas Hilmi, the ex-khedive of Egypt.[65]

Their association, begun in 1911, was renewed in 1922 in Lausanne, where ʿAbbas let it be known that he wished to assist Arslan in meeting the expenses of his activities in Europe by providing him with a monthly subsidy of £30. Once Arslan was assured that the subsidy was not intended to bind him to any particular political position, he agreed to accept it. The arrangement proved to be an awkward one. When the French government, during Henri Ponsot's period as high commissioner in Syria (1926–1933), appeared willing to consider the establishment of a Syrian monarchy as a way to bring effective government to the Mandate, ʿAbbas revealed his aspirations for the Syrian throne. He was disappointed when Arslan announced that the Syro-Palestinian delegation was only concerned with the achievement of Syrian independence and would make no effort to support the ex-khedive as king.[66] Additional disputes arose between the patron and his independent-minded client until the subsidy was discontinued sometime in 1931.

Arslan had been damaged by the relationship. Not only was he accused of selling Syria for £30 a month, he was also seen as a co-conspirator for the return of ʿAbbas to the Egyptian throne, a view which caused King Fuʾad and then Faruq to regard him with considerable suspicion. Arslan's need for funds had driven him into an association which he knew he should avoid. More public disavowals became necessary. After the subsidy was discontinued, he sent Rida some documents he hoped would prove that "the relationship between me and that man ['Abbas] is not what they think. It was initiated at his insistence, but he had ulterior motives. . . . In spite of my desperate circumstances, I am pleased that our association is ended, for it damaged my reputation and caused me trouble."[67] Arslan's peculiar situation ensured that this was not the last relationship which caused him trouble.

Others contributed to the activities of the Syro-Palestinian delegation and the maintenance of its leading spokesman. King Faysal probably provided occasional aid. Ibn Sa'ud, the Arab leader most admired by Arslan, although far from being the oil-rich potentate of later years, nevertheless offered the Amir what financial assistance he could.[68] He also gave him a gift more precious than money. Another of the conundrums which the Ottoman collapse caused men like Arslan to face was the question of citizenship. It was supposedly resolved by the Treaty of Lausanne (1923), which granted a two-year period within which the sultan's former subjects could opt to become citizens of Turkey or one of the new Arab states. Arslan chose to keep his Ottoman passport for several months past the deadline. When he tried to obtain Lebanese citizenship before the French consul in Lausanne (in itself an irritating experience), he was told that the deadline for making a choice had expired—he was a man without citizenship and therefore without the right to acquire travel documents.[69] However, Ibn Sa'ud's Kingdom of the Hijaz had citizenship to offer; Arslan and his family accepted it, and he traveled on an Arabian passport for the rest of his life.[70]

The pan-Ottoman Druze from the Shuf had become a Hijazi citizen and a recognized spokesman for the Syro-Palestinian cause at the League of Nations. It was a world turned upside down. Yet Touma's observation that "instead of dying with one cause, Arslan decided to live with another" is too glib and smacks of a cynicism which is hard to accept.[71] Certainly, Arslan possessed an instinct for political survival and a need for public acclaim. But there was a strength to him, a sense of mission that went beyond the kinds of compromises associated with mere survival. The postwar years were terribly difficult for Arslan, and if his vanity drove him to seek the limelight in order to be certain of his own worth, he also suffered in order to establish the reputation by which he wished to be judged and to serve the cause which he believed was correct. He managed, in the mid-1920s, to establish a position of influence and to regain and expand his Arab audience. Now he had to convey to that audience the means by which the Arab-Islamic world could define its identity and assert its dignity in a world deprived of political sovereignty and caliphal authority.

CHAPTER FOUR.
ADVOCATE OF ISLAMIC
NATIONALISM: THE ARAB EAST

*It is a disgrace for Muslims to leave their former caliph
wandering in foreign countries, powerless to set foot in any
Islamic territory.*   —Arslan[1]

WITH THE failure of the Syrian revolt in the East and the
capture of ʿAbd al-Krim in the Maghrib, European imperial control
settled firmly on the Arab-speaking world. Those Arab leaders who
had held hopes for an immediate reversal of the postwar settlement
now modified their expectations and prepared for a period of uneasy
coexistence with European occupiers. Although the Syrian elite began to build political organizations, they remained divided against
themselves, and their factionalism was encouraged by French administrative practices. No significant steps toward independence
were taken until 1936. In Palestine, the complexities of the impossible Mandate obligation to encourage a national home for the Jewish people while not damaging the rights of the Palestinian Arabs
were becoming obvious. The venom spilling from that tragedy poi-
soned relations between Arabs and Britain as between Palestinians
and Zionists. In its other Arab possessions, Britain was able to adopt
a more positive policy and to grant Egypt (1922 and 1936) and Iraq
(1932) a nominal independence. However, it was a sovereignty severely limited by treaties binding the two states to Britain and ensuring that British imperial needs were secure.

As he surveyed the wreckage of the Ottoman system from Geneva,
Shakib Arslan felt a bitter hopelessness:

I am in the depths of despair these last few days. Feelings of pain and
weariness are piling up and know no source of treatment. . . . Why

not despair when every day we are subjected to shame. We look at Syria and find France clinging to it in order to transform it into a colony, hoping to destroy its patriotic freedoms by delays and lies. We look at Iraq and find it crippled by England which grants it independence in name only. We look at Palestine and find England pouring in Jews and pouring out Arabs. We turn to Egypt and find England unwilling to grant even a limited, mutilated independence unless she receives the Sudan as outright booty.[2]

These conditions demanded redress, and Arslan intended to effect it. He did not interpret his mission as restricted to the Syro-Palestinian cause, nor did he accept the circumstances which made him an exile. Countering his occasional despair was a tenacity which drove him to extend his mandate and to continue his protest: "The excuses of those who accept the present conditions are invalid. If they cannot serve their religion with their swords, they can do so with their pens; if not with their pens, then with their voices; if not with their voices, then with their hearts."[3] Arslan adhered to his own admonitions. The scope and intensity of his anti-imperial struggle propelled him into greater prominence than ever before, enhancing his reputation as an exemplary activist and, in Julien's memorable phrase, making his Geneva residence "the umbilical cord of the Islamic world."[4]

Arslan's efforts to direct the interwar Arab resistance after 1925 concentrated on the following four major activities: keeping alive the Syro-Palestinian issue at the League of Nations; enlisting North African Arabs in the common Islamic anti-imperialist struggle; acting as a religious reformer by commenting on the contemporary Islamic scene; and negotiating a great power alliance for the Arabs against Britain and France. He engaged in these tasks simultaneously, creating a formidable but mixed impression. To some, he was a self-sacrificing *mujahid* demonstrating admirable qualities of personal fortitude and intellectual vigor. Others saw him as a meddling agitator, a paid political agent, a vain and ambitious schemer. He was a bit of each of these, and the composite picture correctly reveals a complex man operating in complicated circumstances. It also reveals an individual who accumulated vast influence, both real and perceived. In gaining his reputation and in exercising the influence which went with it, Arslan became a dominant figure of the interwar years.

The remainder of this study examines Arslan's performance of these four roles. This chapter treats his role in pursuing issues related principally to the Arab East during the decade beginning in 1927. It begins with a discussion of the means by which the Arslan legend was built.

As suggested in the preceding chapter, Arslan's status as an exile in Europe created the circumstances for his first involvement in the Arab cause. In one sense, he gained an advantage simply by being in the right place at the right time. Moreover, the continuing ban on his presence in territories controlled by Britain and France removed him from direct participation in domestic politics and enabled him to become accepted as a universal spokesman. This was an advantage which he sometimes squandered with his aggressive and manipulative political style. However, he did use his position in Europe to develop a breadth of concerns that was unusual. Other talented and dedicated contemporaries were often associated so closely with a particular region—Zaghlul with Egypt, Riyad al-Sulh with Lebanon, ʿAllal al-Fasi with Morocco—that they had neither the inclination nor the opportunity to reach a wider audience. Arslan, on the other hand, lent his name, his prestige, and his physical presence to a variety of political and cultural movements from Morocco to Arabia, from Bosnia to Palestine. In the words of one of his contemporaries: "Shakib Arslan lived his life as a *mujahid* in the cause of freedom and independence; the freedom of the Arabs in every region, and the independence of Muslims in every country. His *jihad* was not limited to his own homeland, but was elevated beyond it to an extensive *jihad* refuting every injustice, resisting all oppression, and aiding the weak everywhere."[5] The overblown rhetoric of eulogy may still capture the essence of what a particular individual meant to those who associated with him.

Arslan's mission during the interwar period was to internationalize the issues facing the Arab-Islamic lands under European domination and to galvanize Arab-Islamic opinion into a recognition that only through mutual assistance based on their common Islamic bonds could they gain independence and restore the proper social order. His principal medium was the periodical press. As he had been part of the new field of Arab journalism before the turn of the century, so he became, in the interwar decades, part of another new process which saw the emergence of the colonized pamphleteer on the European continent. His Arabic articles numbered between eighty and one hundred per year in the 1930s and were often reprinted in several different publications, thus giving him the exposure of a syndicated columnist.[6]

During the 1930s, Arslan also acquired a francophone audience through the journal *La Nation Arabe*, probably his most cherished publication. Beginning as a monthly in 1930, *La Nation Arabe* claimed to be the organ of the Syro-Palestinian delegation and was jointly edited by Arslan and Ihsan al-Jabiri. They also served as its major—and usually only—contributors. The objective of the journal was "to present to the Western world the claims of a nation which has projected its civilizing light across the darkness of the Middle Ages and the ruins of the Greco-Roman world and thus served as one of the principal agents in the formation of the modern world."[7]

The journal was printed in Annemasse, France, and appeared until late 1938. It was an ambitious undertaking and acted as a further drain on Arslan's personal finances. Although he may have used some German and Italian funds to keep the journal afloat, it appears that he tried to produce it entirely from subscription revenue, Arab contributions, and his own income. This severely hampered the venture, and within a year of the journal's appearance, Arslan was apologizing to subscribers for late issues. By 1936, when Italian funds were most certainly passing through Arslan's hands, the annual numbers of *La Nation Arabe* actually declined, and it became an irregular quarterly. Even though the journal defended Italian policy, Arslan was determined to keep it independent of Italian financing. In all, thirty-eight numbers were printed.

In effect, *La Nation Arabe* became Arslan's personal mouthpiece. He dominated its pages, setting a tone of anti-imperialist polemic and politicized Islamic rhetoric. He also used the publication to denounce his opponents, both European and Arab, and to defend himself from the multitude of accusations which were leveled at him. In making the journal his own forum, he succeeded in linking his concerns with the larger issues of the day, giving *La Nation Arabe* an impact exceeding its irregular appearance and its limited circulation. After less than a year of publication, Arslan could claim: "Our review, *La Nation Arabe*, is read everywhere with growing interest and is regarded as the official organ of the Arabs. In Parisian political circles, the review has numerous subscribers and elicits great interest."[8] It also attracted attention in London, where the Foreign Office acknowledged "receiving it regularly."[9] As shown in chapter 5, when the right issue became available, Arslan could make his journal a powerful mobilizing force.

Arslan was more than a polemicist. He supplemented his journalism with a prodigious outpouring of books which ranged in subject matter from biography to poetry, from religious commentary to historical narrative. This literary effort brought him a modest income but substantial fame.

Another of Arslan's methods of influence building was to be on the spot, to associate in person with this worthy congress or that nascent independence movement. He was an indefatigable traveler, and his often arduous journeys to various parts of the world reinforced his image as an indomitable *mujahid*. For example, in 1927, he spent four months in the United States and attended a conference in Moscow; during a six-month span in 1934, he toured the Balkans as far as Budapest, mediated a dispute in the Yemen, met twice with Mussolini in Rome, and lunched with the British high commissioner in Jerusalem. He was like a latter-day al-Afghani, roaming the Islamic world and Europe, attracting new disciples, causing alarm among some Arab rulers, and eliciting expressions of concern from the British and French officials who tracked his wanderings. It seemed, his daughter once told me, that wherever there was a single Muslim, he went to offer advice and encouragement.

To the extent that these journeys defined Arslan's purpose and strengthened his influence, they deserve consideration. One of the most significant was his pilgrimage to Mecca in 1929. It was a venture which had objectives beyond the performance of a basic Islamic ritual and which served to crystallize the Amir's views on the issues of Islamic solidarity and Arab leadership.

By the latter half of the 1920s, the attention of those Arabs who sought to alter the imposed imperial system was focused on a search for leadership from the competing rulers who had been set upon their thrones by the dismemberment of the Ottoman system. To those who approached social organization from an essentially Islamic perspective, the question of political authority was also tied to the fate of the spiritual caliphate, an institution which had been abolished by Atatürk in March 1924.

With Syria divided and its political elite scattered, domination of the spiritual and temporal politics of the Arab core appeared likely to fall to the Hashimites buttressed by their British supervisors. Sharif Husayn was recognized by the British as king of the Hijaz and dared to assume the title of caliph two days after Atatürk abolished it. The sharif's son ʿAbdullah became amir, later king, of Transjordan, and another son, Faysal, was installed as king of Iraq in 1921. Such dynastic aggrandizement was alarming to King Fuʾad of Egypt, who had his own regional ambitions and personal aspirations for filling the caliphate.[10]

By the time Arslan prepared to make his pilgrimage, a third contestant had been added to the leadership struggle. In a remarkable saga for any time and place, ʿAbd al-ʿAziz Ibn Saʿud had risen from the obscurity of an insignificant shaykh in 1910 to achieve official recognition by Britain, France, and the Soviet Union as "King of the

Hijaz and Sultan of Najd and Its Dependencies" by 1926. To Muslims everywhere, he was acknowledged as the protector of the holy cities of Mecca and Medina and the guardian of the pilgrimage.[11] Ibn Saʿud's very triumph intensified inter-Arab dynastic rivalries. His defeat of Sharif Husayn and his occupation of Mecca in 1926 turned the erstwhile caliph of Islam and king of the Hijaz into a forgotten exile on Cyprus. It also made Ibn Saʿud the object of a "Hashimite vendetta" and embroiled him in a continuous series of clashes with the sons of Husayn along his fluid northern borders.[12] Moreover, as King Fuʾad became suspicious of a rival claimant for Islamic leadership, Egypt withdrew its support of the new prince and refused to grant his state diplomatic recognition until after Fuʾad's death in 1936.

On the surface, the contest among Ibn Saʿud, King Fuʾad, and the Hashimites was primarily over borders, dynastic preservation, and other temporal matters. However, it occurred at a time when the Arab-Islamic community was engaged in a lively debate over the restoration of the caliphate, and to some, the outcome of the secular contest would have a bearing on the question of spiritual leadership. At stake for the community at large was the issue of whether Islamic political principles could be effectively instituted as a solution to the grave crises which confronted all Muslims. On more narrowly conceived grounds, ambitious men saw an office with immense prestige going begging, and they maneuvered for position. In the wake of Sharif Husayn's abdication, Fuʾad's supporters organized a Congress on the Caliphate which met in Cairo in 1926. The Egyptian monarch was hardly pleased with the results. Unable to agree on a specific candidate for the office, the delegates could only affirm the necessity of the institution and resolve that it must remain unassigned for the moment.[13]

Not to be outmaneuvered by his Egyptian rival, Ibn Saʿud also convened an international gathering in 1926. Termed the Congress of the Islamic World, it brought together in Mecca official delegations from several Islamic governments to discuss issues of concern to all Muslims.[14] Although the resolutions of the Mecca Congress on the issue of the caliphate were similar to those passed in Cairo, it had more ambitious intentions of becoming an ongoing body, and its delegates selected a permanent standing committee. By granting the absent Arslan a place on the committee, the Congress not only confirmed his status among Muslims, but also legitimized his position.[15] If he needed encouragement to promote his views, he now had it.

The outburst of activity following the abolition of the caliphate reveals the centrality of the caliphate problem to Muslims of this period. The issue was fully politicized. For men like Shakib Arslan and

Rashid Rida, the future of society was at stake, and they would not be silent. Rida, who was aroused to "a pitch of indignation" at Sharif Husayn's claim to the caliphate, felt that the office was not only obligatory, but should be held only by one who possessed all the qualifications established by the classical jurists.[16] However, Rida did concede that until such an individual was trained and selected, a "caliph of convenience" might be considered; for this office he favored Imam Yahya of the Yemen.[17]

To some extent, Arslan shared his friend's views. During the 1920s, he was not prepared to concede that a world without a caliph was possible for those who called themselves Muslims. He later modified this position and came to believe that two or three sovereign, Islamic-oriented monarchs could serve the purpose the caliphate had. This attachment to Islamic government, preferably in the form of constitutional monarchy, was a central component of Arslan's political thought. A continuation of his commitment to the Ottoman sultan-caliphs and to an Islamic social order, it was a position from which he never wavered and for which he campaigned relentlessly.

In the immediate aftermath of the abolition of the caliphate in Turkey, Arslan, like Rida, accepted the notion that the office should be restored and that its holder must possess both material and spiritual power. At the same time, he did not agree with Rida that the restored caliph should meet all the conditions required by the jurists. Such an exercise would be useless, for "there is not in the lands of Islam a single individual who fulfills all the necessary canonical conditions for the caliphate."[18] Arslan was prepared to compromise on the qualifications of Qurayshite descent and Qur'anic learning in exchange for one overriding requirement—power.

For a time, he felt that if the deposed Ottoman caliph, 'Abd al-Majid, could be provided with a principality, perhaps in Basra or the Yemen, then he might be enveloped with sufficient trappings of power to continue in office. However, Arslan soon dropped that idea and turned his support to a monarch whose power was more tangible: "The most suitable throne for the caliphate is unquestionably the throne of Egypt."[19] It was not a concern for Qurayshite descent or Qur'anic skills that prompted Arslan's support for the Italian-educated great-grandson of an Albanian adventurer. Islam required a locus of power, an assertive capability which only Egypt could provide. This capability would become fully apparent when Egypt obtained unconditional independence and began building an army corresponding to the size of its population. When Muslims saw this state with a mobilized force of 1.5 million soldiers and a fleet equal to those of the second-level European powers, then "even the Tartars and Turks among them will rush to pledge allegiance to the King of Egypt."[20] Arslan was no particular friend of ʿAbbas Hilmi's successors, but he recognized that Egypt had the best opportunity to provide Islam with the material strength which would enable it to contest European supremacy and so provide men like himself with their rightful place in the world.

That his affinity for an Egyptian caliphate could be quickly transferred to another monarch did not alter the basic test by which he judged an Islamic ruler. It merely meant that the trappings of power had been acquired by one whom he considered more deserving. Ibn Saʿud's final victories in the Hijaz led Arslan to rediscover the virtues of an Islamic leadership less tainted than those offered by the king of Egypt. By the time he prepared for his pilgrimage, he proclaimed the man he had once dismissed as a petty amir to be the most likely candidate to demonstrate to the West that "the Arab nation is not dead."[21] In his own way, Arslan intended to further Ibn Saʿud's reputation. The pilgrimage of as noted a figure as Arslan, with all its attendant publicity, would, if completed smoothly, enhance Ibn Saʿud's prestige by showing that he could keep the pilgrimage open and safe. It would also show that the famous and influential could, in the future, perform the *hajj* without concern for their safety.

Indeed, Arslan had less difficulty once in the Hijaz than he did getting there. His major obstacle was obtaining permission from the Egyptian government to disembark in that country in order to transfer to a ship bound for Jiddah. King Fuʾad was not anxious to ease the passage of a notorious associate of ʿAbbas Hilmi to the state of Ibn Saʿud. After a discouraging period of revised plans and uncertain promises, Arslan gained the authorization he sought. Delegations of welcome were formed, the Islamic press began to promote his visit, and Rida, to ensure that the ultimate objective of the journey was properly accomplished, informed Arslan, "I am sending you a copy of a manual on the ritual ceremony of the *hajj* for you to study during your voyage."[22]

From the perspective of a certain segment of the Egyptian elite, Arslan's arrival at Port Said on 7 May 1929 and his transit to Suez the next morning was an event of some significance. Rida wrote that he could not keep back his tears of joy at seeing his old friend. An impressive list of other figures came to pay their respects to a former associate and to demonstrate the solidarity of like-minded men.[23]

The Eygptian government, apparently concerned by the attention Arslan was receiving, accelerated his departure from Suez the next day. It was an abrupt conclusion to Rida's carefully prepared plans for receptions and discussions; he was nonetheless determined that the Amir's *hajj* should be ritually correct and hastened into the suqs of Suez to buy him an *ihram* garment.[24]

There was no governmental hostility when Arslan reached his final destination. Ibn Sa'ud was aware of the possibilities Arslan's pilgrimage contained for legitimizing his regime and solidifying his hold on the holy places of Islam. As Arslan wrote, and all second-hand accounts were careful to repeat, the king himself met Arslan at Jiddah and accompanied him in the royal automobile to Mecca.[25] Throughout Arslan's stay in the Hijaz, Ibn Sa'ud lavishly entertained him, publicly praised him, and even offered to bring his family to the kingdom if Arslan would accept a position in his administration.[26]

For his part, Arslan did everything he could to enhance the reputation of his host. He transferred to the underdeveloped Kingdom of the Hijaz all the achievements that were denied the Arabs elsewhere: "From the moment I set foot on the quay at Jiddah, I felt like a free Arab in a free Arab country. I felt I had escaped the oppressive foreign rule which weighs so heavily on all Arab countries. . . . I felt that I was a citizen of a pure Arab government, the way Lloyd George is a citizen of England or Clemenceau is of France."[27] Of equal importance to Arslan's concept of good government, the Arabian peninsula had remained "subject to the Islamic *shari'ah* in all its principles."[28]

Arslan attributed the existence of this admirable state of affairs to the new ruler of the Hijaz: "I found him to be a man of uncommon intelligence and energy with a remarkable keenness of eye, breadth of mind, strength of will, and sense of self. Should God grant him the continued success in the future that He has given him in the past, then Islam and the Arabs will have a true awakening. . . ."[29] Arslan had found his hero for the Arab future. Ibn Sa'ud was not only a sovereign Arab monarch governing on the basis of Islamic principles, he was also a daring warrior who fulfilled Arslan's romantic taste for courageous military exploits.[30] As he had been drawn to Abdulhamid in that ruler's roles as imperial sultan and Islamic caliph, and as he had been fascinated by the heroic qualities he saw in Enver Pasha, so he was attracted to the warrior prince of the Hijaz, in whose domains "the hand of the foreigner is not raised above that of the Arab."[31] Arslan's welcome in the Hijaz was such a contrast to the prohibitions that confronted him in British- and French-controlled Arab states that he was led to confuse independence with power. In summarizing the tone of his speeches in the Hijaz, the British consul in Jiddah reported that the Amir went so far as to express the hope that Mecca would become the political as well as the religious capital of the Muslim world.[32]

As an exercise in public relations and self-promotion, Arslan's *hajj* was successful. However, as a venture for a sedentary sixty-year-old, it proved excessive. Exhausted by his voyage from Geneva, he became very ill only a few days after his arrival in the holy city. He was taken to Taif, the summer retreat of the Hijazi chieftains, but his recovery was slow, and it was not until mid-September 1929, after nearly four months in Arabia, that he was well enough to begin the return voyage to Europe. His passage through Egypt was marked by public receptions and intensely personal moments. His mother had made the journey to Suez, and Arslan's meeting with her was a painful reminder of the restrictions placed on his own movements. Ahmad Shawqi was also awaiting him at Suez. This fleeting encounter with his old friend again underscored Arslan's feelings of loneliness, and he remembered telling Shawqi: "I cannot invite you to Syria because I have not been allowed to set foot there . . . nor to Palestine, nor to Egypt which I can only enter after much difficulty. So I invite you to Switzerland where you can spend the summer and we can be together."[33]

Exiles had to make the most of their rare opportunities. Arslan, with Rida, ʿAzzam, and a dozen or so others, passed the evening in Port Said. The correspondent of *al-Shura* captured the atmosphere of nostalgic reunion which pervaded the Hotel Casino as aging comrades and their disciples, united in a common cause but separated by time, distance, and imperial decree, captured a precious evening in one another's company. All the ingredients were there, including a young Egyptian singer who happened to be performing at the hotel that night. When Arslan's friends pressed him for his reaction to the rising star, he replied in impromptu verse that even graying heads could not but be touched by the voice of Umm Kalthum.[34]

Seeing his friends accentuated Arslan's sense of separation from them, and a few months later, in the midst of the Swiss winter, he published an aggressive yet plaintive article on how he had been singled out for special treatment by Great Britain. He was proud of his prewar record of anti-imperialism, but now that Britain had made peace with Germany and Turkey, why should he be the subject of such animosity that he could not even visit his mother in Palestine? Only the Hijaz and the Yemen had sovereigns who, because they were independent, dared offer him a haven. "Thank God," he wrote, "there remains to us the banner of Ibn Saʿud."[35] It was a banner to which he gave the allegiance of a citizen and the support of a propagandist for the rest of his life.

As long as the restrictions on his travel to Arab lands remained in force, Arslan's effectiveness as an exiled agitator rested with his ability to attract attention to his activities, to publish frequently in the Arabic press, and to maintain contact with influential groups within the Arab states. Several of his other journeys served these purposes. One of the most unusual of them found Arslan in the United States for the first four months of 1927, attending the second annual Conference of the Party of New Syria in Detroit. His purpose in attending the Conference was to provide the Syrian community in the United States with information on the recent revolt, to raise funds for refugees, and, implicitly, to generate support for himself as the legitimate representative of all Syrians before the League of Nations.

In that he addressed the convention and collected donations for the Syrian cause, the journey was satisfactory.[36] However, he failed to dampen the suspicions of the large Christian element among Syro-Americans that he was anything but a Muslim supremacist. Four hundred protestors from the Syrian Christian Association of Detroit gathered to denounce his "presumption" in claiming to speak as the official representative of Syria, and the New York–based paper *al-Sa'ih* branded him as a foreigner with an insatiable appetite for pompous ceremonies.[37]

Despite the hostile reception from the Syrian Christian community, Arslan's reputation as an activist in the cause of independent Syria was nurtured in the Arab East through the favorable coverage accorded his American trip by *al-Shura*, which ignored the controversy and focused on the fanfare.[38] As revealed in the datelines of *al-Shura*, Arslan embarked on a grueling and not immediately comprehensible itinerary at the close of the Detroit conference, with stops in such places as Fort Smith, Arkansas, and Shawnee, Georgia. Arslan did not record his own impressions, and his later writings are nearly devoid of references to this particular episode. All in all, it was a curious and expensive journey, but one which showed his eagerness to assert his presence wherever he felt it might be useful.

The same motive led him, in November 1927, to attend the celebrations in Moscow marking the tenth anniversary of the Bolshevik revolution. He found irresistible his selection as an official delegate of any group, this time serving as the Arab representative of the Berlin-based International Committee for the Struggle against Imperialism. But he was no more attracted to a Communist revolution than he was to capitalist America. However, by now his presence mattered as much as his views. The Moscow trip proved to one British diplomat that Arslan "was almost certainly working under Soviet direction."[39] It was a charge which he could never completely shake and which added to the complex reputation he was building in the files of various foreign ministries.

Whether responding to invitations or generating them, Arslan was constantly traveling. Not every journey achieved its objectives (the trip to the United States being a prime example), but each could be chronicled by the Amir and reported by the press as evidence of his dedication to his mandate in Europe. Around 1930, he began to expand his interests beyond the Syro-Palestinian cause and to shape the reputation which credited him with the orchestration of the entire Arab-Islamic protest movement. He inaugurated this phase of his career innocently enough with a trip to Spain in the summer of 1930. It was one of his most satisfying postwar experiences. The fascination for al-Andalus which had inspired his translation of Chateaubriand in 1898 now led him to compose several of his own volumes on the glories of the Arabs in Spain.[40] In this he was not alone. Other contemporary Arab writers, beginning with Shawqi, also sought in Spain reminders that European Christians had not always dominated Arab Muslims.[41] In this spirit of linking past achievements with current potential, Arslan dedicated his book on the Arab conquests in Europe to the development of cooperation between Faysal, Ibn Sa'ud, and Imam Yahya, a process which would renew the glory of the Arab nation and "restore the days of its might."[42]

From Spain, Arslan crossed to Tangiers and began what was to become his most successful anti-imperialist campaign, studied in the following chapter.

Arslan did not confine himself to the most obvious historical parallels or the most pressing colonial situations. Unique among major Arab Muslim figures of his era, he sought to cement ties with the Islamic leaders in central Europe who had, in his opinion, been abandoned by their coreligionists and left to fend for themselves in a sea of Christianity. In the late summer of 1932, and again in the first two months of 1934, he traveled through the Balkans as far as Budapest. This concern may further reflect his ties to the Ottoman past. He did not, for example, devote as much attention to the Muslims of India as he did to those of Bosnia. Feeling he had tapped a rich lode of Islamic sentiment, Arslan called on the ulema of the Arab East to visit the Balkans regularly so as to incorporate the Muslims there into the mainstream of the Islamic struggle for cultural independence.[43] He alone acted on this suggestion; his willingness to do so endeared him to the Muslim leaders of the Balkans and enabled him to count them among his admirers.

He showed them in other ways that they were not abandoned. If he could not persuade the ulema of the East to organize their European coreligionists, he would do so himself. His tactic was the usual one of the period—holding a congress. Although Arslan did not originate the notion of a congress for the Muslims of Europe, he became one of its leading advocates and principal organizers.[44] When the Islamic Congress of Europe was finally held in Geneva from 12 to 15 September 1935, it was a more modest event than Arslan had predicted. Plagued by low attendance (there were "nearly" seventy delegates) and tainted by accusations of Italian financing, the Congress attracted more attention from outside observers than it did from the Muslims for whom it was convened.[45]

Arslan placed his stamp on the gathering and made sure that the issues which concerned him were aired. He used his position as president to deliver an inaugural address calling for the restoration of the caliphate and to read a telegram in which the deposed caliph, ʿAbd al-Majid, named Arslan as his personal representative to the Congress. This position created a certain resentment among the delegates, one of whom sourly noted that not all present shared such sympathy for the caliphate.[46] Nor did they share the president's prestige. Remarks by the mufti of Budapest or the president of the Warsaw Association of Muslims would hardly shake the imperial establishment in Beirut or the Christian one in Belgrade.

Yet the Congress should not be regarded as an empty charade. It may not have been decisive, but like so many of Arslan's activities, it had a symbolic value. As the delegate who reported his disapproval of the procaliphate sentiments also wrote, the Congress appeared to be the beginning of a movement. Arslan had gotten the leading Islamic dignitaries of Europe to Geneva, he had managed the endorsement of a few petitions to the League of Nations, and he had assured his control over the standing executive committee by becoming its president and arranging to have al-Jabiri selected as vice-president. In the circumstances, the gathering could be considered an achievement. It was also a testimony to the breadth of Arslan's concerns and to the magnetism of his name. Without his sponsorship and presence, it would not have taken place.

Arslan's devotion to Ibn Saʿud as the ideal monarch, his involvement with the Muslims of Europe, and his absorption with al-Andalus were all part of his conception of the politics of Islamic nationalism. He wished to show that issues involving Muslims were not confined to a particular region, but involved all other Muslims. In the Arab East the problems of the Palestine Mandate provided him with the best opportunity to exploit Islamic nationalism.

From the Balfour Declaration of 1917 to the Wailing Wall riots of 1929 to the rebellion of 1936, all the threats to the Arab-Islamic sense of worth were present in Palestine: Jewish immigration into a

Muslim territory contravened the social order ordained by revelation and sanctioned by practice; British possession of the Mandate showed the duplicity of the European states and emphasized their power over the Arabs; and the factionalism of the local Palestinian leadership revealed a disturbing political weakness which was present in Syria and Iraq as well. Perhaps the Arabs were unsuited for self-government after all.

Nobody who claimed to be the voice of Arab protest could ignore these dangers. Arslan used the multiple roles he had created for himself to become an active participant in the Palestinian cause. As a representative to the League of Nations, he showered the PMC with a continuous series of petitions, trying to keep the subject of Palestine from being pushed aside.[47] As a prominent public figure, he felt empowered to negotiate with the Zionist leadership. In September 1934, David Ben-Gurion visited Arslan and al-Jabiri in the Amir's Geneva apartment. During discussions which lasted until the early morning, Arslan confirmed the Zionist leader's belief in his intransigence, and Ben-Gurion confirmed Arslan's belief that Zionism was expansive and determined.[48] The inconclusive meeting was a microcosm of Zionist-Arab relations throughout the interwar period.

As a polemical journalist, Arslan not only understood the significance of the international arena for the Palestine question, he had, as much as any Arab publicist, access to it. Although his writings were generally in keeping with the anti-British, anti-Zionist tone which was prevalent in Arab circles at the time, he had his own special perspective. He showed the sensitivity of a member of the Ottoman-Arab aristocracy when he observed that the British felt they could transform Palestine into a Jewish state because of their contempt for the Arabs. It was, he noted bitterly, an attitude that had some basis in reality as inter-Arab bickering prevented a united front against Zionism.[49] In addition, Arslan may have been more perceptive than some in seeing the imperial configurations of the Palestine question, noting that Britain's support of a Jewish state would put that state at the service of British goals and would prevent an Arab great power from forming.[50] He understood clearly that Zionist objectives were to create a Jewish majority in Palestine and accurately foretold what might happen: "Once they have a majority, c'est fini pour les Arabes."[51]

If the Arabs of Palestine were to thwart Zionist ambitions and expel the British, they required assistance. Although Arslan recognized the importance of Great Power support and attempted to obtain it from Italy and Germany, he also felt that Muslims throughout the world were morally obligated to defend Palestine. It was part of the larger cause of Islam under attack; failure to recognize this fact and to act on it was to deny Islam itself. Muhibb al-Din al-Khatib set the tone with a statement in *al-Fath* upon which Arslan elaborated again and again: "The Islamic world is Palestine, and Palestine is the Islamic world."[52] As he did with the Berber *dahir* in Morocco in 1930 and 1931, Arslan set about to internationalize the Palestine question.

In the wake of the Wailing Wall riots of 1929, Hajj Amin al-Husayni convened a General Islamic Congress in Jerusalem to focus attention on the Islamic dimensions of the Palestine problem.[53] It was the most successful of the several interwar congresses; over 400 delegates attended the meetings, which took place from 7 to 17 December 1931. Although Arslan was not present, he shared in the euphoria of the moment, writing that the Congress was an affirmation that "Islam lives and flourishes, that its unity is not tarnished by the abolition of the caliphate."[54] *La Nation Arabe* proclaimed the Congress to be "the spiritual and social parliament of Islam," and expressed the hope that it would lead to a new Muslim awakening.[55]

One of the resolutions passed by the delegates called for the establishment of an Islamic university in Jerusalem. Arslan was fascinated by the prospect; the cultural splendor of Harun al-Rashid's Baghdad would be re-created on the heights of the Haram al-Sharif:

Let us have a higher Islamic university in which the modern sciences are pursued side by side with the pure Qur'anic faith, a university which nurtures confident Muslim students, not ones who are sick at heart. Let us have a modern university the language of which is Arabic (which the sick at heart are today attacking); let this language be the language of scientific Islam as it is the language of religious Islam.[56]

This was a heartfelt appeal for an idealized order; it did not address the question of the dispossessed peasants of Palestine or the British occupation of the territory. It often seemed that Palestine, or any other region, served only as a catalyst for Arslan's vision of a revitalized Islamic society. The Islamic Congress of Jerusalem had given him hope that there was substance to his dreams and support for his beliefs. It did not hold. By 1933, the standing committees of the Congress had dissolved and the plans for a Muslim university were dropped. Nevertheless, the sentiments which the Congress had generated and the broadly based representation of its delegates sustained Arslan in his belief that pan-Islamic solidarity was a realistic response to imperial occupation and a viable source for internal regeneration.

The high point of pan-Arab concern for Palestine occurred during the 1936–1939 rebellion. Here was a genuine revolt against the imperial state which had occupied Egypt, betrayed Sharif Husayn, and opened the way to Zionist immigration. It captured the attention of Arabs everywhere. Arslan again tried to guide the response: "I have said, and I continue to say, that the Palestinian problem is not a problem for the Palestinian Arabs or the Arab world alone; it is a general calamity for the entire Islamic world."[57] In this crisis, Arslan portrayed Palestine as the crucible in which Arab-Islamic determination would be tested; it was the measure of whether the Arab nation was willing to transform itself through sacrifice and to become in the future what it had been in the past.[58] Although other publicists wrote in a similar vein, Arslan's visibility was such that he became closely associated with events in Palestine. He contributed to the general Arab awareness of British imperial designs and Zionist goals, he linked Palestine as an Islamic cause to North Africa and North Africa to Palestine, and, as shown in chapter 7, he carelessly allowed himself to become a factor in local Palestinian politics.

Palestine seemed to be a cause demanding inflammatory prose and heroic sacrifice. The preservation of peace among Arab heads of state was no less critical a factor in furthering the politics of Islamic nationalism, but it required a moderating influence. In his commitment to the creation of a solid Islamic front, Arslan was willing to exchange the role of ardent propagandist for the more demanding task of patient negotiator. In doing so, he surrendered neither his centrality nor his tendency for the dramatic gesture.

In 1934, the expansion of Sa'udi power collided with the irredentism of Imam Yahya's Yemen to provoke a full-scale war between the two peninsular states. Although a Shi'a Muslim, Imam Yahya (ruled 1904–1948) possessed several qualities which earned him the admiration of Arab publicists like Arslan. (It will be recalled that he was Rashid Rida's choice as the temporary "caliph of convenience.") He was a vigorous Islamic ruler who attempted to implement the shari'ah throughout his fragmented kingdom. He had, moreover, gained the cachet, so important to Arslan, of recognition by European powers as an independent monarch. While his extreme isolationism may have had detrimental effects on his domestic programs, it was an anti-European stance which seemed meritorious at the time.[59]

Much attention was focused on Yahya's conflict with Ibn Sa'ud.

What might, over half a century later, appear as harmless skirmishing between two tribal states whose independence was permitted because of their insignificance was seen by Arab activists of the time as deplorable warfare between two of the three sovereign Arab states. Once he had adopted Ibn Sa'ud, Arslan would not let him be diminished any more than he would allow Yahya to be humiliated. When Hajj Amin al-Husayni, acting in his capacity as president of the General Islamic Congress of Jerusalem, invited Arslan to serve on an Islamic peace delegation, he immediately accepted and arrived with the delegation in Mecca on 16 April 1934.[60]

That the General Islamic Congress had charged the delegation with its mission was evidence of the growing internationalization of Arab issues among Arabs themselves. Ibn Sa'ud's warm reception of the group was proof of his calculated understanding of the publicity surrounding the mission. The delegation spent nearly two months in Mecca, Taif, and finally San'a while Ibn Sa'ud and Imam Yahya exchanged notes and bullets. The Treaty of Muslim Friendship and Arab Fraternity between the two rulers concluded on 20 May, although drawn up under "the scrutiny" of the delegation, was due far less to its presence than to the imam's acknowledgment of the superiority of Sa'udi arms and to Ibn Sa'ud's recognition that his total defeat of the Yemen would probably provoke European intervention.[61] But the mediation commission had gained respect for its members and its cause. Arslan wrote that the treaty gave the entire Muslim world reason for celebration. Although he credited the cessation of hostilities to the noble character of the two monarchs, he could not refrain from reminding his readers that he had been a part of it all: "Because of the close personal relations I have had with the two rulers since the end of World War I, and the correspondence I have exchanged with each of them, I am in a better position than anyone to know about these matters."[62] Rida provided further encomiums, publicly extolling the delegation and praising Arslan personally for "your success as a *mujahid* in the path of God and your service to Islam and the people of Muhammad."[63] Propagandists like Arslan and the mufti reasoned that if war over the obscure province of Asir could prompt such significant attention, then surely the more central problems of Palestine and Syria could do so as well.

They had both tested the waters before. Because of British leniency, they were able to test them again on their return from Arabia. In March 1934, Arslan had requested permission to reside in Palestine; the request was firmly denied, but the Colonial Office and Foreign Office did agree that he could visit the Mandate in order to see his mother (her longevity suited her second son's political career nicely) provided he signed a pledge not to engage in political activity while there.[64] Arslan consented to the condition and accompanied Hajj Amin from Jiddah to Jerusalem; it was his first visit to the Arab Levant since 1917.

His behavior was audacious; he may have kept to the letter of his pledge to British officials, but he certainly violated its spirit. In the company of Hajj Amin, Riyad al-Sulh, and al-Jabiri, he attended receptions, received congratulations for successfully mediating the dispute between Ibn Saʿud and Imam Yahya, and attracted more attention to himself than was prudent. It was too much for the French authorities in Beirut. High Commissioner de Martel complained that the presence of Arslan and al-Jabiri in Palestine was "attracting a swarm of agitators" and was, in effect, permitting "the surreptitious organization of a veritable nationalist congress." He requested the British to expel them.[65] The Foreign Office in London had been sensitive to French feeling from the moment it agreed to permit Arslan to visit Palestine, and British High Commissioner Arthur Wauchope responded to his French counterpart's request in the only way possible; he summoned Arslan to a meeting and invited him to leave Palestine on the first available boat. On 5 August 1934, Arslan found himself heading away from his homeland, banished once again.

Three years later, with the French Popular Front in power, Arslan was invited by de Martel to return to Syria. It was a remarkable about-face both in France's attitude toward Arslan and in the diplomatic positions of the two European powers who controlled the Levant. Because Arslan's return coincided with the Palestinian rebellion, Whitehall became as upset over his presence in Damascus as the Quai d'Orsay had been at his entry into Jerusalem three years earlier. But France had not invited Arslan to Syria in order to embarrass Britain over Palestine; rather, the invitation stemmed from French perceptions of his influence and a belief that it could be exploited to their advantage. Events would show that Arslan was not an easy man to manipulate, but his personal needs were such that he was driven to take advantage of the opportunity to return to Syria. The years of exile were taking their toll, and for all his inflamed rhetoric about European imperialism, the Amir also wanted to go home.

Arslan's financial situation had continued to deteriorate in the first half of the 1930s. The issue of his possible sources of Axis income is discussed in chapter 7. For the moment, it is sufficient to record his continuing record of financial inadequacy and his growing personal disillusionment with his lot. These are important, not just as additions to the biographical record, but as items which, to some degree, determined the Amir's behavior. That in itself was of import to highly placed officials and prominent political figures in several different countries.

More than any other activity, travel depleted Arslan's financial resources. The summer spent in Spain discovering the glorious Arab past had increased his indebtedness to Dr. Bayda by an additional £200.[66] He constantly tried to raise income through the manipulation of his Lebanese properties, but his directives generated more confusion than revenue.[67] He received short-term cash by remortgaging his Berlin apartment house at every opportunity, but these transactions were not very profitable either. At the end of 1930, he wrote: "I am deeply in debt, so I came to Berlin to find someone else to mortgage the building to, but for a five year term. Perhaps God will bring relief in these times, but for now you will find Dr. Bayda and me going from broker to broker."[68] A few years later, he complained that life in Switzerland was simply beyond his means: "How are we to manage? I sold the farm in Syria; I mortgaged the house in Berlin, and would acquire no cash if I sold it." He contemplated selling the family olive groves in Shuwayfat, but paused when he faced the troubling question, "What will then be left for the children?"[69]

As Arslan's health and finances declined, his parental responsibilities increased. He and Salima had what almost amounted to a second family when two daughters, Mayy and Nazimah, were born in 1928 and 1930. Arslan may have been a caring father, but his lengthy absences precluded being a very attentive one. His wife told Professor al-Sharabasi that Shakib spent so much time reading and writing that he had no time for the children and did not even concern himself with their education.[70] This gave him particular troubles with his son Ghalib, who passed his teenage years without knowing Arabic or caring to learn it. This infuriated and frustrated the prince of eloquence: "I am sorely grieved on this matter, and I have given him to understand that if he does not learn Arabic he will not be a true Arab and will not receive any inheritance from me."[71] Finding himself in his early sixties with two infant daughters, an improperly educated son, and a dwindling income, Arslan cast about for another residence. He considered moving to Vienna or Budapest, where life was less expensive, but mostly he thought about the Arab East.

Adding to his sense of personal unease was a sad journalistic task that he had to perform with increasing frequency in the 1930s—writing obituaries. The men of his generation were passing on. This affected Arslan most deeply when he recalled how his exile had deprived him of the companionship of his friends in their—and what he saw to be his—final years. No loss struck him so intensely as the death of Rashid Rida in 1935. His own reflections at the time were of how rarely they had been permitted to be together in the postwar years and of how cruelly shortened their final meeting was. It had taken place on the train from Alexandria to Suez during Arslan's journey to Arabia as part of the 1934 peace delegation. He was subjected to very tight security during his Egyptian transit. A military guard accompanied him for the entire trip, and all conversation with him was forbidden. Rida, who had loyally met his friend's plane and boarded his train, "tasted the bitterness" of the security arrangements. When they met in the aisle of Arslan's car—two men who had for some thirty years shared by correspondence their grandiose plans and their personal intimacies—they could only shake hands in silence.[72] The episode, as related by Arslan, may seem maudlin, but his sadness was as real as the restrictions which caused it.

Grief, age, illness, isolation, and family and financial worries were all matters which might influence Arslan's course of action. Yet his portrayal of himself as a passive and mistreated bystander was inaccurate, and he knew it. In whatever conflict may have taken place within him among his financial needs, his choice of residence, and his anti-imperialist principles, the latter nearly always won. He simply did not give Britain or France an opening through which they might repatriate him. In his 1934 application to return to Palestine, he offered High Commissioner Wauchope no apologies, only the chance to deal with an honorable man on his own terms: "my constant endeavour has been to serve my country according to my conscience and my convictions, regardless of the cost."[73] He wrote to a friend that although his greatest hope was to return to Syria before he died, he understood that because of his activities he would only be permitted entry into the country by an independent Syrian government.[74] Through most of his exile, that possibility appeared remote.

The period from 1928 to 1935 produced little political progress in the Syrian Mandate. Local leaders formed no lasting alliances, and French Mandatory administrators gave few political liberties.[75] During these years, Arslan devoted more public writing to North Africa than he did to Syria. However, he continued to be regarded as a central figure in Franco-Syrian relations, and petitions under his name appeared regularly before the Permanent Mandates Commission. His prominence in Franco-Syrian affairs stemmed from the role he had played in the negotiations with de Jouvenal in 1925. Unlike his relations with other occupied Arab territories, his Syrian interests encouraged him to attempt more than the inspiration of local leaders who would, under his general guidance, formulate their own specific programs. Arslan was himself a local Syrian leader, and he had his own plan for a resolution of Franco-Syrian differences. He had presented it in 1925, and he continued to endorse it without modification for a decade. His vindication came in 1936.

In January of that year, riots broke out in Damascus and soon spread to the major cities of the north. In February, martial law was declared, and French tanks again entered the capital. Arrests numbered in the hundreds, but a replay of the bombardment of 1925 was prevented by High Commissioner de Martel's sudden concessions to the nationalist leaders. At the end of March, a delegation of six Syrians traveled to Paris empowered to negotiate a treaty of independence on the basis of an agreement they had drawn up with de Martel. A Lebanese delegation followed. The election of Léon Blum's Popular Front government in June improved the negotiating climate, and a draft treaty was signed in September. At this point, the figure of Shakib Arslan came center stage. The issue facing all parties to the treaty was how to involve him in a constructive manner.

Arslan's support could not guarantee the treaty's passage in the Syrian chamber but his opposition could sabotage it. Several tactics were employed to gain his endorsement. During the course of the negotiations in Paris, members of the Syrian and Lebanese delegations visited him in Geneva, thus keeping him involved in the discussions and committing him to the decisions which were being taken.[76] Once the draft was initialed, the signatories took great pains to ensure that the Amir's voice would not be raised against the still-fragile document. Pierre Viénot, Blum's undersecretary for foreign affairs, held a long dinner meeting with Arslan in Geneva, and the Syrian negotiating team passed through the city en route to Damascus. They thanked Arslan for his efforts toward Syrian unity and bestowed on him the title "Father of the Muslims," which confirmed the image he had created for himself.[77]

Arslan's political judgment, long-standing principles, and personal aspirations were all consistent with his statesman-like response to the draft treaty. To his obvious satisfaction, it was nearly identical to the agreement he had concluded with de Jouvenal a decade earlier, and he drew on this similarity to justify his public support for the new proposals and to make clear the consistency of his position over time.[78] He was critical of portions of the treaty, but for the most part he glossed over its unsettled details and argued that it was the best that could be expected under the circumstances. With Olympian grandeur, he pronounced, "I am satisfied," and, relying on his usual cultural reference point, reminded Syrians that they should adopt the initialed draft because the Qur'an called on Muslims to honor their agreements.[79]

The French were also satisfied. Viénot wrote de Martel that Arslan's attitude had been correct and that his intervention with other Arab states during the course of the treaty negotiations had been effective in discouraging outside agitation.[80] Arslan's moderation, and the French desire to encourage it, produced the circumstances which enabled him and al-Jabiri to return to Syria in June 1937.

At last he had a chance to be received by the Syrian people in whose name he had carried out his mission. They did not disappoint him. Even with his reputation somewhat clouded, Arslan, as symbol, as personality, as legend, remained a powerful attraction. What he had been, what to many he still was, permitted him a final, glorious moment. As described by French intelligence, "The return of the Druze Amir to the Levant was triumphal."[81] It was as though his presence, so long denied, signified the reality of independence.

In their triumphal tour through Beirut, Damascus, Homs, Hama, and Aleppo, Arslan and al-Jabiri were met by huge crowds.[82] National and municipal leaders turned out to receive them, and the Syrian government made their entry into Damascus a lavish ceremony. Muhammad ʿAli al-Tahir wrote that he would need fifty pages to describe the wondrous receptions accorded the returning heroes.[83] Arslan's own feelings were expressed more simply during his first hours in Beirut: "I am so happy, after 21 years, to return to this country, and my heart is filled with joy at seeing the national aspirations finally realized."[84]

His incessant politicking nearly destroyed the whole ritual. The speeches he delivered at every opportunity were conciliatory on the subject of Franco-Syrian relations and enthusiastic about the possibility of Arab unity. These sentiments, while not shared in all quarters, were not in themselves inflammatory. During his stay in Aleppo, however, he delivered one of the most ill-advised addresses of his career. With the Umayyad mosque as his venue, Arslan proclaimed to a region of the Arab world experiencing increasing tension over the future of confessional liberties: "He who is not a Muslim cannot be a patriot."[85] Arslan struggled to recover in the stir which followed. He asked the archbishop of Aleppo for permission to speak in a church in order to explain to a Christian audience what he had really meant— that atheism does not imply patriotism and that religious faith is a necessary component of, not an impediment to, nationalism. The context of the speech shows this to have been Arslan's message, but he was careless in expressing it. Although he did not speak in the church, he did offer modifications and clarifications of his views. Age had not altered his style.

Although marred, his return was not destroyed by the speech. In the best tradition of Lebanese notables, he passed the summer of 1937 in Sofar, where he met frequently with Hajj Amin al-Husayni. It was even rumored that he would be a parliamentary candidate in the forthcoming Lebanese elections. His visit was capped—and probably terminated—by his attendance at the Bludan Congress in September.

Formally called the Arab National Congress, the meeting was held at a Syrian summer resort near Damascus and was called on the initiative of Hajj Amin al-Husayni in the wake of the Peel Commission's recommendation to partition Palestine into Jewish and Arab spheres. Although it was organized rapidly and without official auspices, the Bludan Congress attracted 411 delegates and was "a landmark in the increasing involvement of the Arab world in the Palestine problem."[86] From the moment of his arrival in Beirut in June, Arslan had asserted his own continued involvement in that problem. His remarks to the welcoming crowd had contained these words: "In our national joy, we should not forget Palestine. . . . Can concessions be made on such a vital issue? Right is on our side, and none can violate our right. Syria will not exist if Palestine is lost. The Arabs cannot dream of progress if they allow themselves to lose Palestine."[87] As much as he wanted to remain in the Levant, he could not prevent himself from speaking out. If he thought that embarrassing Britain would please the French, he was wrong.

The attention, both local and European, which surrounded Arslan's arrival in Syria accompanied him to Bludan. The delegation honored him with yet another office (second vice-president) and with the privilege of addressing the gathering. His remarks went somewhat against the Arabocentric tenor of the Congress. While he acknowledged the usefulness of Arab solidarity in the defense of Palestine, he reminded the assembly that the religious impulse of Islam, and even of Christianity, should also be employed in this regard.[88] Arslan's much-noted presence at a Congress which resolved that "it is the duty of the Arabs and the Moslems everywhere to fight as one man for the liberty, deliverance and the unification of Palestine with the Arab lands, and to bring to nought the colonizing and Zionist endeavors to establish a Jewish state" did not augur well for his continued residence in Syria.[89] When, a few days after the conclusion of Bludan, he delivered a widely circulated speech on Arab unity to the Arab Club of Damascus, he expended his credit.

In December 1937, Arslan abruptly sailed from Beirut to Alexandria. No explanations have been given for his departure, but it was surely requested. The Foreign Office in London was displeased by his presence in the French Mandate. French officials also began to question whether his usefulness as a supporter of the draft treaty was not outweighed by his outspokenness on other matters. The French intelligence report on his activities notes that his speech in Aleppo, his attendance at Bludan, and his address to the Arab Club "attracted the attention of the Mandate authorities in the Levant."[90] That, apparently, was sufficient to end his stay. While al-Jabiri was pardoned by France and remained in Syria to serve as governor of Latakia, Arslan was expelled and then further humiliated when the Egyptian government refused to let him disembark at Alexandria. He had no choice but to return to Geneva. The Syro-Palestinian delegation in Europe had been reduced to one.

In the course of the next year, Arslan viewed with growing disenchantment the gradual repudiation of the Syrian treaty by the French chamber. He knew that as long as France remained in control of Syrian affairs, he would be denied permanent residence. For the damage he was perceived to have inflicted single-handedly on the imperial edifice in North Africa, he could not be pardoned.

CHAPTER FIVE.
MENTOR TO A GENERATION:
NORTH AFRICA

The remedy for this problem is a general campaign . . . with protests to France itself, to the League of Nations, and to the French ambassador in Cairo. Let them not say about religious problems, these are strictly internal affairs. —Arslan [1]

For the full twenty-one years of his voluntary exile, Shakib Arslan has never ceased to incite North Africa. Let us not forget the Berber Dahir Affair. —J. Desparmet [2]

SHAKIB ARSLAN's life and writings traversed the political and cultural turmoil convulsing the Arab East in the fifteen years following the outbreak of the Syrian revolt in 1925. He commented on virtually all issues, great and small, experienced many of them directly, and, if he determined the final resolution of but a few, he most definitely had an impact on the opinion of his time. However, he was something of a latecomer to Eastern Arabism. Consequently, he had always to confront his earlier Ottoman associations and to fight for political survival among his factious peers. No such limiting circumstances existed in his relationship to the North African independence movements, where his intervention was welcome and decisive. It was in the Maghrib that his influence was most pronounced, there that his reputation as Islamic spokesman and political strategist was most secure. Charles-André Julien has written that "it was the inexhaustible spring of his thought which nourished Maghribi nationalism, most of whose leaders were formed or inspired by him." [3] He brought to the emerging political elite of North Africa, men often two generations his junior, his respected presence as an activist commentator on the issues of the Arab East and his ability to make them feel part of the total Arab-Islamic entity. He also publicized their struggles to his Eastern associates, working to create feelings of a common endeavor bound by fraternal ties of Arabism and Islamic solidarity. This effort, marked by some major achievements, constituted another component of Arslan's justifiably unique reputation. No other interwar Arab spokesman was so intimately associated with both the Maghrib and the Mashriq, no other linked the two halves of the Arab world in his person as did Arslan. That Arslan, consummately a man of the Mashriq, came to occupy so central a place in the Maghrib was due to his already high standing among the urban elite of the region, the timing of the new North African movements, and, once again, his own location in Europe.

All three countries of French North Africa had found in Eastern pan-Islam an attractive doctrine through which to offer resistance to France before and during World War I. The formation of nationalist political organizations during the interwar years, usually headed by men born between 1890 and 1910, has tended to obscure the continuities between their movements and earlier patterns of resistance. Thus, while it is true that the Moroccan protectorate treaty was signed only two years before the beginning of the Great War, and the Berber tribal areas were not pacified until 1934, it should also be recognized that the Sharifian court, the tribal leaders, and the urban merchants and ulema repeatedly, if often in fragmented fashion, opposed the French takeover of their country. In their opposition, they became accustomed to looking toward Egypt and the Ottoman Empire for external assistance and intellectual inspiration.[4] This tendency was intensified after 1908, when the Young Turk regime came to power in Istanbul, and German and Ottoman interests coalesced to generate a variety of semiofficial efforts to embarrass France in Morocco and to attract Moroccan resisters to the pan-Islamic orientation favored by Enver Pasha. Al-Ittihad al-Maghribi, mentioned in chapter 1, recruited Moroccan students at Cairo's al-Azhar university, made plans to support a Moroccan uprising in 1911 and 1912 and, through the efforts of Shaykh ʿAli Yusuf, encouraged the dispatching of al-Muʾayyad and other Egyptian journals to Morocco. During the war, Enver Pasha's security service, Teşkilat-i Mahsusa, worked with German experts to send agents to Morocco and to establish propaganda centers in Istanbul, Lausanne, Berlin, and Madrid from which materials were distributed throughout the Maghrib. Thus, firm connections were established between some members of the Moroccan elite and Eastern pan-Islamic activists before the Ottoman collapse in 1918.

In Algeria, the possibilities for clandestine agitation were less promising: the tribal elite had been destroyed in the aftermath of the resistance of the 1840s and 1870s, the urban bourgeoisie was displaced by European *colons*, and the religious establishment was dispossessed. Nonetheless, as shown below, there survived among the Islamic leadership the impulse which sent ʿAbd al-Hamid Ibn Badis to Cairo and Bashir al-Ibrahimi to Damascus in the early years of this century and so produced a group of scholar-politicians which was acquainted with and attracted to the Near Eastern style of pan-Islam.

Similarly, the Young Tunisians of the 1890s and early 1900s were not just liberal assimilationists; men like the brothers ʿAli and Muhammad Bash Hanba and ʿAbd al-ʿAziz al-Thaʿalibi produced journals in Arabic as well as in French, and in the perplexing effort to rescue their country from subservient status, looked to the wider sphere of pan-Islam as well as to the possibility of assimilation with the colonizers. In 1910, ʿAli Bash Hanba proclaimed in *Le Tunisien*: "Every Muslim is a supporter of Muslim union, and the Tunisians, to a man, are partisans of this policy and are attached to pan-Ottomanism, which is a consequence of such an idea. . . . The Turks and Egyptians inspire us with feeling as much as our nearer neighbours in Algeria or the peoples in further Asia."[5]

Of the figures who circulated around Enver Pasha and ʿAbbas Hilmi, who moved through the clandestine groupings in Berlin, Lausanne, Istanbul, and Cairo, and who propagated pan-Islam from personal belief and political commitment, none was more consistent, available, or prominent than Arslan. Although his direct involvement cannot always be fully documented, his personal associations are known, and in a world of conspirators and small elite groupings, such associations reveal much. Arslan did not suddenly discover North Africa as part of the larger Islamic cause in the postwar era; he was affiliated with all the movements to integrate the Maghrib with the Mashriq during his Ottoman career.

With his associate, ʿAbd al-ʿAziz Jawish, Arslan had participated in the attempts to organize a pan-Maghribi union at the time of the Italian invasion of Libya in 1911. He probably prepared pan-Islamic propaganda during the war; he is reported to have used his connections with the CUP to secure a high position for ʿAli Bash Hanba, the Tunisian who headed Enver's information office in Istanbul in 1914;[6] and he was allied to the figures in the Lausanne office, ʿAbbas Hilmi and Muhammad Bash Hanba. His missions to Berlin during the war and his activities there after the Ottoman surrender brought him into close association with German civilians who believed in the viability of a pan-Islamic rising against Britain and France.[7] And it was in Berlin that Muhammad Bash Hanba, "one of the most outstanding men of the Islamic world," died in Arslan's arms in 1919.[8]

Arslan's pan-Islamic ideals, his widespread contacts, and his personal magnetism provide the connecting thread which runs across time and space from the Ottoman Middle East to the Maghrib, and from postwar Geneva to Cairo, and back to the Maghrib. As Edmund

Burke has noted, Arslan's influence on a later generation of North African nationalists should come as no surprise, "for he played an important part in converting many of their fathers to pan-Islam."[9]

As had been the case with their fathers, this new generation, whose members had reached adulthood after the First World War, was informed by a knowledge of events in the Arab East. Through his prominent role in publicizing those events, Arslan had become an admired and established figure. He was available for Maghribi activists to turn to and was only too willing to embark on new ventures. Arslan's role in the Maghrib of the 1930s is best studied through a separate examination of his relationship to the four regions of Morocco, Libya, Algeria, and Tunisia, with no intention of reviewing in full the evolution of each independence movement, but rather to demonstrate the circumstances of Arslan's association with them. His appeal in North Africa reveals much about the content of interwar Maghribi protest as well as about his own special role and aspirations.

His first contacts with the younger generation of Maghribi activists were made among Moroccan students in Paris. They were attracted by his reputation and he, in turn, found the religious orientation of the Moroccan cultural awakening in accord with his own social and political views. In the early 1920s, groups of urban Moroccans had accepted the need to revitalize Islam in order to revitalize their society as a whole. They sought to accomplish this task through an educational system which was outside the control of the French authorities. In the early 1920s, a series of so-called free schools was established in Fez, Rabat, and Tetouan. Imbued with Salafiyyah ideals, these schools offered a curriculum designed to generate pride in the Islamic past and hope for a modernized Islamic future free from the undesirable influences of European culture.[10]

With the entry of France into the war against ʿAbd al-Krim, graduates of the free schools engaged more overtly in political activity by founding secret societies intended, like the schools themselves, to spread the ideas of Islamic reformism among the urban elite. One of the leaders of such a society founded in Fez in late 1925 was Muhammad al-Fasi; instrumental in organizing a similar group the following year in Rabat were Ahmad Balafrej, Muhammad Hassan al-Ouezzani, and Mekki Naciri.[11] They were to become Arslan's closest associates among the Moroccan nationalist leadership. The first three soon went to Paris to continue their education and to become, in 1927, prominent among the founders of the North African Muslim Students Association (AEMNA). Originally established to provide a variety of housing and counseling services to the growing number of

Maghribi students in the French capital, the organization quickly became involved in political concerns. Thriving in the exhilarating atmosphere of students abroad on the Left Bank, AEMNA brought together young men from the three North African countries, showed them their common identity and their common problems, and served as a base from which pamphlets could be distributed and meetings arranged.[12]

But even as Moroccans went to the *écoles* of Paris, they remained true to the Islamic reformist ideals with which they began their protests against French cultural imperialism. Politics and religious reform were to go hand in hand; the original free school movement was sufficiently influential, its graduates, both those who went to Europe and those who obtained more traditional Islamic higher educations, sufficiently committed, that "Salafiyya became the wellspring of Moroccan nationalism."[13] As secondary students in Fez and Rabat, these "proto-nationalists" had been nurtured on publications emanating from Cairo, most notably *al-Manar*, *al-Fath*, *al-Zahra'*, and the verses of Ahmad Shawqi.[14] When the young Moroccans, on the verge of political commitment in Paris, actually met Arslan, an author of the doctrines which had so inspired them, an individual who was a pupil of ʿAbduh, a friend of Rida and Shawqi, and a protagonist committed to a cause resembling their own, the effect was powerful and immediate; their youthful activism found direction in his willing counsel.

Arslan's entry into the circle of students was probably provided by Balafrej and Muhammad al-Fasi. They both told Halstead that they visited Arslan in Geneva several times during their student years in Paris (1926–1932) and that he treated them like sons.[15] They accompanied him during the latter part of his trip through Spain and were instrumental in arranging the dramatic conclusion to that journey when, for the first time, Arslan set foot in Morocco. He made the crossing to Tangiers on 9 August 1930. By the nineteenth he was back in Cadiz. His stay in the Maghrib was brief and closely supervised. Yet from it developed the most enduring of his political friendships and the most effective of his anticolonial protests. "From this moment," wrote Lévi-Provençal of the visit, "a closer and more permanent relationship would be assured between Shakib Arslan and the *foyers d'intrigues* of Tetouan, Rabat, and Fez through which he would inspire and coordinate the campaigns directed against France. . . ."[16]

As so often happened during Arslan's travels, his presence in a region and the associated requirement for local dignitaries to pay homage to him brought together groups which might not otherwise have openly associated. During his overnight stay in Tangiers, and the several days he spent in Tetouan, delegations from several Moroccan cities gathered to greet him, giving Arslan the opportunity to inaugurate his role as mediator among those who were to guide the Moroccan independence movement for the next two decades.[17]

In Tetouan, he was a house guest of the venerable Bennouna family, with which he established a particularly close relationship. The patriarch among the family's activists, Hajj ʿAbd al-Salam, had founded a free school and a secret society in his native city in 1923 and 1926, respectively, and was among the most prominent personalities in the Spanish zone. He came to serve as one of the principal liaisons between Arslan and the nationalists in Fez and Rabat.[18] While in Tetouan, Arslan gave a series of public lectures and sought, generally, to build links between the Moroccans and the Eastern Arab world. His hosts had an uneasy sense of inferiority toward the Eastern centers of Islamic learning and political activism. In an interview which revealed as much about Maghribi attitudes as it did about Arslan's, he, as "the greatest writer of the East," was asked by Ahmad Balafrej a series of questions which seemed to contain a quest for affirmation: What is your opinion of the people of the Maghrib? Do you feel there is an awakening in the Maghrib? What is your opinion of the Arabic of the Maghrib? What are the virtues of the Maghrib? Arslan's replies, complimentary and reassuring, were intended to elevate the Moroccan cause in the eyes of its own adherents as well as to bring it to the attention of Eastern readers.[19] In the mind of at least one Moroccan figure, the visit fulfilled the Amir's hopes: "it opened wide the door of contacts with our brethren [in the East]" and formed "a pure pearl in the historical chain of the emerging Maghribi awakening."[20]

In this vein of mutual admiration, Arslan was feted during his last evening in Tetouan at a painstakingly prepared banquet during which such future nationalist leaders as ʿAbd al-Khaliq Ben Torres and Muhammad Daʾud delivered speeches, Thami al-Ouezzani read a qasidah congratulating the Maghrib for its good fortune in receiving the visit of such a distinguished guest, and, as the culminating gesture, Muhammad Bennouna presented the Amir with a Moroccan jallaba and burnus.[21] One does not want to read too much into a eulogistic account of the honors done to an esteemed visitor. On the other hand, it would be overly cautious not to suggest connections between Arslan's appearance in Morocco and his involvement in later developments. A closely watched figure, he had made a personal and very public gesture to the Moroccans to show that they were not isolated. Bennouna's reportage, although overindulgent by some journalistic standards, has about it the same excitement that Arslan himself once expressed in describing Muhammad ʿAbduh's presence in Beirut. There was both symbolic value and practical substance to this visit, and the contacts initiated by it were not inconsequential.

When Arslan passed through Suez on his return from Mecca in 1929, he had worn Bedouin dress. Although one doubts that he arrived back in Cádiz in his Moroccan *jallaba* and *burnus*, events showed that he accepted seriously the homage of the Tetouanese and interpreted accurately the stirrings of the young Moroccans who saw in him a channel for their growing discontent with French rule. He advanced their cause beyond what they could have envisaged and within months made it an international Islamic crusade. He was aided in doing so by a major blunder on the part of the French protectorate administration.

In May 1930, the decree which came to be known as the Berber *dahir* was signed by the young Moroccan sultan.[22] From the beginning of the protectorate, French authorities recognized a distinct judicial regime in the Berber areas of Morocco where local customs predominated over certain regulations of the *shariʿah*. The decree of 1930 extended this concept and increased the scope of the Berber tribunals in civil law while imposing French law in criminal cases. The decree was based on the divide and rule principle and was intended to separate the Berbers administratively and culturally from the Arabs; it is unlikely that Resident General Lucien Saint and his advisers had as their foremost consideration a full cultural transformation of the Berbers. However, by placing about half the Berber population under the jurisdiction of French courts in the area of criminal justice, the *dahir* could be interpreted as a direct attack on the authority of the sultan's government, on the rule of Islamic law, and on the very integrity of the Islamic faith. It could also be seen as an attempt to detach the Berbers from their fragile loyalty to the Moroccan state and so facilitate their assimilation to French customs. To make the *dahir* appear even more threatening, its promulgation coincided with a period in which several special Berber schools with entirely French curricula were established and in which limited, but alarming, efforts were made to encourage Berbers to renounce Islam for Christianity.

The response to the decree shows how deeply the Residency had misjudged the extent of Islamic sentiment among both its Arab and Berber subjects. The nascent movement of cultural affirmation now had a concrete issue around which to coalesce and, in Arslan, an international spokesman through whom to voice its grievances. Within Morocco, the young men Arslan had met in Paris, Geneva, and Tetouan organized various forms of nonviolent protests—communal prayers of mourning, formal delegations to French authorities, and occasional street demonstrations. None was in itself successful, and the organizers suffered jail terms, exile, and, in the case of Muhammad al-Ouezzani, a public flogging for their efforts. Yet the cumulative effect of the public manifestations was to arouse the communal conscience of Morocco in a defense of Islam under attack.

This was Arslan's type of issue. When the movement inside Morocco was restricted by the French, he carved out a role for himself in Geneva. Working closely with Balafrej, Muhammad al-Fasi, and Mekki Naciri, he coordinated an international propaganda campaign against the *dahir*. He provided the Moroccans with a channel of communication to the Islamic world at large—most notably through *al-Fath*, *al-Manar*, and *La Nation Arabe*, offered them a set of tactics which they largely adopted, and donated his considerable experience as a polemicist to the protest. It became a legendary effort and a major factor in shaping Arslan's image among North African activists and French officials.

Shortly after Arslan's return from Tetouan, *La Nation Arabe* launched what was to become a continuous commentary on the decree. In the time-honored method of a true propagandist, Arslan was sometimes careless with his facts but always relentless in presenting his version of them. To him, the framers of the *dahir* had a single basic objective in mind—the detachment of the Berbers from Islam and their eventual conversion to Christianity. He portrayed the regulation as the culmination of the evangelizing efforts of Cardinal Lavigerie and as a deliberate anti-Islamic act which violated, among other things, Berber wishes, the terms of the 1912 protectorate treaty, and universally accepted tenets of religious freedom.[23] The following is typical of his arguments:

It may be asked if the practice of Berber justice, according to the objectives of the Residency, means the conversion of the Berbers to Catholicism. We reply: yes. It means the initial application of measures long contemplated to attain this goal. First, Muslim legislation, even the exercise of Muslim law in personal status, is taken from the Berbers. That is the first step in detaching them from Islam. Next is the prohibition of Muslim religious education and of the Arabic language which, for Muslims, is like Latin for Catholics. That is the second step. The third step is to send missionaries to preach Christianity among the Berbers at a time when no Muslim religious education can interfere with their propaganda. It is noteworthy that the French have not waited for the completion of the first step before beginning the second and third. They do all three at the same time.[24]

By carrying out this policy, "M. Saint may thus justify his name and be noted in this century as having completed the work of Ferdinand and Isabella."[25] By attributing the most sinister intentions to Resident General Saint and his advisers, Arslan was able to present the Berbers as innocent victims whose fate was linked to that of the entire Islamic community: "The brutal hand of military force has now attacked the Islamic religion itself and the freedom of conscience of its people."[26]

This extension of the Berber cause was at the heart of Arslan's appeal. It is evident from his articles in *al-Fath* that he was seeking something more substantial than the mere castigation of the French. By persuading his coreligionists that the *dahir* represented a policy of monstrously threatening proportions, he hoped to shock the international Muslim community into forceful action. "This issue," he warned, "is not confined to the attack on the Islam of the Berbers, but includes the entire world of Islam."[27] As he had done in his press campaign of 1912 against the Italian invasion of Tripolitania, Arslan called on Muslims to draw the line against imperial threats to the faith. Other Muslim communities had watched from the sidelines while the Ottoman Empire fell (still Arslan's greatest regret), and now most of Islam was under European domination. If the French succeeded in implementing the *dahir*, "depriving the Muslim Berbers of the Qur'anic *shari'ah*," would not England and Holland be encouraged to pursue like policies? If Muslims did not act now, "they will lose their religion as they lost their kingdoms and their empires." The *dahir* was not, then, a question confined to France and Morocco: "Every Muslim in the world has a right to involve himself in this issue."

He endeavored to orchestrate that involvement. His plan called for a massive outpouring of letters, telegrams, and petitions to the League of Nations, to all branches of the French government, and to the chancelleries of the Great Powers so as to create "a continuous, deafening cry which France will be unable to ignore."[28] This was similar to the strategy of protest he had been practicing before the Mandates Commission on behalf of Syria and Palestine. What made the campaign against the Berber *dahir* so distinctive was the enthusiastic international Muslim response to Arslan's appeal. Protest committees were established from Sumatra to Berlin, from India to Paris. In Java, a Muslim Defense Committee for the Berbers was formed and in Cairo, Prince ʿUmar Tusun headed a similar organization which worked closely with ʿAbd al-Hamid Saʿid's Muslim youth groups in circulating petitions and collecting signatures. Rashid Rida placed the prestige of *al-Manar* behind the campaign, and the rest of the Arab press, from Tunis to Damascus, joined in the outcry against the injustice done to the Muslim Berbers.[29] As an example of the expanding awareness among Muslim public figures of the broad character of the imperial menace to Islam, and of the propaganda value of that issue, the Muslim Congress of Jerusalem passed a resolution on "the de-Islamisation of the Berbers" in which the delegates condemned a policy designed, in their view, "to turn the Muslim Berbers from their religion and to impose Christianity on them."[30] Probably surprised, and certainly delighted, by the extent of the emotional support generated by Arslan's press campaign, Muhammad al-Ouezzani exclaimed, "The movement has exceeded all expectations, all hopes. . . ."[31]

While it is likely that the international Muslim agitation was more narrowly based than Arslan's presentation of it would indicate, the campaign against the *dahir* must be judged a success. Within Morocco, its impact, including the local resistance, led the Residency to modify the most controversial elements of the decree in 1934 by returning the administration of Berber justice to the sultan's tribunal and thus to the domain of Islam.[32] More dramatic was the effect of the campaign in broadening the scope and solidifying the organization of the nationalist movement itself. Arslan's role was central to this development. He managed to place the assault on Moroccan cultural identity implied in the Berber *dahir* within the larger context of an imminent imperial threat to the right of all Muslims to practice their beliefs. Morocco and its plight became a cause in Eastern Arab Islamic circles, and Moroccans, in turn, gained a new awareness of the issues confronting other Islamic countries and new allies in furthering their own cause.[33]

Arslan's conduct of the campaign demonstrated once again his preference for action based on the principle of Islamic solidarity as opposed to more narrowly focused national loyalties. It was not national independence *per se* which determined his choice of symbols—he expressed no concern for a change in the protectorate relationship between France and Morocco—but rather a conviction that the universal community of believers, when presented with a danger to the faith, would respond decisively. Despite its diversity, the community shared a common Islamness; by recognizing this bond and acting on it, Muslims would achieve liberation from their current oppression and restoration of their glorious past. Woven into Arslan's articles of protest were bittersweet evocations of the lost grandeur of al-Andalus and the vanished power of the Ottoman era; reminders of recent noble failures, of ʿAbd al-Krim and the Syrian revolt; and warnings of a present darkened by the Wailing Wall incident, the Eucharistic Congress in Carthage, Italian brutalities in Libya, and atheistic Kemalists in Ankara. His appeal touched a deep chord and demonstrated the attractiveness of Islam as a political weapon. As Le Tourneau has written, "because of Shakib Arslan, Morocco seized the limelight of the Muslim question."[34] It was the Muslim question that he sought to capture, and it was on the basis of the Muslim question that his tactics were, in this case, vindicated.

Nor would he let the issue rest. In the midst of his commitment to the Moroccan cause, he also undertook a campaign to rally the Muslim world in yet another common protest, this time against what he called Italian atrocities in Tripoli and Cyrenaica.[35] From his own direct involvement with the Ottoman forces in 1912 until his death, Arslan's public reputation was closely tied to his responses to Italian ventures in Libya. Initially enhancing his image as an implacable anti-imperialist, the Libyan connection ended by diminishing him. When he made his peace with Mussolini in 1934, he was terribly compromised, not least because of the vehemence of his previous opposition. In this earlier phase, which is our concern here, Arslan was never more outspoken than in his condemnation of General Graziani's brutalization of the Cyrenaican population. He wrote to Rida that when he learned of the deportations, executions, tortures, and sexual humiliations inflicted on the civilian population of Jabal al-Akhdar, "I let my pen loose on those dogs."[36] In article after article, he enumerated the horrors committed by the Italian forces and condemned fascist Italy as being beyond the pale of humankind. He patterned his imagery of protest on that used in the campaign against the Berber *dahir* and cast his opposition to imperialism and human suffering in Islamic symbols. He told his readers that when the Italian forces captured the oasis of Kufrah, they "turned the great Sanusi *zawiyyah* into a tavern where they drank toasts to the extermination of the Muslims of Tripoli; and they threw the holy Qurʾans beneath their horses' hooves and then used them to light the fires of their cooking pots."[37]

Just as the Berber *dahir* had implications far beyond the language of the decree, so did the Italian abuse of Islam and the population of Libya mean more than the atrocities themselves. The real objective of the fascist government was the extermination of Islam from the entire region, in this case by exterminating the native population and replacing it with Christian colonists. Using the historical analogy which he favored at the time, Arslan saw the fascists in Libya acting as Ferdinand and Isabella had done toward the Moors of Spain. To forestall the fate that befell al-Andalus, the Muslims had to act in concert. When the Italians executed ʿUmar Mukhtar, that magnificent old warrior whose spirit and tactics had formed the heart of the resistance in Cyrenaica, Arslan wrote: "His blood will always cry for vengeance and that cry will be heard by all the Muslim world."[38] It was not an exclusively Arab cause as defined by Arslan. It had to be Islamic. No other focus of communal loyalty was sufficiently powerful to withstand the onslaught: "If Tripoli and Cyrenaica become totally Italian, then Egypt stands in the greatest danger. In this event, Pharaonic pride will be of no use to her whatsoever nor will the claims of some of her sophists that she occupies no place in the Islamic world or that she is not an Arab country."[39] What would save Egypt, and possibly Tripoli, was the same kind of concerted response that was being made against the *dahir*.

Although Arslan proceeded to map out a similar schedule of telegrams, boycotts, and the like, the Libyan protest did not generate the same level of support as the Berber cause. Circumstances were simply too unfavorable. The indigenous urban elite, such as it was, had neither organization nor backing, and Graziani's retribution against the remnants of Mukhtar's followers broke the Bedouin resistance and began dismantling the tribal system itself.

Yet, if internal circumstances prevented the campaign against Italy from becoming the same kind of launching pad for Libyan nationalism as the *dahir* had been for Moroccan, it nevertheless attracted similar attention from the colonial power involved. Italian legations and consuls reported that Arslan's attacks on their Libyan policy had been reprinted in Beirut and Damascus papers, that his *al-Fath* articles had been reproduced as pamphlets and distributed to Muslim pilgrims in Arabia, and that his call for a boycott of Italian goods had the potential to cause commercial difficulties.[40] Sensitive to the impact if not the substance of Arslan's criticisms, the Italian Foreign Ministry issued instructions on how to counter his charges and concluded, as their British and French counterparts had done, that he was the principal cause of the anticolonial agitation which confronted them in the Arab world.[41] But Arslan's capacity to influence Arab opinion intrigued as well as irritated Rome. A top secret memorandum recommended that despite all the evidence portraying the Amir "as an absolutely intransigent and utterly disinterested individual," his concern for Syria might make him amenable to an overture suggesting he support Italian pressures on France's position in the Levant in exchange for a modification of his aggressive stance on Cyrenaica.[42] Even as his prestige reached new heights, the groundwork was laid by which it would be tarnished.

But for the moment, his position had been stated in the most unambiguous terms. Arslan's courage and, in the Moroccan case, his achievements in orchestrating these protest movements reinforced his position as a champion of Islam throughout the community as well as his reputation in the eyes of French officialdom as a dangerous troublemaker. Resident General Lucien Saint of Morocco complained to a correspondent about the way in which his intentions had been misrepresented by the perfidious campaign conducted in certain foreign publications. Arslan proudly took the reference to mean La Nation Arabe, since it "has taken the lead among those publications which have strongly attacked the Berber policy of M. Saint and his collaborators."[43] This was true enough and was widely recognized by both admirers and opponents. Never had Arslan's reputation been more luminous, his influence more pronounced.

As the young Moroccans moved to consolidate their gains through the establishment of organized political groups and the formulation of coherent demands, they continued to seek the Amir's guidance. While he was more instrumental in directing the strategy of protest than he was in shaping the content of ideology, his role was of sufficient dimensions to prompt agreement among Halstead's informants that he could be called the tactician of the Moroccan nationalist movement.[44] The leaders of that movement were seldom out of touch with him during the 1930s: Muhammad al-Ouezzani served as his secretary in Geneva from the fall of 1932 to the summer of 1933; Ahmad Balafrej obtained his assistance in bringing together the financial backing and the advisory board which led to the appearance in 1932 of Maghreb, the first journal of the new movement; and his mediation was sought in the leadership dispute between al-Ouezzani and ʿAllal al-Fasi in 1936 and 1937.[45]

Nor was political leadership all that Arslan offered to his Moroccan friends. His paternal relationship to their movement extended to them as individuals, and he helped them personally whenever he could. For example, when Ahmad Balafrej was taken to a sanatorium in Switzerland to be treated for tuberculosis, Arslan tenderly reassured him that he should concern himself only with his recovery, not with his medical bills: "Each time a bit of money reaches me, I will keep a little for myself and the rest will be for you. I will send it to you. . . . There is nothing for you to do. You will be my son and every minute I will take care of you."[46] There is every reason to believe that he made similar gestures to other North Africans in Europe.

Arslan also maintained the ties he had forged with the nationalists in the Spanish zone during his visit to Tetouan. He returned briefly to that city in 1936 when it appeared that the Francoists and the Popular Front were in agreement on substantial autonomy for the zone.[47] In a fascinating example of the cumulative effects of personal influence, Rézette reports that at Arslan's insistence, ʿAbd al-Salam Bennouna sent one of his sons to Nablus in Palestine for his secondary education. As a result of this act, a certain prestige came to be associated with study at Eastern Arab institutions, and the notables of Tetouan, following Bennouna's lead, abandoned Qarawiyin in favor of enrolling their sons at Egyptian universities or Palestinian madrasahs, where they were exposed to the more intensive political activities of that region of the Arab world.[48] Further evidence of the growing integration of Morocco into the affairs of the Mashriq was provided by an event which occurred at the opening of the Bludan Conference in Syria in 1937, when Moroccans took to the streets in organized demonstrations of solidarity with their Palestinian brethren.[49] This gesture, whether specifically encouraged by Arslan or not, represented a certain triumph for the policy he had initiated in 1930.

Arslan's ties to the Moroccans and the enthusiasm with which they accepted him led him to expand his range of associations with other groups concerned with North African affairs. At some point in the immediate postwar period, he penetrated the circles of the French Socialist party and established personal friendships with two of the senior leaders, Pierre Renaudel and Robert Longuet, whose positions were usually on the doctrinal right of the SFIO.[50] He also kept up a correspondence with Gabriel Peri, editor of the Communist paper *L'Humanité*, to which he and al-Jabiri contributed occasional articles. Arslan was well aware that the strains within the Socialist party were such that it was unable to take a consistent position on the colonial question, but he did not hesitate to remind its adherents of their essential obligation. At the time of the protest against the Berber *dahir*, he demanded that the voice of the European left make itself heard: "We do not ask the socialists to undertake Muslim propaganda—far from it. But we do call on them and on those radicals who deafen the world with their cries of '*laïcité*' to attack the governmental policy which aims at Christianizing the Berbers. . . ."[51] The alliance between a landed Muslim aristocrat and the grandson of Karl Marx was purely tactical but occasionally fruitful. Arslan provided the liaison which brought Renaudel, Longuet, and the latter's son, Robert-Jean, to the advisory board of *Maghreb* and so made possible its appearance.[52] Edited by Ahmad Balafrej, *Maghreb* was published in Paris from 1932 to 1934 and, with contributions from its French patrons as well as its Moroccan editors, took a stand in favor of the independence of Syria, Tunisia, and Morocco.[53] Although, as Halstead notes, it was not always clear in this peculiar alliance who was using whom for whose ends, Arslan's own association with the SFIO provided further evidence to those who were determined to see him as a major threat to the continued existence of *France outre-mer.*

Arslan's triumph with the *dahir* protest, the obvious intensity of his commitment to Maghribi affairs, carried over into Algerian and Tunisian circles and helped to solidify his role as mentor among leaders from those two regions. His range of contacts was continually broadened through the activities of the AEMNA. Whether issuing pamphlets, organizing annual congresses, or providing a forum for widely divergent approaches to questions of unity, independence, Islam, and Arabism, the student organization was a fertile breeding ground for the exchange of ideas and the establishment of intra-Maghribi contacts. There may be some exaggeration, bred by colonial paranoia, in the report from the Quai d'Orsay stating that "the leaders of the AEMNA did not conceal the fact that they received their instructions from Shakib Arslan."[54] However, Arslan's personal influence among the students was pronounced, and he, in turn, probably enjoyed the role of a mentor whose suggestions were more often than not wholeheartedly adopted. It was a welcome change from the bitter struggle required to maintain a position among the factious Syrian exiles.

In Algeria, Arslan's guidance of political and cultural revival existed at two poles of the political spectrum—the reformist-oriented Association of Algerian Ulema on the one hand and the populist socialism of the various parties of Messali Hajj on the other. The third major stream of indigenous Algerian activism during the 1930s, the assimilationist *évolués* who sought continued association with France on the basis of equality, did not attract the Amir's sympathy.

The organized expression of Salafiyyah ideals in interwar Algeria was embodied in the Association of Algerian Ulema and its journal, *al-Shihab.* Founded in 1931, the Association was led by 'Abd al-Hamid Ibn Badis, a Zaytuna-trained *'alim* of exceptional character and abilities. A man of intense piety who could write, "my reason for being is Islam," Ibn Badis was a magnificent orator, an effective propagandist, and a master of Islamic reformist thought.[55] At Rashid Rida's death in 1935, Ibn Badis was ready to be acknowledged as the spiritual and intellectual leader of Western Salafiyyah Islam. His major biographer has written of him: "He was of a passionate temperament, burning with an extraordinary religious ardor, feeling himself called to serve Islam—the Islam of the Salafiyyah, of Muhammad ʿAbduh, of Rashid Rida, of the *Manar* school—at all levels of social life and to carry the reformist message from one border of Algeria to the other." [56] Forging an organization which emphasized the restoration of the dignity of Islam and Arabic through a revived educational system based on progressive Qurʾanic schools, which exalted Arabic as the vehicle of cultural exchange between the Maghrib and the Mashriq, which recognized Algeria as both distinctive and as part of the total Arab-Islamic heritage, and which possessed a discrete political consciousness, Ibn Badis and his lieutenants espoused a program which embraced most of the causes to which Arslan had given his energies since the war. He could not avoid the appeal of their mission, nor could they, in need of external counsel, resist his availability.

On one level, the organization acknowledged Arslan as a master of Salafiyyah principles and Arabic style, awarding him a place in the domain in which they were functioning. Of equal importance, they also embraced his more secular role. The Algerian ulema, hindered by monolingualism and a terrible naiveté about European politics, found in Arslan their interpreter of the European scene and allowed him to act as their political strategist. [57]

Arslan also served as a conduit for the penetration of ideas and events from the Eastern Arab world into Algeria. News of the social, cultural, and political evolution of the Mashriq, with which the Algerian Muslim leadership came to equate their own renaissance, was most frequently conveyed to them through the pages of *al-Fath* and *al-Manar*. Through a desire to place themselves in the mainstream of the currents emanating from the source of their inspiration, the Algerian reformists embraced cultural Arabism and came "to salute the Mashriq as their second *patrie*." [58] Ibn Badis felt the reputation of *al-Shihab* was enhanced by reprinting the articles which Arslan wrote for *al-Fath* and other Eastern journals as well as by occasionally publishing his correspondence. [59] Moreover, in an action which surely corresponded to Arslan's advice, the Association sent delegates to the various Islamic congresses held in the 1930s.

As the recipient of the prestige associated with the multiple roles of European expert, Salafiyyah spokesman, and Mashriqi symbol, Arslan's moral and political influence among the Algerian elite of Arab culture was such that he became, in Merad's view, "a veritable oracle. Mentor for some, director of conscience for others, counselor whose opinions were received with humble gratitude, orator whose speech moved sensible men to fall in ecstasy, writer whose pure and fluid prose was delectable to all those enamored of the beautiful classical Arabic language, Shakib Arslan was all this at once, and more."[60]

Nevertheless, Arslan's direct imprint is not always discernible. Ibn Badis was an original thinker and went his own way in the matter of doctrine. While the reformists' position on the caliphate and their struggle against maraboutism reflected Arslan's own predilections, he was less attracted by theology than by the potential for Islamic political action inherent in the Association. Many of his special preferences were a part of the reformists' general outlook. He certainly encouraged the orientation of the ulema toward cementing Algeria's place in a larger Arab-Islamic framework. For example, as he had found in Ibn Sa'ud an exemplary Arab-Islamic leader, so did the Algerian ulema and their younger followers develop an admiration for the ruler of Arabia. They could not accept the strand of fanaticism they saw in Wahhabism, but, following Arslan, they could admire Ibn Sa'ud's energy, his independence, his application of strict Islamic orthodoxy, and could go so far as to refer to him in al-Shihab as "the king of Islam."[61]

Given its prestigious leader, an impressive network of schools, and its organization of the Algerian Muslim Congress in 1936, the Association of Ulema might justifiably have anticipated continued growth and influence. However, other forces in the political arena also sought to command the loyalties of that segment of Muslim Algeria which was prepared to express its dissatisfaction with colon society. At the second session of the Muslim Congress in 1936, a dramatic figure made an unscheduled appearance during which, with the flair for which he was known, he grasped a handful of earth and proclaimed before an audience of several thousand: "This land is not for sale. All of its people are its heirs. One does not sell one's country."[62] The man was Messali Hajj. In political style and social outlook, he stood in marked contrast to the Algerian bourgeois ulema. In his competition with them for public support, he became the most popular interwar Algerian spokesman. One of Arslan's major objectives during the mid-1930s was to reconcile these two forces and to harness the energy of Messali Hajj to the cause of militant Islam instead of militant socialism. The significance of the undertaking must be seen in the light of what Messali originally represented.

The first of the several parties which came to be known as Messalist, the Etoile Nord-Africaine, was formed in the depressing environs of Paris inhabited by migrant North African workers.[63] Messali, imbued at this stage of his career with radical socialism, became head of the Etoile in 1926 and, in association with the French Communist party, attempted to organize the migrant workers. Although aiming at the creation of class consciousness, the Etoile, with its café meetings and its medium as a haven of contact for homesick men wrenched out of largely rural family settings to the slums of Paris, may actually have served more as a working man's version of AEMNA. Even though the party associated its message of proletarian liberation with political emancipation from colonial rule, it was seemingly far-removed, both socially and ideologically, from the concerns of Shakib Arslan in Geneva. Nevertheless, the Etoile and its fiery leader attracted the Amir's attention, and by 1933 the Sûreté Générale reported that Arslan was funding the organization.[64] Moreover, during this period, Messali himself was gradually moving the party from a position which stressed the importance of class struggle to one which emphasized the more narrowly focused, and more patriotic, emancipation of Algeria from France. That he eventually went even further, making the full ideological journey from Marxism to Islamic nationalism, is often directly attributed to several months he spent in Arslan's company.

The circumstances which finally brought the two men together arose from Messali's existence beyond the limits of what French authorities would permit to an *indigène* activist. In and out of French jails for much of his life and learning of yet another impending arrest, he fled Paris for Geneva in early 1936. Exactly what transpired during the time he took refuge with Arslan is not known. One can imagine an intellectual confrontation on a huge scale, a battle between two independent personalities and two substantial egos, one a determined master, the other a strong-willed pupil. Or there may have been no clash at all, but a more restrained discussion of political options. Whatever the nature of the exchange between the two men, when Messali returned to Paris in June 1936, he was a different man. In place of his European attire, he wore a *burnus* and sported a flowing beard. Encapsulating the thoroughness of the apparent transformation, Julien has remarked that "the revolutionary gave way to the Muslim."[65] From this change has come the widely held view that Arslan "converted" Messali during the latter's stay in Geneva.[66] This interpretation was given credence by the program of Messali's new party, the PPA, founded in 1937, which touted "the indestructible moral force" of the Arab people and placed on the masthead of its journal the slogan, "The will of the people emanates from the will of God. The will of God is unassailable."[67] A somewhat contrary view of the whole affair is presented by Jean-Claude Vatin, who argues that Messali was not actually converted by Arslan, but that he consciously incorporated strains of Islamic patriotism into his political

program, and presumably altered the symbols of his personal appearance as well, because he sensed the appeal such doctrines would
have.[68]

The two interpretations are not dichotomous. Arslan, himself not
averse to tactical positions, would not need to make of Messali a de-
vout ʿalim to feel satisfied with his program. If, in the months that
they spent together in Geneva, he could convince Messali that the
most suitable strategy, both for the movement and for the future of
Algeria, was to pledge support for the Arab-Islamic roots of Algerian
society, then that would be sufficient. Messali's own reading of the
political moment and Arslan's advice were probably similar—the Algerian, to gain adherents, modified his political platform; the Amir,
to ensure that the populist skills of Messali were directed toward the
service of Arab-Islamic solidarity, encouraged the modification.

Messali's new-found moderation should not be over-emphasized.
After all, the PPA retained the Etoile's original emphasis on social
equality, justice, and, most distinctively, total independence. Nevertheless, whether Messali's was a calculated conversion to Islam or a
genuine one, his own appeal, both personally and doctrinally, was
enhanced by the legend of his months at the side of the Amir, and
the PPA's adoption of Islamic symbols contrasted with the Etoile's
earlier position. When Messali proclaimed in 1938 that "a people
which demands to be assimilated to another people breaks the bonds
which tie them to God as they break with their history, their ancestors, their posterity," he sounded very much like the Association
of Ulema's famous assertion that Muslim Algeria "is a nation far removed from France by its language, its customs, its ethnic origins,
and its religion."[69] And both resembled Arslan: "Islam is the fortress which protects the Arab from complete assimilation to the
foreigners."[70]

Yet even Arslan's affiliation with them could not bring the two
groups to cooperate. Messali had too sharp a vision of the immediate
struggle to blend with the more prudent, more long-term policy of
cultural revival envisaged by the Badists. Arslan both gained and lost
by his physical distance from the various movements he sought to
manage. He could persuade, he could mediate, but he could not compel. In the end, he had nothing to offer but his reputation and that,
while inspirational, was not always sufficient.

While Arslan's tendency to view politics through the prism of Islam might appear to limit his choice of allies, the episode of Messali
showed that he would not refrain from supporting men of talent
whose outlooks were more secular than his own. Whether, in doing
so, he ever sought to use his prestige as a bargaining point is not

One *mujahid* confers with another: Habib Bourguiba and Arslan, 1946.

known. However, by the mid-1930s, he was in a position to argue that the association of his name with a movement would give it instant visibility. Not all wished to take advantage of this opportunity, but it may have constituted part of his attractiveness to the Neo-Destour party of Tunisia.

More naturally inclined himself to the program of al-Thaʿalibi's original Destour, Arslan continued to praise that party even after its organizational base had eroded and its leader had embarked on a difficult exile. But al-Thaʿalibi's concerns for the restoration of the Islamic past and the maintenance of pan-Islamic solidarity were subsumed by the Neo-Destour's emphasis on a distinct Tunisian personality and its attention to the social problems of the Tunisian people.[71] Habib Bourguiba favored an essentially secular state, but was nevertheless attracted by the demagogic potential of political Islam. While he argued for secular constitutionalism, he also, in the late 1920s and early 1930s, seized the initiative on Islamic issues by defending the veil as symbolic of Tunisian cultural identity and by criticizing the ulema for neglecting their religious responsibilities to the Tunisian people on the question of French citizenship.[72] Similarly, he embraced the aura of Arslan. Recounting their first meeting, which occurred in 1937 at a banquet in Paris hosted by the AEMNA, Bourguiba noted that before all else, Arslan impressed him as a great

Muslim who felt for him, as he did for the Amir, the natural affinity of two fellow Muslims meeting in a foreign land.[73] Although one does not wish to place too restrictive an interpretation on Bourguiba's account, it should be pointed out that his praise of Arslan, published several months after their encounter, came at a time when the Neo-Destour was faced with the crisis of al-Tha'alibi's heralded return from fourteen years of exile. A public association with Arslan, the supporter of his rival, would have been particularly useful to Bourguiba at that moment.

Another opinion suggests that the two men were simply too different to have a close relationship.[74] The Neo-Destour, building as it did on the political consciousness already generated by al-Tha'alibi and his associates in the 1920s, did not need Arslan in the way that certain Moroccan and Algerian militants did. Although his approval was certainly worth obtaining—and Bourguiba did write to him for advice upon occasion—his association with the Neo-Destour was less intimate and less influential than with certain other parties of the Maghrib.

When viewed as a whole, the effects of Arslan's pronouncements and personal relationships gave him the appearance of manipulating the rebellious sentiments among the North African elite and produced a current of French scholarship which saw in his activities a major source of Maghribi discontent. This impression was conveyed, not just by obstinate defenders of empire like Robert Poulaine of *Le Temps* (*Colonial*), but also by more sympathetic observers who, although they wrote for that organ of empire *L'Afrique Française*, brought some measure of scholarship and understanding to their interpretation of North African affairs.[75] But the memory of the broad-based response to the campaign against the Berber *dahir* was etched deeply in their minds, and they were, in the final analysis, compelled to view the growing strains between France and its North African possessions as threatening. Reluctant to concede that the awakening Islamic consciousness which they so carefully chronicled could blossom because of a felt need on the part of the indigenous Muslim communities, they preferred to see it and its implied affinity with pan-Arabism as unnatural and to seek external sources for the provocation. They found them in *al-Fath*, *al-Manar*, Rashid Rida, Syrians, Ibn Sa'ud, and the pilgrimage, all of which contributed to creating "mysterious affinities" between the Maghrib and the Mashriq. But the single most important source for the infiltration of Eastern ideas into the Maghrib was, in the collective opinion of these authors, Shakib Arslan, "the publicist celebrated in all of Islam as the political counselor of the Muslim community."[76] Traces of Arslan's influence were detected everywhere. He was, somehow, "the Arab Lawrence," spreading the contagion of pan-Arabism and Wahhabism, shaping the opinions of Tunisian and Moroccan students in Paris, defending the dream of unity, and issuing directives from Geneva which were followed in Rabat and Constantine.[77] He was at once "prophet and tribune of pan-Arabism," and his statements were taken as the bellwether of Arab-Islamic opinion.[78]

Arslan was both flattered and affronted by the elevation of his reputation to such heights. He wanted to claim his role and to deny it. On the one hand, he welcomed the French coverage of him as a chance to affirm that he did speak out, that he did "rise up against injustice and inhumanity wherever they are encountered."[79] If the French wished to classify him as the spokesman against such wrongs, it was a role he would proudly accept. One suspects that he was not, in fact, altogether displeased at the attention his efforts received and that he took a certain satisfaction in being able to produce a list of 133 French articles which had attacked him in the course of a single year.[80]

On the other hand, he was disturbed that his activity had earned him the often used title of "the ancient and eternal enemy of France."[81] He was not, he proclaimed, an enemy of France, but an enemy of the policy which permits "the Muslims of North Africa, with whom I hold ties of blood, language, and religion, to be treated as a class inferior to the French, to all Europeans, to the Jews, and even to the Maltese."[82] He tried to distinguish between his abhorrence at the practices of French imperial administrators and his willingness to compromise the moment France demonstrated a readiness to change its policies. He had done this in the instance of the Syrian treaty; he would do it in North Africa as well: "I am not afraid to be a friend of France, or of any country which does not exploit my Muslim coreligionists."[83]

As important as Arslan felt this clarification of his position to be, his main point in responding to the French journalists and scholars was to show them that in selecting him as the sole cause of Maghribi restlessness, they were missing the thrust of his criticism and blinding themselves to the realities of the North African situation: "If the native Algerian cries out at being déclassé, humiliated, deprived of the most basic human liberties, at being treated by French justice as an absolutely inferior being . . . then it is Shakib Arslan, fierce enemy of France, who has taught him to speak up simply in order to blacken the name of France."[84] Attempts to credit him with what were internal responses to repression were, he felt, ridiculous: "The Algerians are told that they are not oppressed, and if they believe themselves to be, then it is because Shakib Arslan put the idea into their heads. Otherwise, they would be very happy."[85] The awakening of the Maghrib was not caused by Arabs from the outside, but by France itself. It was not Shakib Arslan, but the deportations, the expropriations, the attacks on Islam, the imprisonments, the censorship of the press, the biased fiscal policy, which were creating the ferment among North African peoples. In passages of scathing eloquence and unhappy prescience, he claimed that the French must understand that the true enemies of their country were not people like himself, but French citizens, the chauvinists and the racists, "the blind who do not wish to see the light, the deaf who do not wish to hear the voice of reason," these were the individuals responsible for betraying the French cause and leading it to an end which could only be catastrophic.[86]

In denying any role for himself in North African events, he was more disingenuous than convincing: "I do recall having met two or three Moroccan students in Paris for whom I had a high opinion because of their brilliant education, but I never exchanged views with them on political affairs."[87] However, his arguments that France must take responsibility for the Maghribi reaction to its policies constitute some of the best writing in La Nation Arabe. He used to good effect the attention which was focused on him. He would probably rather have been on the inside negotiating with Léon Blum than condemned to the thankless rank of noble enemy, but he at least had the knowledge that his efforts were making an impression, that as one regarded as "the professional enemy of European 'colonialism,'" he not only attracted a new generation of anticolonialists, but also the attention of his opponents.[88]

As his French critics correctly observed, Arslan's North African associations were not isolated from his concerns for the Arab East. His personal mission was to bring the two halves of the Arab world into contact with one another. When Robert Montagne wrote in 1936 that the bombs of Palestine exploded in Tunis and Tetouan, his imagery provided evidence of the growing integration between Maghrib and Mashriq.[89] And when Habib Bourguiba seated himself next to Arslan at the AEMNA banquet a year later and saw his Neo-Destour colleague, Dr. Thameur, in animated conversation with an Egyptian while a representative of the Algerian ulema discussed affairs with a Syrian, he was struck by the "charming atmosphere of fraternity" generated by the presence of Arslan.[90]

The decade of the 1930s, particularly the first half, formed the apogee of Arslan's career. For a time, he seemed to embody the entire pan-Arab, pan-Islamic, anti-imperial crusade. His influence was exercised mainly through his contact, personal and epistolary, with individual militants. Although their grievances were rooted in their specific regional circumstances, Arslan persuaded them of the common ties which united them and so enlarged their perspectives, their hopes, and their sense of what was possible. As an itinerant man of action who appeared at crucial moments in disparate regions of the Arab-Islamic world, he gained respect from all quarters. To Mekki Naciri, the Moroccan, he was "the man of the hour in the Arab-Islamic world," while to Rashid Rida in Cairo, "Amir Shakib is one of the greatest statesmen among the leaders of the Arab nation and one of her most famous writers; he is the protector of her lands, the defender of her rights, and the agent of her welfare."[91] Public praise need not, of course, mean full private agreement. Arslan, even in his triumph, faced bitter opposition. Yet so extensive was his exposure, so valuable his apparent sense of accomplishment, that it was almost necessary to favor him in order not to undermine the cause which he represented.

While Arslan accumulated plaudits from both the Maghrib and the Mashriq, his place in the political history of the two regions was quite different. He may have been head of the Syro-Palestinian delegation to the League of Nations, but he could not be called the tactician of the Egyptian or Syrian independence movements. But in the Maghrib, and especially in Morocco, the religious overtones of politics, the absence of the native Christian communities which caused a man of his insistent Islamic orientation such difficulties in the Mashriq, and the general youth of the militants coincided perfectly with Arslan's public views, accumulated experience, and political availability to give him a special role. The immediate success of his achievements in the protest against the Berber *dahir* made the Moroccans' choice of political strategist appear well founded. This success increased Arslan's attractiveness as a mentor and, more than in the Mashriq, extended it to figures beyond his natural audience of Salafiyyah reformers. His closest Moroccan associates were those most thoroughly Gallicized. For example, Halstead discovered in his interviews that al-Ouezzani, for all his immersion in the French university system, learned more from Arslan than from his formal education. And the alienated demagogue of the people, Messali Hajj, accepted, whether through persuasion or personal preference, Arslan's view of political Islam. Even Bourguiba, so often portrayed as the epitome of political rationalism and secularism, found it useful to associate himself with Arslan's reputation. Arslan did not attempt to define the content of national ideology in the three countries, but sought to direct the energies of their various spokesmen in a way that would have the most political effectiveness and at the same time would ensure a place for his cherished Arab-Islamic principles within the society of the future. It is to a closer examination of those principles that attention is now directed.

CHAPTER SIX.
THE INTEGRITY OF TRADITION

Political ideas make their own realities. Often in defiance of logic, they hold men and are in turn held by them, creating a world in their own image, only to play themselves out in the end, shackled by routine problems not foreseen by those who spun the myth, or living past their prime and ceasing to move people sufficiently. —Fouad Ajami[1]

On the basis of the evidence I have presented, it is clear that the ties of Islamic solidarity are stronger and of greater import than the bonds of patriotism. —Arslan[2]

DURING THE interwar years, Arslan assigned a central place to politicized Islam in reviving society and rendering it capable of resisting European imperialism. He took the several major controversies of the time and Islamicized them, showing less concern for any specific Arab region than for the Arab-Islamic world as a whole. He also became a participant in these controversies and created a special place for himself as international organizer and inspirational force.

In conjunction with his tactical responses to a variety of imperial situations, Arslan offered an examination of the internal problems of the Islamic world and prescribed remedies for the ills which afflicted Muslims. Neither an original nor a reflective theological thinker, Arslan nevertheless commanded a wide readership for his Islamic commentaries. His scathing treatise, *Why Are the Muslims Backward While Others Are Advanced?* is an enduring contribution; it went through three Arabic editions during his lifetime and was reissued in 1965 and again in 1981.[3] This book and Arslan's many articles on the subject of Islam's place in modern society belong to the apologetic stream of Salafiyyah reformism.[4] While Arslan's point of departure was identical to that of ʿAbduh and Rida, his methodology, if it may be called such, differed from theirs. He did not provide a critical review of the classical jurists, he constructed no *tafsir*, he offered no reexamination of *hadith*. It is fair to Arslan to conclude that his technique was more akin to al-Afghani's than to ʿAbduh's. Arslan had no time for theological finesse, and his writings on Islam were never far removed from the political events he watched so closely. If his lack of doctrinal sophistication caused him at times to engage in the most shallow of apologetics, he also touched the most sensitive of social issues.

Although Arslan gradually evolved a vague political program for Arab unity, his belief in the primacy of Islamic solidarity predominated. Social regeneration and the assertion of dignity in the international arena would come more naturally from the bonds of Islam than from those of Arabism. His vision of the future did not rest in the construction of a new order, but in the reinvigoration of the old. In the tradition of Salafiyyah reformism, this required an evaluation of what constituted the authentic components of Islamic society and why that society was in such disarray.

Using the same point of departure as ʿAbduh and Rida, Arslan admitted the present backwardness of the Islamic world in relation to Western Europe and Japan. That such an unfortunate situation existed was due to a failing of Muslims, not to any defect in their religion. Proof of this premise was found in evidence from the past, and Arslan defended the validity of the Islamic experience by calling forth the historical record, pointing with pride to the heroic epoch of early Islam when the Arabs "conquered half the world in half a century."[5] They were able to do so because of their adherence to the regulations of the Qurʾan, their willingness to sacrifice their lives in the cause of the faith, and their fortitude in the face of hardship and danger. It was a time of brave men, when "a single Muslim could stand up to ten, and sometimes even a hundred, non-Muslims."[6] Arslan's treatment of the conquests and the development of high Islamic civilization was always presented in this manner. He extolled the virtues of men and avoided discussing the complexities of doctrine. In action lay achievement. When a people possessed "ardor, courage, and resolve," they could succeed in anything.[7] No further analysis was necessary.

Similarly, in his frequent discussions of the achievements of urban Islamic civilization, Arslan drew no connections between the content of the religious message and the society which it shaped. He asserted the greatness of the past by describing the grandeur of buildings, by listing the large and embellished cities, and by measuring the extent of martial conquest. He was not so much reconstructing the past as lending psychological support to his readers, and to himself, by presenting them with irrefutable evidence that their religious system had once possessed temporal dominance and glory.

But why had the greatness, so universally recognized, sunk to the current depths of degradation? In addressing this question, Arslan was not interested in establishing a historical continuum of Muslim decline, not concerned with a cause-and-effect analysis anchored to specific events or general trends. It was the present crisis of Islam that affected him, and it was that crisis which he wished to explain and whose perpetrators he wished to excoriate.

The direct rule of Europeans over Muslim lands was an obvious manifestation of the crisis. But the West had always been there and had, until recently, been successfully repulsed, even defeated. Hence, Muslims had to bear the major responsibility for their current decline. The success of the Western powers in subduing the Islamic world was made possible by internal maladies gnawing away at the body politic. For Arslan, they were easily identified as the ultraconservative traditionalists and the secular Westernizers. The former, through their misinterpretation of Islam as tradition-bound, had scorned all science and philosophy, incorrectly condemning such intellectual pursuits as the heretical practices of infidels.[8] These reactionaries failed to understand that "Islam, from the very beginning, was a revolt against degenerate tradition," and, by their rejectionist mentality, led Islam to a state of stagnation contrary to its nature.[9]

Arslan also condemned fatalists as ignorant people who failed to understand the inherent dynamism of Islam and its demand for a life of action in which the results attained were in direct proportion to the effort expended. Dervishes, the itinerant men of poverty, were to Arslan "nothing but the paralyzed limbs of the body politic of Islam."[10] To those prepared to renounce worldly effort in favor of contemplation of the afterlife, Arslan directed this passage of contempt: "If we are preoccupied, all our lives, with the matters of the other world alone, the earth will meet us with the rebuke: 'You had better go directly to that other world; I have nothing for you here.'"[11]

To prod the apathetic and rouse the indifferent, Arslan tried to show that positive effort went hand in hand with Islamic achievement. He was capable of drawing historical analogies of the utmost simplicity. In one instance, he wrote of the Prophet's despair at his setback in the battle of Uhud, but then commented that because of his faith and courage he was finally victorious.[12] So it could be for Muslims of the twentieth century. If they did not give up hope, if they retained their faith, if they made personal sacrifices, then they would prevail. Long on these kinds of homilies and short on analysis, Arslan did not endeavor to rethink the doctrines of Islam. He did not feel it was necessary to do so.

Doctrinal considerations were for others. He had a direct and pragmatic solution propounded within the tradition established by Muhammad ʿAbduh. It was a bold placement of utilitarianism in association with revelation. "Islam is sufficiently flexible," wrote Arslan, "to come into accord with every situation in the modern age."[13] To ʿAbduh's statement that "Whatever is socially useful is ethical . . . as long as it does not conflict with injunctions specifically revealed," Arslan added his own resounding endorsement that whatever was in the public interest could not contradict the intention of Islam: "Those believers who truly understand Islam are receptive to all things new which do not conflict with the faith; they do not fear the new as a source of corruption. I do not believe that anything which benefits Islamic society can be incompatible with the religion which is based on furthering the happiness of mankind."[14]

In the end, what the community needed, it could acquire; the fact of need made the acquisition justifiable. Arslan was thus receptive to a rational approach to social progress. He did not approve of the secularists' use of this idea, but he was more interested in the application of human endeavor to political ends than was Rashid Rida. By asserting that "man's will is the fundamental means to his ends," Arslan was able to grant a certain amount of revelatory sanction to the cause of independent Syria or to the notion of Algerian revolutionism as defined by Messali Hajj.[15] At times, his concession to the human factor appeared to transgress the bounds of revelation: "Some ask if we must return to the Qurʾan to resurrect our enthusiasm for learning; others suggest that our awakening need not be religious, but should be national—patriotic as was the case in Europe. My own objective is for an awakening, whether it be religious or patriotic."[16] What Arslan said of himself as politician when he endorsed the Franco-Syrian treaty of 1936 could also be applied to him as "theologian": "Let it not be said that Shakib Arslan is a dreamer without a sense of the practical."[17]

This outlook permitted Arslan to make of the religious ethic what he thought it should be at the moment—positive and forward-looking. If the crushing weight of European occupation was overpowering, the Qurʾan stated: "God changes not what is in a people, until they change what is in themselves."[18] Did not al-Afghani show that Islam was suitable to every facet of modern civilization without disturbing the faith of the believer? Therefore, those "geographical" Muslims who neglected action in favor of religion were in violation of their religion; those who were content with the performance of the prescribed rituals were not fulfilling the total range of obligations demanded by the code. They were guilty of apathy, and modern authority refuted them: "I say that the intention of the apathetic is contrary to the intention of Jamal al-Din [al-Afghani]."[19]

In order for Muslims to flourish as God intended them to, they had to work, to sacrifice. Arslan presented to the Muslim community a call for action that may be described as a modern *jihad* ethic in which the individual responsibility of each believer was emphasized: "With constant discipline, with will and determination to march onward, and with a correct understanding of the essentials of the faith taught by the Qur'an, let us strive and continue to strive."[20] This was how Islam and modern civilization were compatible. If Muslims recovered their spirit of positive effort, then they, too, could acquire the technical skills currently monopolized by Europe. Such skills were merely the product of the effort which the Europeans had applied and the Muslims had neglected, and "Europeans, like Muslims, are only men."[21]

Arslan was a reformer without offering a reformulation; he conveyed a sense of Islam's possibilities without exploring very deeply the potential limits of revelation. He asserted that Islam was a positive, dynamic force; he denounced those who said or acted otherwise; and he employed reason to countenance the action he encouraged, arguing that such action was permitted because reason demanded the prosperity of the Islamic community. But in the end, religion was its own justification for being: "Each righteous man knows that when religion is founded on its proper pillars, it is the source for outstanding morality; nothing can replace it as a revitalizing force in the souls of the people."[22] All that was needed was already permitted. Adherence to the *jihad* ethic would restore Muslims to their rightful place in the world.

While Arslan gave broad scope to what was permissible for Islamic society as a whole to achieve progress, his encouragement of freedom of action was not unbounded. If blind adherence to misinterpreted traditions sapped the inherent vitality of Islam, an even greater threat was posed by those who "abandon all traditions and think that they are leading the caravan of progress and success."[23] These were the misguided "apostates in the name of progress"; they were exemplified by Taha Husayn, Muhammad Husayn Haykal, Dr. Shahbandar, and, above all, Mustafa Kemal Atatürk.[24] These enemies also had to be faced, their challenge repulsed.

At issue was the place of Islam in generating the new social awakening. The influential circle of Egyptian liberal intellectuals saw Islam as a barrier to the only process by which society could be reinvigorated, namely, "the infusion of secular values based on nineteenth century European liberalism."[25] In transmitting such values, they criticized outmoded literary styles (one of Taha Husayn's targets was Shawqi), renounced Egypt's Islamic identity, and subjected the religious literary heritage, including the Qur'an, to the scrutiny of new critical techniques. They were anathema to Shakib Arslan.

It might at first appear inconsistent for one as dissatisfied with the status quo as Arslan to oppose groups committed to changing it. He was not himself without traces of positivism; the society which he called forth was created by the spirit of human endeavor and a belief in progress. It might also be expected that a man with Arslan's experience of Europe would have favored the adoption of selected Western practices by Islamic society. However, it was the experience of a man in, not of, Europe. Unlike Haykal or Taha Husayn, both of whom had advanced degrees from the Sorbonne, Arslan had not participated in the acculturation process which transmitted an admiration for European values. His assertion that "it is necessary for the East to remain Eastern" was a defiant rejection of those who conceived of renewal as the copying of foreign ways.[26] Arslan used his fluency in French to convey to a francophone readership an Easterner's distaste for Europe, not to absorb its intellectual currents. His urgent propaganda and his contemptuous denunciations were more than a defense of a particular society at a given historical moment. They were Arslan's defense of his world and of the al-Afghani/'Abduh/Ottoman legacy to which he, in his own way, was a faithful heir. He had to resist the West for what it had done to that world, for the threat it implied to the legitimacy of that legacy. He closed the world in, asserting that revival would come from a rational application of its own traditions, not from imported ones.

Arslan believed that indigenously evolved traditions were preferable to alien ones because they were right for the societies which possessed them. He maintained that the distinctiveness of world cultural systems was desirable; Europeans operated effectively within Christendom, the Japanese flourished under their complex religious structure. This was as it should be. Cultural pluralism within a given system was decidedly inappropriate.

Hence, the dynamic Islamic legacy encompassed cultural and moral values which, because they were suitable for Muslim society, had to be preserved. In Arslan's opinion, the proposals of the liberal Westernizers would destroy Islam as a social system by depriving Muslims of the traditions which were their assurance of distinctiveness.

To Arslan, tradition meant an accumulated cultural heritage which served both morally ethical and socially cohesive ends. His *jihad* ethic was framed by an Islamic moral order:

Whatever scope the *shariʿah* gave for the acquisition of science and the arts, for the achievement of power and glory, it must be the opposite when it comes to issues of propriety, personal modesty, and moral purity. . . . We believe the *shariʿah* had, and should continue to have, the strongest prohibitions against immorality, prostitution, and licentiousness; freedom must be bound with chains of propriety. What some of the Westernizers among the Easterners designate as civilized and socially necessary is neither civilized nor necessary.[27]

It is jarring to read from the pen of a cosmopolitan man who lived in Europe for over twenty years that mixed dancing should continue to be banned because it involved holding close, and "holding close is the first stage of fornication."[28] But Arslan saw the disintegration of *shariʿah*-inspired moral commandments as a prelude to the disintegration of Islamic society itself. The general good demanded protection of what was distinctive even as it permitted rational progress:

The cultural nihilists seek to Europeanize the Muslims and other Easterners and to make them disown their distinctive characteristics and their historical traditions so that they will become, in the manner of a chemical compound, dissolved and transformed into a different substance. Only the mean and low-minded can entertain the idea that man should disown his heritage. . . . They act in contravention of the inherent instincts manifested by every nation in its desire to preserve its special characteristics in matters of language, faith, customs, architectural style, and cuisine.[29]

In his campaign to preserve the full range of Islamic cultural authenticity, Arslan collided with the secular liberals. He opposed them by asserting the validity of the arguments for cultural authenticity reviewed above and by subjecting them to *ad hominem* attacks, an intellectually weak but no doubt personally satisfying technique. He would have none of Taha Husayn's questioning of the authenticity of Jahiliyyah poetry or his dissection of the Qurʾanic suras. Accusing the Egyptian of plagiarizing the Jahiliyyah criticisms from the orientalist Margoliouth, Arslan claimed that Taha Husayn was just trying to make a big name for himself.[30] Convinced of the rightness of his own version of the Islamic past, Arslan permitted no tampering with it by the "Ifranj" of Cairo. What they wrote was only ill-considered opinion; what he endorsed was factual history. He branded Salama Musa and his circle as "the *shuʿubiyyah* of our age," anarchists intent on diminishing the excellence of

Arab achievements; for their insolence, they should be regarded as enemies.[31]

But there was an even greater enemy. In Arslan's view, the most pernicious force among the Westernizing secularists was Kemalist Turkey. The errors of the liberal nationalists in Cairo paled beside the crimes committed in Ankara. No Islamic issue so exercised Arslan as the Kemalist reform program, and he devoted more of his writing in the late twenties and early thirties to this subject than to any other. It was as though Atatürk was burying Arslan's past, and he responded with sustained outrage. His most fundamental beliefs were challenged, his concept of the proper social and moral order was threatened. His treatment of Kemalism encapsulated his full counterattack on Westernization.

Arslan denounced virtually everything that "the atheistic Kemalists" proposed.[32] He contended that the government in Ankara (which he carefully distinguished from the Turkish people) was undertaking a direct and ruthless attack on Islam; and his writings were filled with such phrases as "the destruction of the pillars of Islam by the Kemalists," "Ankara's destruction of the spirit of Islam in Turkey," and "the elimination of the very foundations of Islam by the Kemalists."[33] To Arslan, the menace of these policies was such that they could be summarized as "the revolt of Ankara against the caliphate, against Islamic principles, against Eastern traditions, against even Allah Himself."[34]

The spread of these ideas would contaminate all of Islam, and Arslan's mission was to contain the epidemic and show its evil: "Compassion for the unity of the Muslims and for the preservation of Islam itself demands that we combat this extravagance and carelessness with all our might."[35] Some, he noted, were cowed into silence by the ruthless dictator of Ankara, but Arslan charged into the fray, proclaiming: "I feel no fear or shame in defending Islam."[36] He mounted his defense by demonstrating the basic unsuitability of Atatürk's social reforms for the situation at hand. In so doing, he also defended his own views of the proper order of things. The following examples suggest the nature of Arslan's charges. The adoption of the Latin alphabet merely served to render the Turkish language alien to its own people and to prevent the Turks from being able to read the Qur'an. Insistence on unveiling only exchanged purity for licentiousness and was accompanied by such signs of moral depravity as the mingling of young people of both sexes even to the point of allowing them to dance together. And the termination of religious instruction threatened to create a generation which would know Islam only as something other people practiced, the way they might know about Buddhism.[37]

Arslan also responded to policies which endangered the outward symbols of cultural continuity. A man of impeccable European attire, he launched from Switzerland a vigorous defense of the fez. He scorned those who debased themselves by wearing hats only as an imitation of European practice. When Amanullah, the king of Afghanistan, visited Lausanne in 1928, Arslan refused to meet with him because the monarch had worn a hat during his state visit to Egypt a few weeks earlier.[38] In one of his rare comments about the United States, Arslan pointed out that the Shriners wore the fez and thus showed more respect for the rituals they had adopted than the Kemalists did for indigenous tradition.[39]

To Arslan, Kemalist legislation went beyond the administrative separation of religion and politics and constituted a direct attack on the faith itself. So intense were his feelings on this matter that at one point he dared question in print the value of Turkey's independence and suggested that had Turkey not been victorious over the Greeks, then the heresy which came to afflict it would have been avoided. The Allied occupation would still be in effect, and Mustafa Kemal would be speaking in Arabic about Islamic alliances and the need to preserve the caliphate.[40]

Arslan also accused the Egyptian liberals of directly attacking the faith through their claims that nationalism was incompatible with religion and that, since nationalism was the ideology of the advanced nations, religion and modernity were incompatible.[41] It was essential for Arslan to refute these contentions and to demonstrate that modernization was not synonymous with the rejection of religion. This was his major effort, his principal theme. His arguments, repeated in dozens of publications, were based on the premise that progress, wherever and whenever it occurred, took place in association with the religious ethos of the society concerned; that renewal was only genuinely achieved within the framework of historical tradition. His favorite method was to cite examples of how Europe and Japan achieved advanced levels of civilization without abandoning their traditional religious and cultural values.[42] Whether it was official government sponsorship of proselytizing missionary activity or the prayers the English said for their king, Arslan found evidence of religious symbolism throughout contemporary European society. His arguments lacked substance, but they were clever. Do not, he asked, the kings and presidents of Europe invoke Christianity in justifying their national policies? Does not the archbishop of Canterbury occupy a position second only to the king of England in ceremonial processions? He could utterly misinterpret, or perhaps see only in the light of his own hopes, the Lateran Accords concluded between the papacy and Mussolini's government in 1923. He chose to emphasize the agreement as a magnificent affirmation by a modernizing regime of the role of religion in the state. "Listen," he demanded, "you who are so diligent for modernization, you apostates in the name of progress, the Italians decided for a return to religion, but this does not delay their path to advancement." Then, in a direct slap at the Kemalists, he warned: "O you Easterners who use sophistry in the method of separating church and state, we give you this example so you can remember and be wakeful."[43]

Japan fascinated Arslan because of his belief that it had attained a level of modernization equal to that of Western Europe without surrendering its authentic belief and cultural systems. He stated that as the Japanese had learned Western science and technology while continuing to honor their religion and uphold their traditions, so all Muslim nations could achieve the rank of the powerful nations without throwing their religion and traditions overboard.[44]

Why is it, Arslan demanded, that we Muslims are so slow to comprehend these developments? Do we not understand that if, as the Kemalists urge, we break with our history, discard the Qur'an, and cast to the wind our beliefs, our values of right and wrong, we will be destroyed? Arslan called forth his warning: "If you, O Islamic world, want to learn and to progress, then there is the example of the European world. Just as it achieved progress while remaining fundamentally Christian, so can you remain Muslim and move ahead to the degree that you exert effort. Your betterment does not depend on heresy."[45] These and countless other examples showed the compatibility of religion and progress.

Arslan was determined to prove that whatever success Turkey had enjoyed was in spite of, not because of, Kemalist secularism. While he could not deny the achievement of Turkish sovereignty, he could show that there was an Islamic base to this praiseworthy development. Thus, he consistently maintained that Turkey was still Muslim, that the popular belief in Islam remained unshaken, and that "despite their government's irreligious policy, the Turkish people retain their faith in the indissoluble bond of religion."[46] In support of this contention, Arslan directly challenged Atatürk to recall certain events surrounding the war of independence against the Greeks. Had the Kemalists forgotten how the Ankara Assembly claimed it was fighting to free the caliph of Islam from the hands of non-Muslim states? Had Mustafa Kemal forgotten how he used to go to the Ankara station to greet Sayyid Ahmad al-Sharif al-Sanusi and kiss his hand in front of all the people? During this time, did not the Ghazi go back and forth to the mosques repeatedly? Well, demanded Arslan, if Islamic beliefs were such an impediment, why then did the Kemalists take refuge in them to save their country? [47]

Safran has written of the Egyptian liberal nationalists: "Reason came to be sufficient for validating any socially relevant conclusions." [48] This characterization also applied to Arslan. He seemed on the surface to be as secular as those he tarnished with that term. However, he differed markedly from them in the sources of his rationalism and in his resistance to the application of European-derived models to the Islamic world. A man like Haykal felt that members of the Westernized elite like himself had to take command: "The means for placing Egypt on the path taken by Europe lay in the presence of those intellectuals educated according to European principles." [49] Arslan, on the other hand, tied his sense of superiority and worth to the Ottoman-Islamic order in which he had achieved distinction. He was the spearhead of Islamic consciousness in a hostile world, the preserver of a cultural and social system which should be invigorated but not forsaken. Yet that order, too, had been one in flux, one which encouraged in a man who had Arslan's opportunities the acquisition of European languages and the attainment of a new mobility. He faced a dilemma in the changing world of the 1920s and 1930s; he was not against progress, but at the same time he wanted to retain authentic tradition. His resolution and his disorientation, his affirmation and his confusion, were expressed in this response to Kemalism:

> Whenever the Muslims try to protect their religion, their morals, and their virtue, whenever they try to fight heresy, licentiousness, and moral depravity, the men of Ankara say: these people want to use religion as an instrument of politics. . . . But this is a question of belief, honor, and rights, of morality, education, and a heritage to descendants. Whenever someone tries to protect these principles, he is met with those who say: this is mixing religion with politics! [50]

Yet, one who insisted, as Arslan did, on the application of reason to *taqlid* and who framed his call for the preservation of traditions with the qualification "except when they run counter to the general welfare and to certain knowledge" had in mind change of some sort. [51] It was not, however, defined in the form of specific programs. Arslan usually confined himself to general exhortations supported by his insistence that concerted human effort could produce whatever conditions society required. In the realm of education, he did offer more sharply defined recommendations. While he tolerated no interference in cultural matters, he acknowledged the Muslim world's need to acquire advanced technical skills. The natural sciences possessed an almost magical allure for him, and he studded his writings with examples of his own awareness of microscopy, chemistry, and the theory of relativity. It was "absolutely essential" for Muslims to gain knowledge of these subjects by studying in Europe; it was even more important that they not succumb to the dangers of free thinking and atheism while there.[52] Arslan could voice his satisfaction at the growing numbers of Syrian and Egyptian students who spoke European languages and at the same time maintain that the full process of acculturation could be prevented by fortifying Arab youth with religious instruction before they were sent to Europe.[53] He held tenaciously to this simple view of a complex problem. He found his solace in the Japanese model, which he repeatedly displayed as evidence of the possibility of selectively borrowing technical expertise without modifying the spiritual or social bases of society. In endorsing the phrase "Nous tenons à nous moderniser tout en restant nous-mêmes," Arslan revealed the awesome dilemma of one who was at once cultural preservationist and progressive idealist.[54]

The ability of a society to determine for itself what it should borrow and what it should reject was, for Arslan, a function of political sovereignty. Kemalist Turkey presented him with a conundrum which he treated with direct polemical assaults; Ibn Saʿud offered him a resolution which he accepted with alacrity. Arslan's support for a modified caliphate, reviewed in chapter 4, was less on the grounds of religious necessity than of political power. The survival of the Islamic order was dependent on a strong, independent ruler who cherished the heritage of the past while making the adjustments necessary for prosperity in the future. Arslan concluded that Ibn Saʿud was such a ruler.

Other Arab-Islamic spokesmen shared Arslan's quest for an Islamic power-base and echoed his admiration for Ibn Saʿud's achievements. Rashid Rida wrote that Ibn Saʿud's independence from Europe made him "the greatest Islamic power on earth since the fall of the Ottoman state and the rise of a non-religious government in Turkey."[55] ʿAbd al-Hamid Ibn Badis of Algeria also praised the Arabian monarch's independence and his adherence to Islamic law.[56] Ibn Saʿud was attractive as an antidote to Kemalism. Mustafa Kemal, by his relentless secularism, refused to make himself available for acclaim as a successful Islamic ruler. However, Ibn Saʿud's barren and undeveloped domains hardly seemed evidence of anything more noteworthy than the fact that no foreign power was interested in his territory at the moment. Arslan recognized the existence of this attitude and endeavored to change it by surrounding his ruler with a positive image and making him acceptable for a larger leadership role. He thus initiated a campaign to show that Ibn Saʿud was not only as independent as Turkey, that he was not only concerned with enforcing the rules of the *shariʿah*, but was also a modernizer. This led Arslan to draw a strained portrait of the Wahhabi monarch as an advanced development planner eagerly introducing automobiles, electricity, a new postal system, and other attributes of modern civilization into the Hijaz.[57]

However misleading this propaganda may have been, the motivation behind it is clear. It was a direct response to the assumption in Atatürk's reforms and in the programs of the Arab Westernizers that modernization and Islam were incompatible. Ibn Saʿud was successful in introducing selective modernization because "he battled [his opponents] with the sword of the *shariʿah* itself; he showed them that the Qurʾan and the *hadith* did not prohibit modern inventions. . . . He quoted to them evidence of permissibility from the words of God, not from the words of Ankara."[58] Such wisdom coupled with such success showed the errors of those who claimed that progress required Islam to be discarded.

This message, so prominent in Arslan's writings, was carried into the arena of inter-Arab politics. Arslan hoped to harness Ibn Saʿud's religious purity and political sovereignty to the materially advanced states north of the peninsula and thus create an Arab power which would become "one of the pillars on which world equilibrium would rest."[59] Although he reluctantly came to accept the existence of several states in the Eastern Arab world, he continued to encourage defensive alliances among them and to support the creation of a confederation centered on Syria, Iraq, and Arabia. He left no doubt about his candidate for the leadership of such a confederation: "I prefer no one over Ibn Saʿud, not even Faysal."[60] Always, the Islamic fact represented by Ibn Saʿud swayed Arslan's judgment.

Arslan's encouragement of these Eastern Arab confederations and his coterminous involvement in the Maghrib have prompted some to see him as a tribune of pan-Arabism. This is one of the principal arguments made by al-Sharabasi and al-Dahhan.[61] During his lifetime he was called "the fortress of Arabism and the pillar of Islam," and his obituary notices included numerous testimonials to his efforts on behalf of Arab unity.[62] Arslan certainly saw Arab alliances as desirable, and he was deeply conscious of the central place of Arabs in the Islamic community. However, he was not, strictly speaking, an

Arab nationalist. The factors of group loyalty and personal identity which he saw as most effectively binding continued to be primarily Islamic ones, and it was those to which he appealed in his anti-imperial campaigns. French Berber policy in Morocco was portrayed as a violation of the integrity of Islam; Zionist immigration to Palestine constituted a threat to the holy shrines of Jerusalem. It was the duty of the entire Islamic world to respond to these perils on the basis of a shared sense of community. Unity, to Arslan, was the mutual acceptance of the Islamic cultural heritage and the mutual obedience to the moral commands which made Islamic society distinctive. He did not espouse a politically unified Arab nation, nor did he pursue his search for a locus of Islamic power by demanding a unitary Islamic state.

Although Arslan employed from time to time the vocabulary of political Arabism, he tended to do so in a religious context. He was not, for example, precise in his use of the term *ummah*, and it is evident that he intended it more as the community of believers (even if confined to the community of Arab believers) than as a secular nation. In fact, he was inclined to use more frequently the terms *al-ʿalam al-islami* (the Islamic world) or *al-bilad al-islami* (the Islamic countries). His widely circulated Damascus speech of 1937 received more attention for its moderation and pragmatism than for its conception of Arab unity. Arslan proposed a staged process of alliance-building among distinct states culminating in an organization not unlike the Arab League as created in 1945. His distance from the cultural nationalism of al-Husri is evident in his selection of Austria-Hungary as his historical model and the Little Entente between Czechoslovakia, Rumania, and Yugoslavia as his contemporary example. Despite his persistent use of the term *al-wahdah al-ʿarabiyyah*, Arslan sought confederation based on enlightened self-interest, not integral union: "This political, economic, and military unity does not require administrative unity or the complete merger of one kingdom with another. Arab unity is something that is possible without undue difficulty, something that will allow Iraq, Syria, and Saʿudi Arabia to remain independent kingdoms in their internal administrative structure."[63] Moreover, Arslan denied the possibility of anything other than communal solidarity between the Mashriq and the Maghrib: "Our unity with them does not extend beyond religious, linguistic, cultural, and social unity."[64] This stance brought criticism from Libyan patriots who felt Arslan had abandoned his anti-imperial campaign in exchange for Italian gold.

Arslan's political program concentrated on the need for harmony among the jealous Hashimite monarchs and the two major rulers of the Arabian peninsula. He did not conjure up a vision of the integral national state, nor did he have recourse to the German romantic nationalists who served as Satiᶜ al-Husri's models. Indeed, whereas al-Husri endorsed the popular poem of the pan-Arabists, "One nation from Iran to Tetouan," Arslan denied the politics of Arab unity: "The Arab movement is not a pan-Arab movement attempting to unite all those who speak Arabic into a single unit. The Arab movement is not so utopian as that; Arab intellectuals are sufficiently realistic not to imagine an Arab empire stretching from the frontiers of Iran to the shores of the Atlantic as some would suggest."[65]

This was a realistic position which gave Arslan more room to maneuver. It also showed his inclination to avoid dealing with political Arabism. He preferred the communal bonds with which he was familiar, and those were Islamic. He feared that nationalism would undermine the communal religious solidarity he considered so essential to rebirth. Seared into his memory was the unforgettable, and unforgivable, truth that the Ottoman Empire had fallen partly because of the Arab revolt against it. Thus, while he seemed to perceive that individual Arab states would come into political existence, he continued to emphasize that what they had in common was not so much Arab nationalism as Islamic communion. When he said Muslim, he usually meant Arab; when he said Arab, he always meant Muslim.

Nationalism further disturbed Arslan because of its secular connotations. Islamic solidarity, in his view, was a stronger barrier to European ambitions than was secular nationalism. It was the religious, not the patriotic bond which commanded correct moral behavior and which provided believers with the comforting knowledge that whatever the present situation, they were, as followers of the commands of Allah, inevitably to succeed.[66] Imperialists, in tandem with their Westernizing accomplices among the Muslims, found nationalist movements easy targets in their efforts to undermine the moral fiber of the community. Alcohol and narcotics, the well-known corrupting devices of imperialism, were not forbidden by nationalist movements, but "Islamic solidarity is an impregnable fortress in the face of drunkenness."[67] Only Islam, in all its aspects, could prevent the assimilation of the believer into the grasp of the alien other. Like his mentor al-Afghani, Arslan's, too, was "an Islamic response to imperialism."[68]

Further evidence of Arslan's inability, or unwillingness, to come to terms with the root concept of Arabism is seen in his relations with the Christians of the Arab East. He may have been quoted out of context in his famous Aleppo speech with its phrase "he who is not a

Muslim cannot be a patriot," but his conviction that Islamic concepts of state and society should predominate in the Arab world was
so well known as to cause the speech to be taken as the true measure
of his sentiments.[69] The suspicion with which the Arab Christians
had regarded him during World War I was not moderated, despite his
service to the cause of Arab independence. This was largely because
Arslan himself regarded this service as inseparable from the cause of
freeing Islam from foreign dominance and ensuring that Islamic society would then dominate the Middle East as it had always done.
His backhanded compliment to his first colleague on the Syro-
Palestinian delegation was an indirect dismissal of the entire Arab-
Christian community: "Those Christians such as Sulayman Kin'an
who seek their community's interest in accord with the interest of
the Arab Muslims are rare."[70] His list of those who confused regeneration with the spirit of Atatürk's reforms included the Christian Arab journals of North America; he also stated that the Assyrians were not true sons of Iraq; and he never masked his distrust
of the Maronite community in Lebanon for what he saw as its encouragement of French intervention, its support for the continued
presence of the French, and its adoption of imitative cultural Westernization.[71] The same attitude of Muslim superiority which had
governed his behavior toward the Christians during the epoch of
Abdulhamid remained with him through the interwar years.

A revealing example of Arslan's uncompromising stance on Islamic principles of social organization and his sectarian view of Arabism
appears in an article which al-Sharabasi has reproduced in an attempt to show the Amir's support for integral Arab unity.[72] In fact,
the article suggests something quite different from al-Sharabasi's interpretation of it. It shows Arslan groping for a definition of nation-
hood and concluding that there was really no need to submerge primary religious identifications in the mystique of a secular state.
Drawing on Islamic religious literature and early Islamic practices
for his references, Arslan argued that since Muslims obey the Qur'an,
and since Qur'anic injunctions demand that Muslims treat Christians with equality and justice, Christians need have no fear of living
with the Muslim majority in a single state. Arslan avoided secular
Arabism and asked Christian Arabs to trust in the Muslims' un-
swerving adherence to the divine commands to protect them in a
Muslim-Arab state.

For all the directness of his Islamic orientation, Arslan was more
agitator than theoretician, and his intellectual contribution to interwar thought was tempered by his political involvement. He had

some claim to a place as Islamic reformer, but his observations on Islam were oriented more toward a justification of action in the material world than toward reformulation in the spiritual one. For this very reason, he could not aspire to the position of intellectual leadership held by his mentor ʿAbduh or his colleague Rida. He could, however, command a wider audience than either of them.

In presenting the main themes of Arslan's thought, the issue is not the failure of the thinker; rather it is why he and the ideas he propounded were so popular and, within limits, so effective during the interwar period. Of his influence, there is no doubt. Arslan was a phenomenon of the time, ingrained in the epoch as an international public figure as few other Arabs were. Of the many tributes paid him by his admirers, Kurd ʿAli's attempt to explain him to another generation best captures the moment: "None of us had such worldly fame as did Amir Shakib. Respected in the field of politics as in literature, he was known equally by the West and by the East; he was the unequaled measure. . . ."[73]

Tributes merely attest to influence; and the political actions which demonstrate influence, such as the campaign against the Berber *dahir*, are but one dimension of an individual's impact on his time. It remains to be seen if Arslan's association with the intellectual positions presented in this chapter contributed to the esteem in which he was held.

Commenting on the consistency of his attitude toward the European imperial threat to Islamic sovereignty, Arslan wrote in the late 1930s: "If you read my publications from before the war, and then read what I am writing now, you would think you were reading the grandson of the earlier Arslan."[74] This did not make Arslan an archaic pan-Islamicist in an age of secular Arab nationalism. The Arab-Islamic world had not yet accepted secular nationalism as its organizing principle, and many of its activists were prepared to endorse Arslan's use of Islam as a political and cultural weapon unencumbered with theological justifications more complex than the basic assurance that activism was permitted. That Arslan was to gain popularity for espousing this doctrine—or, more precisely, this tactic—was because he touched the existing sentiment of his time. Part of the appeal of his message was its very representativeness. He clearly carried with him the outlook of an earlier era, but the ideals of that era had not entirely vanished. Arslan served as a conduit for the expression of hopes and fears which had existed before 1914 and which, far from being dissolved in the crucible of war, were exacerbated by it. Islamic sovereignty, threatened under Abdulhamid II, was extinguished after 1919 except for the thread of hope attached to the kingdom of Ibn Saʿud. There was thus a climate of receptivity to activism organized around principles of Islamic solidarity and dedicated to the goal of Islamic liberation. The twenties and thirties were filled as much with efforts to restore revised versions of old forms of association as with preparations for the new ones.

The tendency to view the interwar period as one of preparation for the triumph of Nasserist pan-Arabism overlooks the dominance of Islamic sentiment at the time. Movements such as the Young Men's Muslim Association and the Muslim Brotherhood in Egypt, the secret societies and free schools in Morocco, and the Association of Algerian Ulema, while they did not always win political power in the postindependence era, expressed the dominant orientation of the 1930s. Arslan not only represented that orientation, he directly inspired it.

Although Arslan's use of Islam in his call to action struck a responsive chord, his notoriety exceeded that of a polemicist, and one must look beyond the content and even the frequency of his writings to explain his prominence. A major factor in his ability to gain a position of mentorship among younger Arabs, to retain his stature among his peers, and to earn the respect of the Europeans who dealt with him directly was his commanding personality. Charming and intransigent, audacious and persuasive, he possessed an array of interpersonal skills which he used to great advantage. Although not a demagogue in the manner of Messali Hajj—he was no more than an adequate public speaker—Arslan was very effective in small group situations.[75] The frequent gatherings of students and exiles in his Geneva apartment allowed him to use the drawing room as a complement to the printed page as a channel for the transmission of ideas and the exercise of influence. Al-Jabiri, his colleague of twenty years, was awed by Arslan's boldness and referred to him as a man possessed of "un courage terrible."[76] During his lengthy meeting with Arslan in 1934, David Ben-Gurion first noticed his host's physical frailty, but was quickly struck by his "vigor and fervor" once he began to speak.[77]

Others, from quite different vantage points, have furthered the impression of Arslan as a formidable individual. Syrian High Commissioner de Jouvenal continued negotiations with him on the Syro-Lebanese question in 1925 to the point of proposing specific clauses because he sensed in the Amir a personality of sufficient proportions to ensure that the document, if agreed to, would be signed by others. And in a profile prepared for the German Foreign Ministry, Arslan was described as "especially proud" and "socially very adroit."[78] He was a self-confident man possessed of substantial personal presence. His capacity for influence-building embraced direct contact as well as journalistic output.

Arslan was aware of his image and nurtured it through constant association with the new Arab royalty. Ibn Saʿud and Imam Yahya were public friends. He regularly visited King Faysal during that monarch's summer holidays in Switzerland, and at one point the ruler of Iraq was reported to have dined "dans l'intimité" at Arslan's residence.[79] In pursuing these contacts, Arslan was, in some respects, simply behaving in the manner expected of one who had been accustomed to audiences with the Ottoman sultan and the Egyptian khedive. But he also knew what he was about, and he cultivated his role even as he fulfilled it.

As a result, his reputation was expanded by others' perceptions of his ability to control events and to shape opinions. To read Louis Jovelet's summary of developments in the Arab world for the years 1930 to 1933 is to gain a sense of how much Arslan dominated the thinking of some French observers of the Arab world; he was synonymous with the Arab opposition.[80] French opinion on Arslan's impact on the Maghrib has been analyzed in chapter 5. It ranged from the sense of alarm and accusation by the *Afrique Française* school to the feelings of respect on the part of men like Julien and Le Tourneau. The latter, writing from the perspective of 1950, concluded that Arslan was one of the four most influential Arab personalities of the interwar period.[81] Arslan did not found a movement which lived after him, but his impact on his own age was substantial. One exaggerated dimension of it was expressed by Paul Allard of *Paris Soir* in his proclamation that Arslan was "one of the most extraordinary international adventurers of modern times."[82]

Officials of both Britain and France saw Arslan as the single source which aroused Arab agitation and defined Arab aspirations; and they accorded him an organizational capability he did not really possess. However, for those who preferred the simple act of attribution to a single source rather than the difficult task of social analysis and policy review, Arslan was a natural target. It was far easier to blame the discontent of Algerians or Palestinians on the strings he was allegedly pulling from Geneva than it was to alleviate the conditions of the plaintiffs.

By portraying Arslan as a dangerous figure whose ability to manipulate Arab anti-imperialist movements was more extensive than it may really have been, Britain and France enhanced his reputation in the Arab world. In this way, Arslan's prestige was fed from two opposing sources—Europeans who exaggerated his real control over events, and the Arab public, which, partly as a result of the European press reports, saw him as a brave *mujahid* striking fear into the hearts of imperial administrators by his independent activities in their own capitals.

Yet Arslan was not a mere figment of a nervous imperial imagination. Nor, for all the cloying praise directed at him by his supporters, was he a hollow creation of the press. He was a *mujahid*, an exiled and persecuted patriot, a representative at the League of Nations, a commanding and appealing figure. For a moment in the interwar period he captured the hearts of the politically active and the religiously inclined. As publicist, he defined the issues by which Arab-Islamic society measured its wrongs—the Berber *dahir*, the Mandate system, Zionist settlement in Palestine, rampant secularism—and claimed that they could be righted. He also fulfilled the rituals through which an older world sought to preserve itself; by his pilgrimage, his rich literary style, and his elegant manner, he celebrated the virtues of an aristocrat made activist by a brutal twentieth century. But he spoke not so much to the unachievable past as to the links between past and present. He spoke to that deep-seated human desire to resurrect the familiar order in a time of trouble; but he had in his message action, in his person courage, and for a time he was, as Kurd ʿAli stated, "the unequaled measure." But in his efforts to explore new directions to end Arab humiliation, in his need to use the influence which came his way, he took on more than he could control. At the peak of his popularity and respect, he was accused of corruption and betrayal. As the following chapter shows, his reputation has never fully recovered.

CHAPTER SEVEN.
TOWARD THE AXIS

*I have never been soiled, thank God, by accepting a single
sou from any foreign power.*   *—Arslan*[1]

*In view of the present circumstances, the Amir's presence in
Switzerland appears undesirable for he has always been
considered as an agent of Italy, of Germany, and even of the
Soviets.*   *—The Federal Public Ministry, Bern*[2]

IN ITS EFFORTS to obtain independence from the two
powers which between them controlled most of the territories from
Morocco to Iraq, the Arab movement had achieved few real triumphs
by the late 1930s. Neither violent revolt nor measured negotiation
had altered the fact of British and French domination. Restrictive
treaties with Iraq and Egypt, unenacted Popular Front legislation
for Syria and the Maghrib, and continued Zionist immigration into
Palestine together convinced Arab opinion of the intransigence of
Franco-British imperialism. Faced with this situation, a broad cross
section of Arab leaders concluded that their objectives could be met
only with the assistance of European allies capable of employing diplomatic leverage and potential armed force against the occupying
powers. Other studies have traced these developments in detail.[3]
Here it is sufficient to record the broad pattern of Axis-Arab cooperation as a framework within which Shakib Arslan's writings and activities attained special prominence. Arslan not only welcomed the
new shift toward the Axis, he endeavored to shape it.

Arab overtures to Germany and, to a much lesser extent, Italy
were based primarily on the strategic advantages envisaged in an alliance with European powers "disinterested" in imperial ventures. In
this sense, Germany was particularly attractive as an ally. Neither
the Weimar government nor its Nazi successor considered the Middle
East of sufficient importance to warrant the formulation of a coherent political position toward the region. Berlin's interests were in
Europe, and there seemed little point in antagonizing Britain in the

Levant if concessions on the continent could be gained without doing so. Moreover, with the proclamation of the Axis in 1936, the
German Foreign Office conceded that the Mediterranean was an Italian sphere of influence and reasoned that it would be more useful to
the Reich's objectives to leave Italy and Britain to resolve their differences in the Arab world.

Not that official German involvement was completely lacking.
Contacts with Arab political leaders were established in the late
1930s. Arabic broadcasts began from Berlin in 1939, Arab students
and emissaries were received in that city, and Nazi dignitaries like
Goebbels and von Schirach visited certain Arab capitals. In part, this
interest was generated by increasing tension with Great Britain and
by the realization that in one respect, Nazi Jewish policies might be
self-defeating. If Zionists succeeded in gaining a Jewish state in Palestine as the Peel partition plan of 1937 appeared to permit, then in
Nazi eyes the international Jewish conspiracy would have a concentrated power-base from which to weave its intrigues. Germany therefore had some interest in supporting the Arab world in general as a
potential counterweight to this threat. The Palestine rebellion of
1936–1939 presented an opportunity to embarrass Britain and encourage the Arabs, so modest financing of the rebels was undertaken
and arms were made available to Iraq.[4] Still, these were tentative
steps, and official German interwar policy toward the Arab Middle
East may accurately be described as disinterested.

The same was not true of fascist Italy. Under Mussolini's adven-
turous leadership, Italy made a determined bid to alter the status
quo along the shores of the Mediterranean and the Red Sea.[5] While
the lines of foreign policy were imprecise, certain trends emerged
vis-à-vis the Arab world after 1933. Mussolini, in an attempt to challenge the dominant position of Britain and France, pursued a strategy which aimed at revising the Mandate system which had left Italy
without a Levant possession and weakening the League of Nations,
which prevented it from obtaining one. He also launched projects of
direct imperial expansion, as in the Ethiopian war (1935–1936) and
the mass colonization projects in Libya (1938–1939). To shake Britain from its position on the Red Sea, a large Italian mission operated
in the Yemen, and efforts were made to court Ibn Saʿud. In the Levant, Rome pursued extremely complex and occasionally contradic-
tory policies, at one point supporting both Weizmann and Hajj Amin
al-Husayni, but all aimed to make Britain's position uncomfortable.

These maneuvers were backed by an expensive campaign of cultural propaganda designed to counter the impressions formed during
the Libyan conquest and so to increase Italy's prestige among the

Arabs. Broadcasts from Radio Bari, subsidies to various Arabic news-papers, and the use of a network of informers and agents were the principal means by which a pro-Italian, anti-British message was conveyed to the Arab world.[6] Radio Bari proclaimed that Rome in-tended to redeem the Arabic peoples oppressed by British and French imperialism, that the mother of civilization would reconstitute its great Mediterranean role as intermediary between Asia and Europe. These promises were given some reality by the establishment in Rome of a new Institute for the Near and Far East in December 1933, the opening ceremonies of which coincided with the hosting of a congress of Asiatic students. In subsequent years, an oriental cul-tural club was formed, a permanent office of European-Asian coopera-tion was established, various bulletins were published, and a few Italian works on Islam were translated into Arabic. The image of Rome as a home for Muslim students and a patron of Islam culmi-nated in the proclamation of Mussolini as the protector of Islam dur-ing a state visit to Libya in 1937.

While the attempts to embarrass Britain and the gestures toward Islam conceivably had some appeal in the Arab world, they were never sufficient to overcome Arab distrust of Rome's imperial ambi-tions. Italy was viewed as a successor to Britain and France, not as a disinterested liberator. This "conflict of Italian ambitions with Arab aspirations" even prompted some Arab spokesmen to prefer an ac-commodation with Britain to an alliance with Rome and led others to request that Germany relieve their fears of Italian imperialism.[7]

It is a measure of their frustration with the suffocating presence of Britain and France that, despite well-founded reservations about Ital-ian intentions, various Arab rulers and cultural leaders approached both Rome and Berlin in the years before the war.

In the two years preceding the outbreak of war, regimes and indi-viduals maneuvered for position, utilizing the flexibility presented by a choice of allies to enhance their bargaining position with both camps. For example, Ibn Saʿud, attempting to break away from his dependence on Great Britain, embarked on a series of negotiations with the two fascist powers which led him, in 1938 and 1939, to rec-ognize the Italian annexation of Ethiopia, to establish formal diplo-matic relations with Germany, and to conclude arms purchase agree-ments with both Rome and Berlin. Similarly, the Iraqi regime of the first coup d'état (1936–1937) arranged to purchase weapons from Germany and initiated with Ambassador Fritz Grobba the close liaison which survived the rise and fall of governments in Baghdad and culminated in the anti-British uprising of 1941. Hajj Amin al-Husayni, already funded by Italy, made his first formal approach to

German representatives in 1937, requesting arms and financial aid for the Palestinian rebellion from the German consul in Jerusalem. Anti-British elements within Egyptian palace and military circles made similar soundings, and in 1938 ʿAziz ʿAli al-Misri, inspector-general of the Egyptian armed forces, visited Berlin, where he conducted negotiations on arms purchases. Other concurrent initiatives were undertaken by nationalist circles in Beirut and Damascus as well as in the Maghrib.[8]

Although the strategic value of Axis ties was more significant than the content of fascism in prompting these initial contacts, there did exist in Arab circles a certain admiration for fascist achievements as such. Like the Arab states, Italy and Germany were weakened internationally and domestically by the war. Unlike the Arabs, they had managed to reverse that status. Mussolini's posturing at least gave Italy the appearance of a great power, and, as Germany won more and more concessions from Britain in Europe, the prestige of the fascist system increased at the expense of the parliamentary one. The imposition of the forms of Western democracy had brought only continued dependence and inefficient government to the Eastern Arab states. Disillusionment with this state of affairs found expression in the formation of paramilitary youth movements such as the government-sponsored Futuwwa in Iraq, the SSNP of Antun Saʿadah in Syria/Lebanon, and the Green Shirts of Young Egypt, each of which expressed varying degrees of admiration for the fascist achievement.

It is against this background that Arslan's dealings with the Axis powers should be examined. He played a central role in orchestrating the interplay between German and Italian desires for a new world order and the Arab search for independence. It was a role for which he has been harshly judged by some. Western historians have found distasteful his final alliances, while contemporaries saw his support for Italy as a betrayal of his previously unambiguous anti-imperialism and therefore a stance for which he must have been paid. This suspicion of collaboration tainted his image in the final years of his life. Yet for Arslan, friendly contact with the Axis was a natural extension of his efforts to exert pressure on Britain and France. In conjunction with his coordination of protest movements and peaceful discussions, he also attempted to manage European rivalries so as to gain a great power ally for the Arabs. His experience in European diplomacy combined with his sense of personal mission and his feelings of self-importance to compel him to assume the role of principal negotiator. Only he could goad a disinterested Germany into an alliance, only he could control an overly ambitious Italy in the best interests of the Arab-Islamic cause. In fact, he could do neither, and he became enmeshed in a situation too complicated for him to manage until, in the end, he lost the flexibility which had given him a certain strength. But for a time, his involvement in European diplomacy discomfited his British and French opponents and thrust him ever more prominently into the international arena in which he delighted.

From the perspective of those European governments which traced Arslan's movements and attempted to determine what his objectives were, he was less a victim of exile than a manipulator. Foreign Ministry archives and public security records painted a different picture of Arslan than did his admirers in Cairo or Damascus. It is the picture of a professional agitator, of an agent in constant motion seeking the best arrangement for himself. Dr. Rosaria Quartararo, after thoroughly reviewing the Italian and British Foreign Ministry archives, admitted that she could not decide whether Arslan was merely an *agent provocateur* or a man with a real cause.[9] I have no hesitation in resolving Dr. Quartararo's dilemma with the assertion that Arslan was far more committed and directed than any *agent provocateur*. Admittedly, there was, as in the First World War, an ambivalence to his position, a principled justification coupled with apparent compromise. Although in his pro-Axis stance Arslan was part of a strong current of Arab opinion, his apparently single-handed manipulation of a vast network of intrigue and his ability to attract publicity ensured that he would be controversial. So much of what Arslan was to his Arab audience and so much of what he chose to do with his considerable influence is tied to the issue of his relations with Italy and Germany that no account of the man is complete without an attempt to explore it. Moreover, the positions which Arslan took had reverberations throughout the Arab world, and he became, more than ever before, the focus around which regional political forces aligned themselves. How this role developed is best examined through his separate contacts with the two Axis powers.

Arslan's special relationship with Germany and with German Foreign Office officials began during World War I and was maintained without interruption during the twenty-eight years he resided in Europe. Berlin had been a haven of refuge for him in the early 1920s, and he made no effort, public or private, to conceal his friendly attitude toward Germany. As he once asserted when trying to get the Wilhelmstrasse to adopt his perspective on a certain matter, he was the most long-standing Arab friend Germany possessed, one who had for forty-seven years been preaching the community of interests between that country and the Islamic world.[10]

Arslan's definition of those interests and why they came to exist was partly due to the image he formed of Germany through associations with particular individuals. From the time of his special mission for Enver Pasha in 1917 to his last meetings in the 1940s, Arslan's Germans were the aristocrats of the prewar Wilhelminian Foreign Service. A small group of men centered around Werner Otto von Hentig, Dr. Curt Max Prüfer, Baron Herbert von Richthofen, and his "très cher ami et frère" Baron Max von Oppenheim comprised the circle through which Arslan formed his impressions of German attitudes toward the Arab Middle East.[11] He even counted the ex-kaiser as "a friend" and made a special visit to him in Doorn in 1934.[12] Never did he appear to deal directly with officials whose careers were built primarily through service to the Third Reich.

Within this small circle of aristocrats, Arslan had his most intimate contact with von Oppenheim (1860–1946). If each used the other somewhat, theirs was nonetheless an enduring and endearing relationship. Von Oppenheim, of Jewish ancestry, served as an attaché in the German Consulate-General in Cairo from 1896 to 1910. He resigned this post to pursue an interest in Hittite archaeology, but was recalled to the Foreign Office in 1914. From Istanbul he formed and directed the Intelligence Office for the East, an organization which aimed at generating a Muslim holy war against the allies. He soon returned to his archaeological pursuits, but surfaced in times of crisis to act as an unofficial agent of the German government, using his contacts with the former colleagues mentioned above to further German political penetration of the Middle East.[13] In mid-career, Arslan and the baron had in common a love of scholarship, language, and the Ottoman Middle East; at the end of their lives, they shared the uncertain privilege of being honorary Aryans.

While these relationships may not excuse Arslan's miscalculations, they at least demonstrate the origins of his conviction that German-Arab friendship had an especially firm foundation. While the Sûreté arrested his Maghribi friends in Paris, and the Quai d'Orsay barred him from his homeland, he was courted by the officials of the old German foreign service, men experienced in and generally sympathetic to the Middle East who, even in their private exchanges, could recognize in the exiled Amir "a highly cultivated man."[14] It was a far cry from the *indigène* outlook of much of French officialdom. Arslan basked in being accepted for what he thought he was.

In terms of courtesies, if not of policy formulation, the impression was mutually reinforcing. To the Auswärtiges Amt of both the Weimar and Nazi eras, Arslan had two particularly attractive characteristics—his unquestioned pro-German sympathies and "the extraordinary confidence and prestige he enjoys throughout the entire Arab world."[15] While Germany harbored no imperial ambitions in the Arab Middle East, the Foreign Office felt it would be useful to curry favor with an individual of Arslan's standing and sympathies. The German consul in Geneva was instructed to assist Arslan with his travel documents during the preparations for his trip to the United States. Personal letters were composed to soothe his ruffled feelings over a published report that Germany would defer to Franco-British interests in the Middle East. As mentioned in chapter 3, the Ministry intervened in the form of a personal letter from Baron von Richthofen during a repossession hearing on Arslan's Berlin apartment house.[16]

While assisting Arslan the Foreign Office also wished to be informed on his political thinking at all times. Thus, in 1926, Arslan's old friend Baron von Oppenheim began the practice he was to continue for the next nineteen years of forwarding copies of the Amir's personal correspondence to the oriental division of the Auswärtiges Amt.[17] The tone of the German archival material suggests that Arslan's knowledge of Arab politics and personalities was more important to his Foreign Office acquaintances than his friendship. He was considered a useful source of information (in this case unknown to him) but, since he could prove an embarrassment, he was kept at arm's length whenever he made a political request. He was never really a party to high-level decision making on German Middle Eastern policy; he never gained the opportunity to present his case at the levels he thought he deserved. He initiated a flurry of protocol activity and a review of Franco-German-Arab relations when he insisted on an audience with the president in 1927. He was no more successful in this demand than in one made seven years later to be received by Hitler. If these slights injured his sense of self-importance, they did not deter him from his persistent efforts to use Berlin for his own cause. Shakib Arslan's attraction to Germany was based on far more grandiose expectations than the exchange of personal friendships and favors.

When Wilhelm II proclaimed in Damascus in 1898 that Germany was the protector of 300 million Muslims, Arslan stood at the kaiser's side.[18] For the rest of his life, his understanding of intra-European and European–Middle Eastern alliances rested on this nineteenth-century pledge. In his mind, its sincerity was affirmed by the German-Ottoman alliance in World War I. Throughout the interwar years, he worked to convince the German Foreign Office to activate this concept and to make it the cornerstone of German Arab policy.

He became convinced of the need for a German alliance because of the inability of Arab leaders to accomplish anything without it. Thus, while he pursued his relations with Germany, he preserved a certain flexibility in dealing with the Mandate powers and responded positively to the 1936 Franco-Syrian treaty. However, the repeated failure of negotiations at any level to bring a substantial modification in the status of the Syrian Mandate or the Maghrib protectorates led Arslan to intensify his negotiations with Germany. Resistance, whether it was at the barricades or the bargaining table, would be unsuccessful unless funds, arms, and diplomatic backing were given by a European power. This was the role Arslan envisaged for Germany; this was at the heart of his "community of interests" affirmation.

He and Ihsan al-Jabiri attempted to prod the Auswärtiges Amt into action with some daring proposals which show the high risks Arslan was prepared to assume in his frustration with the Mandate powers. During the latter stages of the Syrian revolt, Arslan arranged for al-Jabiri to see Baron von Richthofen to discuss a plan for obtaining weapons and a substantial loan from Germany for the Syrian rebels. Von Richthofen assured al-Jabiri and, in a personal letter, Arslan that while an independent Syria enjoyed Germany's sympathy, Weimar's precarious economic situation and its supervision by the Arms Control Commission made any active assistance impossible.[19]

A few years later, Arslan again tried to force Germany's hand. This time, he portrayed a German commitment to the Arabs as having distinct advantages for Berlin. His scenario, presented to Dr. Prüfer, envisaged an inevitable and imminent war between France and Germany. Berlin, he argued, would be well advised to secure allies for the conflict in advance. None would be more natural than the oppressed Arabs of the Maghrib and Syria, whose active rebellion would hasten German victory. Prüfer was not in the least interested in the proposal, feeling it was dangerous and impractical. However, he knew his man, and reported that Arslan, unconvinced by his objections, would surely seek another channel through which to present his scheme. He therefore "urgently advised against the reception of Arslan or Jabiri by leading government personalities."[20]

Distrustful as he normally was of European states, Arslan could take the risk of appealing so openly for German support because of his belief that Germany was the one great power which truly held no future imperial ambitions in the Arab world. If this disinterest could be expressed in the form of a German declaration in favor of Arab independence, then there was hope for liberation. He was aware of the risks inherent in what would be an unequal alliance. In 1939, he wrote to Daniel Guérin that the Muslims sympathized with Germany only because it was the enemy of their enemies; they were not ignorant of the fact that, if they fell under the German yoke, they would only have changed masters.[21] But for the most part, he was firm in his conviction. During the war, he urged the ex-mufti to declare his support for the Axis and explained to him that "I follow the Axis in the hope that by means of their victory, Islam will be liberated from its slavery."[22]

The most detailed of his justifications is contained in a letter to a Balkan acquaintance, Sulayman Agha of Croatia. Although written during the war, the letter serves as an accurate summary of Arslan's feelings over a period of several years.[23] Emphasizing the basic reason for a pro-German position, he explained that Muslims would only recover complete independence through a German victory. Germany "has never subjugated or oppressed a single Muslim" and would, after its triumph, treat the Muslims as allies, not as subjects. In response to the threat of simply exchanging one set of masters for another, Arslan had to rely on what he saw as the logic of the situation: "Germany knows full well that if it wishes to carve out for itself colonies in the Arab countries as the British and French did, there will be no hope for peace, for the Arabs are firmly resolved to live free and independent. Germany knows this and so does Italy." Besides, Arslan could demonstrate that there was no other way. He himself had attempted negotiations with the Mandate powers, and they had failed. "One who holds illusions on the possibilities of any change whatsoever in British, French, or Russian policy is a person deprived of reason or of conscience."

Arslan was a desperate patriot who, in trying to expand his negotiating options, actually found them narrowing. Could he, in his drift toward the Axis, find features of Nazi Germany that were inherently admirable? How did he, as a cultivated Muslim with the attitude of Qur'anic noblesse oblige toward people of the book, comport himself when faced with the anti-Jewish policies of Hitlerian Germany? Like any Semite, he was uneasy at their full implications, and he never sought directly to defend them. More often than not, he placed himself in the awkward position of one who, having chosen a suspect ally, defended that choice by maligning the alternatives. Germany may have suppressed a few million Czechs, but that was nothing when compared to the British and French enslavement of 150 million Muslims. Why did Britain bemoan the forced immigration of Jews from Germany under a totalitarian regime when it, as a democracy, slaughtered Palestinians guilty of no crime other than the defense of their homeland?[24]

In the long run, Arslan chose not to meddle in what he called

German internal affairs (a not uncommon stance in the late 1930s), but he did take some pains to disassociate Islam, and hence himself, from racism. He explicitly denied the existence of Arab anti-Semitism for the obvious reason that the Arabs were a Semitic people, and he attempted to put some distance between Arabism and Nazism: "The Arab national movement is a purely Arab movement which is not racist and which has no need of German national-socialist theories to prompt the Arabs to reject foreign domination."[25] His response to doctrines of race and *Volk* was to cite the Qur'an and *hadith* to prove that individual piety was the sole criterion by which a believer was judged: "If a Jew or a Christian freely becomes a Muslim, he is one of the faithful with the same rights and duties. But if he wishes to retain his Judaism or his Christianity, no one should prevent him from doing so."[26]

Thus, while his own experience with select Germans had been generally pleasant, he found it difficult to expound any view of the country which made it a power to emulate. To Muhammad ʿAli al-Tahir he wrote that Germany, like the Allies, "holds principles I do not share," and he tried to explain to Nuri al-Saʿid, "I do not care for Hitler, nor do I defend him or believe his ideology. . . ."[27] All he wanted was an alliance which would enable Arab-Islamic culture to surface from its oppression and to live independently. Germany was no different from other European civilizations in lacking any inherent attraction as a model. It just happened to be "the enemy of our enemies."

In his interwar relations with Germany, Arslan was not so much an agent spreading German propaganda as he was an Arab plaintiff trying to persuade German policymakers to adopt a certain set of attitudes toward the Arab Middle East. This was not the case in his dealings with fascist Italy, for whose foreign adventures he served as apologist. In order to make Italy appear as an acceptable counterweight to Britain and France, Arslan had to portray the instigators of the Libyan atrocities as the new Western champions of Islam. It was a risky partnership, and it led Arslan into some of the most twisted polemics of his career, subjected him to fierce attacks on his integrity, and deprived him of a portion of the credibility which his own efforts had deservedly brought him.

During the 1920s, the Syro-Palestinian delegation had tried to attract Italian support for Arab grievances.[28] These overtures ceased during the Italian reconquest of Libya. However, when Italy sought to rehabilitate its image in Arab eyes by adopting a conciliatory policy toward the Libyan population, Arslan reassessed his attitude. He was attracted by the fact that the Italians, in the words of one of their severest critics, "were most careful not to offend Arab opinion in religious matters."[29] Rome went on record as opposing proselytization in Libya and took steps to build mosques and to respect the *shariʿah* in the sphere of personal status and inheritance. However superficial these policies may have been, however uncaring and domineering Italian rule in Libya actually was, appearances could be used to advantage by a skillful propagandist.

His sensors finely tuned to the status of Muslims under colonial rule, Arslan saw in Italy's new attitude an opportunity for a closer alliance. In 1933, he published an article in the Jerusalem press expressing his approval of the Italian amnesty in Libya. The Italian Foreign Office reacted with guarded optimism, hoping that "the influential leader" might be tracing a new direction for Italo-Arab relations.[30] Most likely as a result of this article and the attention it received, contact between Arslan and the Italians was reestablished. By Arslan's account, he was invited by Mussolini to come to Rome, but replied that he would do so only after the deported Libyan tribes were repatriated.[31] When this policy was initiated, Arslan appeared at the Muslim Student Congress hosted by Mussolini in December 1933, thus lending that gathering a prestige it would not otherwise have had. Soon thereafter, in February 1934, he had two meetings with Mussolini during which he presented the Duce with his demands for further modifications of Italy's Libyan policy. Although he never directly admitted it, Arslan probably also agreed to mute his criticism of Italian policies if they were adjusted so as to permit some freedom for Islamic religious institutions. Over the years, he expressed his satisfaction that Italy had kept its part of the bargain.[32]

On these tenuous grounds, Arslan added Mussolini to his public list of personal friends and concluded that Italian colonial policy, however deplorable in the first place, was the best arrangement that Muslims could expect from a European power. It was then his task to allay the suspicions of his Arab audience and to persuade them that, appearances to the contrary, Italian declarations were sincere and Italian promises reliable. This restricted him terribly. The aggressive spokesman who pledged, "When it concerns Arab and Muslim interests in general, I have no fear of attacking anyone," found himself admitting, "I cannot attack Mussolini at the very moment I am demanding that he restore the rights of Muslims in Libya."[33] Islam was Arslan's benchmark of freedom. He was, at least in the case of Italy, willing to exchange political liberties for religious ones.

This was most obvious, and most awkward, in his attempts to persuade his fellow Arabs that the Italian invasion of Ethiopia was not an imperial undertaking similar to those which had deprived them of their own independence. His several articles on the subject argued that since Christian Ethiopia had continually suppressed its Muslim majority (he used his own statistics), Italy's action, while it had the unfortunate consequence of destroying the sovereignty of the Ethiopian state, brought with it an enlightened Islamic policy and should thus be welcomed by all who were concerned with the fate of Muslims. He would not condone imperialism, but "our pity for Abyssinia has been tempered by the memory of the terrible suffering which Christian Abyssinia has imposed over the centuries on the Muslims of that and neighboring countries."[34] Rashid Rida warned Arslan that Eastern opinion was firmly on the side of Ethiopia, but the Amir persisted in presenting an admixture of apologetics for Italy's Islamic policies combined with displeasure at the act of invasion.[35]

Arslan could hardly have been deceived by the façade in Libya or by his own rhetoric on Ethiopia. One who had sufficient political acumen to recognize the Popular Front as essentially the government of an imperial power would surely see that Italy's ambitions paralleled those of Britain and France. He admitted as much in the early years of the war, writing that Italian greed would have to be curbed by Germany.[36] He also acknowledged that Mussolini's Islamic policy was more likely based on political considerations than on true affection. But so was Arslan's own pro-Italian stance. As he explained to Rida, "There are certain things I want from Mussolini regarding the Syrian, Palestinian, and Tripolitanian questions."[37] Italy could assist in redressing Arab grievances primarily because of its status. Sounding rather like the fascist propaganda machine, Arslan proclaimed that "Italy is now a power of the first rank . . . and nothing is done on the international stage without her compliance."[38] Thus Italy, a great power, "could aid us in Syria and Palestine by a pro-Arab policy."[39] Faced with the realities of the Libyan conquest, Arslan, "as a practical man," decided that advantages were more likely to accrue to the Arab cause by appeasing a repentant imperial state than by antagonizing it.[40]

The tensions surrounding Arslan's rapprochement with Italy reached a crisis point in the spring of 1935 as he moved from tentative approval of Mussolini's Libyan reforms to full support for Italy's overall Islamic policy in Eritrea and Ethiopia. In March and April of that year, Arslan published a series of articles in the Jerusalem-based paper *al-Jam'iyyah al-'Arabiyyah* praising Italy's pro-Arab voting record at the League of Nations, defending Rome's policy toward the Muslims of Ethiopia, and explaining how an alliance with Italy would benefit the Arab and Muslim cause.[41] With the appearance of

these articles, Arslan unwittingly entered the local arena of Palestinian politics and became a pawn in the struggle between the Nasha-
shibi and al-Husayni factions within the Mandate. What had begun
as an ordinary propaganda venture to justify Arslan's own position
and persuade others to adopt it turned into a vicious smear campaign
with the Amir as the main target. A notorious episode in interwar
Arab politics, the press war of 1935 became fixed in Arslan's life as
"the incident of the forged letter" and resulted in one of the most
damaging public accusations of his career. The weapon which he had
so often wielded to humble his own opponents, the periodical press,
was turned on him with devastating effect. After the publication
of the forged letter, his reputation was never quite as secure as it
had been.

On 18 April 1935, the Nashashibi-oriented paper *al-Jam'iyyah al-
Islamiyyah* published a photostated reproduction of a letter which
the editors alleged had been written by Arslan to Hajj Amin al-
Husayni, the mufti of Jerusalem. The document, dated 20 February
1935, stated in part: "the agreement was concluded to give a start to
the propaganda in favor of Italy in the Arab countries as soon as possible. . . . Perhaps the Ministry of Propaganda in Rome will send to
our newspapers some notices for publication."[42] The mufti's opponents were using Arslan's Italian associations and his well-known
friendship with Hajj Amin to discredit the mufti himself; their purpose in publishing the letter was to show that Hajj Amin and the Supreme Muslim Council which he headed were working closely with
a European power every bit as imperialistic as Britain. Although
Arslan's own pro-Italian leanings were raised only as a means to
undermine Hajj Amin, the Amir was more compromised than the
mufti. As a simple statement in the Esco Foundation report reveals,
all parties to the episode responded aggressively: "The publication of
the letter aroused violent discussion in the Arab press, accompanied
by mutual recriminations, charges and countercharges."[43]

None was more aggressive than Arslan. At the heart of the storm,
he struck back with all the forces at his disposal. He poured forth a
stream of private and public letters and took up his own defense in
the pages of *La Nation Arabe* and whatever other journals would
publish him. In his correspondence with Rashid Rida, Arslan lashed
out at everyone associated with the letter. Dr. Shahbandar was
blamed for approving the forgery, al-Jabiri was condemned for failing
to inform Arslan about the article's publication, and the British were
attacked for refusing him entry to Palestine to launch a lawsuit for
slander.[44] Expert calligraphers were called in to declare the letter a
forgery, internal evidence was produced showing the existence of de-

partures from Arslan's customary form of dating and salutation, and, as proof positive, the prince of eloquence himself pointed out that the letter had fifteen errors in its thirty-eight lines: "Do you think an academician who has composed Arabic for fifty years, whose style is known for its grammatical rigor, is capable of committing errors of syntax and grammar which not even merchants would make?"[45]

Rashid Rida cautioned Arslan that he was carrying his self-defense to extremes. The letter, Rida explained, was generally recognized to be a forgery.[46] Arslan would not be assuaged. What might seem like an overreaction to an incident which could be expected by one who took pride in being an outspoken polemicist was, in this case, justified because of the way Arslan defined the stakes. At issue was his very credibility as an anti-imperialist figure. Instead of being congratulated for bargaining in the best interests of the Arabs, he was accused of spreading propaganda for the benefit of Italy. He recognized the full implications of the damaging phrases expressed in the letter and denied them time and again: "I have not become a propagandist for Italy, and Mussolini did not ask me to become one."[47] Rida, with his own strongly held views on the importance of Arslan's unblemished image to the Arab-Islamic cause, urged him to go further and to "withhold all praise of Italy and all condemnation of Ethiopia at this time."[48] This Arslan could not do. He felt he had made a sensible rapprochement that was being seized upon by those who wished to discredit him for their own causes—the British, the Zionists, and certain Arabs seeking their own advantage.

For all the fuss, the sentiments expressed in the letter could reasonably have come from Arslan. The phrase "I am confident that Italy will not treat us as England and France have treated us" was consistent with his strategy at the time.[49] Nor was the famous letter, forged or not, his final contribution to Italian propaganda in Palestine. Heedless of Rida's admonition, he continued to publish pro-Italian articles in several different journals. No matter how often or how vehemently he disavowed his authorship of the forged letter, his activities only reinforced the notion that he could have written it. Officials within the British Mandate service reported that "there seems to be little doubt that it is still he [Arslan] who very largely works Italian propaganda of this kind in Palestine and Egypt."[50] In this case, Arslan's objectives corresponded to Britain's interpretation of them—to mobilize Arab opinion so that, in the event of a European war, the latent unrest in Syria and Palestine would burst forth against the Mandate powers. So protective of his reputation, yet so willing to use it, Arslan was demonstrably effective in associating his stature with Italian policies and thus giving them a certain credibility. To the British high commissioner's office, he was the crucial medium through which Italian assertions of a progressive Islamic policy became believable to Arab opinion. This prompted added scrutiny by British officials of his movements and of the behavior of those who were suspected of being his agents.[51]

Nonetheless, Arslan's concerns about the ability of his reputation to survive the incident of the forged letter and the questions to which it gave rise were justified. His role in furthering Italian propaganda was so jarring, not just because it seemed such a dramatic reversal of his earlier hostility, but also because most other Arab leaders distrusted Italy so deeply. The principal exceptions were Arslan and Hajj Amin al-Husayni, and even the latter told the German ambassador in Teheran that any Arab leader who worked exclusively with Italy would immediately lose his following.[52] For those who were unconvinced by Arslan's explanations for his conciliatory attitude toward the Italian presence in Libya and Ethiopia, there was only one other possibility—he had betrayed his principles for money.

Throughout the controversial final decade of his life, nothing caused Arslan so much misery as the rumor that he was a paid Italian agent. He could admit and attempt to justify his support for Italy, but he was hurt and outraged by the accusations that such support had been given in exchange for money. The charges came from a variety of sources and served a variety of interests.[53] That they were not immediately dismissed as pure fabrication reveals the Amir's vulnerability in the area of funding.

Arslan's chaotic finances have been mentioned several times in this study. It is necessary to review them here, for, with the publication of the forged letter, they became more than ever a prominent feature of his public image. Moreover, the issue as to whether Arslan's political loyalties were determined by his well-known need for money extends beyond his own example and touches on the efforts of the Axis powers to influence Arab politics through subsidies to other individuals and organizations.

Arslan became implicated in such efforts because he was recognized by those who paid attention to him to have insufficient personal income to do all that he did. His German friend Dr. Prüfer described him as a man "in chronic financial crisis," and the Union Civique of Geneva complained that the Amir had a reputation among the merchants of the city as "un mauvais payeur."[54] Swiss authorities were worried that Arslan's precarious financial situation would make him susceptible to monetary arrangements with other powers and so compromise Swiss neutrality. Speculation over the sources of Arslan's possible supplementary income thus excited friend and foe alike and made him, nearly as much as did his controversial writings on other matters, the object of investigation and rumor.

As one example of the aura of intrigue which surrounded him at this time, the Swiss security service, which was one of the most efficient European agencies supervising his activities, became convinced that in 1936 he had received 500,000 French francs from Pierre Viénot, the undersecretary of state for foreign affairs in the Popular Front government.[55]

However, most of the allegations concerning Arslan's illicit financial arrangements related to his receipt of Italian funds. British and French officials were particularly determined to posit his role as a distributor of monies as an explanation for the continued unrest in their Arab territories. This was a continuation of the trend, mentioned in chapter 5 in the North African context, which labeled Arslan as the sponsor of hostilities which Palestinians (or Syrians, or Moroccans, or Algerians) would not, by themselves, initiate. Himself manipulated by sinister forces in Rome, he must have been the agent through which discontent was fomented and rebellion sustained.

Even before the uprising of 1936, British sources reported that Arslan, al-Jabiri, and their colleagues were in receipt of funds from the Italian government for propaganda purposes in Palestine.[56] By 1937, the sums had been estimated at £75,000 and were assumed to have been distributed over a four-year period beginning in 1933.[57] It is certainly possible that Arslan would have been willing to serve as a conduit for funds designated to purchase arms for the Palestinian rebels. Given the close scrutiny under which he was placed by the Swiss, it would have been an extremely difficult, but not impossible task. However, such a function would not have been especially unpopular in Arab circles. What was more damaging was the rumor that the money he was alleged to have received from Italy was for his personal use. Offended by these allegations, but unable to ignore them, Arslan was forced constantly to defend himself. He often did so with forceful eloquence: "For fifteen years we have defended the Arab and Muslim cause, and we defend it at our own expense. . . . We have made great sacrifices in possessions and money and we will continue to do so. We serve neither Germany nor France, neither England nor Italy nor any other country. We serve exclusively the Arab nation to which we belong and the Muslim world in general."[58] While few would deny his devotion to the Arab-Islamic cause, the charges persisted. Arslan came to feel that the French press was especially vindictive in this respect, complaining that it has "slandered me beyond human endurance."[59] In repudiating the attacks by French journalists, Arslan frequently resorted to paraphrasing their arguments and, by implication, showing how ridiculous they appeared when placed beside his known achievements. It could be an effective technique: "Shakib Arslan did not act for patriotism, pan-Islam, or pan-Arabism; he acted to serve Hitler and Mussolini to whom he is sold. In other words, do not believe that this man defends your cause for love of liberty, justice, Islam, or any other ideal. No, he does it for simple material interests, and you should not concern yourselves with what he writes on your behalf."[60]

In challenging those who were familiar with all that he had given to the Arab-Islamic cause to dare to brand him as a paid Axis collaborator, Arslan was not only engaging in skillful polemic, he was in large measure stating the truth. His pro-Italian sympathies were not given in exchange for personal gain. He certainly received subsidies from Italy and Germany, but they were for defined purposes such as travel, lodging, and the printing of *La Nation Arabe*.[61] As a closer examination of his financial affairs in the late 1930s shows, Arslan did not use whatever Axis money may have passed through his hands for personal gain. Once, when asked by the Swiss authorities if he received money from any government for his work, he replied: "No. I am a free man and I wish to remain one."[62] The intention expressed in this statement was sincere; the practice, given Arslan's circumstances, may be regarded as sufficiently close to the intention to exonerate him from the most compromising charges made against him.

Arslan's income was derived from four principal sources. Arab rulers and princes, Islamic leaders, and Syrian groups in North and South America made irregular contributions to the Syro-Palestinian delegation.[63] Arslan used these funds for their intended purposes, the costs of which were considerable—postage, telegrams, the printing and distribution of petitions to the League of Nations, the publication of *La Nation Arabe*, his own (and probably a large portion of al-Jabiri's) travel expenses in connection with his duties as head of the delegation, and a myriad of associated propaganda activities.

In addition, Arslan received, and assiduously cultivated, royalties from his books and direct payments for articles and introductions which he authored. As his reputation grew and his financial situation worsened, he used the former to help alleviate the latter. He once complained to Rida that Arab publishers, in requesting that he write prefaces and articles without compensation, showed little sympathy for his dreadful economic circumstances. They did not understand that he had a wife and children to support and no time to devote to nonremunerative writing.[64] The prince of eloquence was compelled to compose for the market as well as for the cause.

Until the outbreak of the war in 1939, Arslan also received income from the family estates in Lebanon. Previous references have been made to the correspondence which shows Arslan deeply involved in a variety of detailed income-raising ventures ranging from the sale of land to the construction of buildings. That he would give of his already overextended time and energies to these matters indicates how vital the Lebanese income was to him.[65] Finally, he received some rent from his Berlin apartment house. This was irregular because of international currency restrictions and sometimes nonexistent because of Arslan's habit of remortgaging the building at every opportunity. During the war, he implored von Oppenheim to use his influence to arrange for the apartment's rental income, which had accumulated to some 2,000 RM, to be transferred to his agent in Amsterdam so that he could begin meeting his debt payments.[66] The desperation with which Arslan pursued this relatively small sum ($800) reveals a man in dire financial straits.

His indebtedness was caused by the inadequacy of his own income to meet the private and public demands he placed upon it. He lived both modestly and carelessly. No matter what his circumstances, he never compromised on hotels. He was, after all, an Amir, and one who expected to be addressed as *son altesse* had certain obligations. In addition to Shakib's personal secretary, the Arslan household had a maid, although for seven years she was not an expense simply because Arslan failed to pay her. The issue was finally settled by her solicitors. Although he went to a barber twice a week, there were times when he could not afford coffee and, to the amazement of his Swiss surveillants, he was so impoverished he drank from the public fountains during the winter.[67] His two Geneva addresses, Avenue Hentsch and Rue Marignac, while by no means extravagant, had to be sufficiently respectable to entertain King Faysal and other visiting dignitaries. In addition, Arslan accumulated considerable medical expenses. He also had to pay for the education of his three children and their travel. It all added up to a healthy set of costs for the maintenance of a bourgeois existence in Geneva. During the three-month period from 1 July to 30 September 1938, he withdrew from his bank 8,935 Swiss francs.[68]

He added to his personal expenses by making modest donations to needy Arab students and their associations. His contributions to Ahmad Balafrej have already been mentioned. He also provided sums ranging from 50 to 150 Swiss francs to ʿAbd al-Qadir Hani, another of his "dear sons" who kept alive the Misr society in Switzerland.

Last voyage: Alexandria harbor, 1946.

Always, he apologized to Hani for not being able to send more, but he was at the moment "a l'embarras."[69] Those "moments" embraced most of his period abroad. They existed because in his desire to remain unencumbered by personal obligations to European governments, he refused to accept money for his personal needs from them.

Arslan's combination of financial integrity and financial distress confounded even his German friends. One of the more remarkable documents in his Auswärtiges Amt dossier is a letter from von Oppenheim to von Hentig explaining why the latest communication from Arslan stated that the Amir's banker in Berlin had been instructed to pay 1,500 marks to von Hentig. "It is," wrote von Oppenheim, "undoubtedly the old idea of Shakib that he received money from the Foreign Office and wishes gradually to pay it back."[70] Although this is only one incident, it conforms to the pattern of behavior Arslan followed in the late 1930s. It shows that, in a particularly desperate moment, he must have accepted funds for his personal use from the German Foreign Office. It also shows that, in his strong desire not to be beholden to any European power, he returned the money. He would accept European financial assistance for public activities related to furthering the cause of Arab independence, he might possibly act as a channel for disseminating funds to Arab militants, but he would not receive gifts of money for his personal use.

Arslan was no paragon of record keeping, and it would be unrealistic to suppose that he always distinguished his public from his private resources. But there was no sense of personal aggrandizement or even a very clear sense of financial survival in his sorry economic plight. By contrast, when the mufti and Rashid ʿAli al-Kaylani arrived in Europe in 1941, they received from Berlin a joint subsidy of 200,000 RM per month, free housing, and special payments totaling 250,000 RM. The Italian Foreign Ministry acted similarly, outfitting two splendid villas for their use and requesting that each of them be paid a subsidy of 2.5 million lire in 1942.[71] Had he asked, Arslan could surely have received from Rome and Berlin sufficient funds to alleviate his difficult circumstances. But he did not ask, and, until additional evidence to the contrary can be produced, it must be concluded that he did not receive significant personal subsidies from Italy or Germany. His rapprochement with Italy was purely tactical, his relations with Germany were remarkably correct. For a time, his own income was sufficient to keep up appearances in Geneva. As he wrote, "We have never been very rich, but we have never been poor, and we have always been able to live rather comfortably by our own means, which we have inherited from our parents."[72] However, by the eve of the Second World War, this was no longer true. Like so many others in similar circumstances, Arslan maintained appearances by accumulating indebtedness.[73] By 1946, he was virtually broke.

If Arslan's financial problems caused him certain hardships and embarrassments in his last years, they did not noticeably restrict his ability to capture publicity. In fact, his finances created the circumstances for his final confrontation with the French Mandate authorities.

Unable to afford Geneva, and perhaps feeling that his effectiveness in Europe was waning, Arslan made one last attempt to return to Syria. In 1938, the presidency of the Arab Academy of Damascus became vacant. Arslan desperately wanted the post and campaigned for it openly. It would provide him with an income and would, as a serious academic appointment, conceivably provide the French with a reason to relax the ban on his residence in the Mandate. His supporters within the Syrian government understood his situation and were able to arrange for his selection.[74] Once the announcement of his appointment was made, Arslan informed the readers of La Nation Arabe that he was returning to Damascus at the invitation of the Syrian government and that, while publication of the journal would cease for a time, it would be resumed from the Syrian capital.

Thus, in February 1939, he embarked for what should have been an honorable conclusion to his restless career. Instead, it proved a tantalizing interlude, another bitter disappointment. When his ship docked at Alexandria, he was informed that he could not, after all, continue to Syria. By the first weeks of 1939, the French government had not only completed the cessation of the Sanjak of Alexandretta to Turkey, but had also refused to ratify the treaty of 1936. These decisions were greeted in Syria with riots, demonstrations, and governmental paralysis. The last person the French wanted to enter the country at that moment was Shakib Arslan.

Yet, in denying him entry, the Mandate authorities created the very situation they wished to avoid—Arslan again became front-page news in the Egyptian and Damascus press. The insult to him was an insult to all Arabs, and the mockery which the French made of the independence of the Syrian government was used to illustrate the hollowness of European treaties.[75] Whatever rumors may have attached to Arslan's Italian associations, his capacity to serve as a rallying point for anti-imperial opinion was still with him. So, too, was his personal attractiveness, and he became the personage of the season in Egypt. Finally permitted to exist freely in the country whose journals had carried his articles and whose presses had produced his books for two decades, he was honored at a variety of receptions and banquets. Muhammad ʿAli al-Tahir relentlessly kept him in the public eye during his first weeks in Cairo. Even the monarchy relaxed the hostility which, as much as British pressure, had kept Arslan from Egypt during the interwar years as King Faruq, making sure not to snub a potential entree to the Axis camp, entertained the Amir at Abddin Palace.[76] Arslan had last been so received when, on the eve of another war in a much different world, he had discussed Egyptian-Ottoman relations with ʿAbbas Hilmi in 1912.

After nearly four months of waiting for the situation in Syria to improve, Arslan realized that settling in his homeland would again elude him, and he returned to Geneva in mid-July 1939. Six weeks later, Germany invaded Poland. Arslan was trapped in a Europe at war. Until this moment, he had possessed a certain flexibility in his dealings with Allies and Axis. Now, sides had to be taken. As in the First War, Arslan was drawn by his own predilections and by circumstances to cast his lot with Germany. The associations which had blemished him in the earlier conflict had been overcome through his own unremitting service, but in this instance there was to be no opportunity for rehabilitation—time finally ran out on him.

Arslan made no excuses. With the war barely into its third week, he appeared in Berlin. While there is little doubt that the primary purpose of the trip was to shore up his finances in the face of various wartime restrictions which had begun to limit his receivable income more than ever (he used the visit to remortgage his apartment house), his presence in the Nazi capital at such a sensitive moment also demonstrated his unequivocal support for German policies. It was an appearance which was condemned in the Arab East even as it was publicized by German officialdom. Radio Berlin announced his visit, and, according to some sources, he was even made an honorary citizen of the Reich. It was one of the few honors Arslan ever denied receiving.[77] But the untimely visit gave the impression that he was posing as the representative of all the Arabs (an impression he would have done nothing to dispel), and those who did not share his views, or accept his leadership, denounced him vehemently. In gaining an honor which he surely did not seek, Arslan was stripped of the one which probably meant more to him than any other—the presidency of the Arab Academy of Damascus.

When he returned to Geneva in October 1939, he discovered that his trip to Berlin had repercussions in Switzerland as well. The Ministère Publique informed him that he would have to leave the country by April 1940. Arslan delayed the action by launching an appeal, and eventually the case was decided in his favor. However, he was told that should he leave Switzerland again, he would not be allowed to return.[78] This decision, which he had no alternative but to obey, thrust him to the sidelines. An ailing old man confined to a neutral country in time of war, he was eclipsed by the pace and focus of world events.

Never one to cede the center stage willingly, Arslan behaved as though his advice and counsel were shaping the outcome of the conflict. He provided Baron von Oppenheim with a steady stream of letters on how Germany ought to conduct the campaign on the Eastern front, he told the Italian government how to manage its Balkan policy, he offered advice of a tactical nature to Hajj Amin al-Husayni, and he sent personal bulletins to Ibn Saʿud and Imam Yahya reviewing the world situation and the course of the war. He also sought to recover his public voice by resurrecting *La Nation Arabe*. When the Swiss refused to let him publish it in their country, he turned to his German contacts for assistance. After protracted negotiations, arrangements were made to have Librairie Plon print the journal from occupied Paris.[79] Arslan is not on record as having made any self-congratulatory statements about such a delicious prospect. Instead, he kept pestering Berlin about the details of publication, so that his mentor on the project, von Hentig, came to question the importance of the journal relative to the fuss it was causing.[80] Hence, although Arslan edited at least two numbers of his journal, there is no evidence that it actually appeared during the war.

Arslan complained that without *La Nation Arabe*, he would be "resigned to silence."[81] That was far from the truth. More in keeping with his character, he also pledged: "I will not cease to provide advice. Given my political experience and my complete knowledge of all that is Arab, I am certain to be on the right path in those matters which concern my nation and the entire Middle East."[82] Until illness finally slowed even his pen in 1942, he found public outlets for his opinions in the pro-Axis press of Spanish Morocco, in the Berlin-based *Barid al-Sharq*, and in the Germanophile *al-ʿAlam al-ʿArabi* of Buenos Aires.[83] The two principal wartime issues to which he addressed himself were continuations of themes he had pursued for several years: the need for Arabs to recognize that Germany, by fighting the powers which enslaved Muslims, was worthy of their support; and the need for Germany, in turn, to make an unequivocal declaration in favor of Arab independence. On the level of inter-Arab politics, Arslan was also involved, though only marginally, in the bitter competition between Hajj Amin al-Husayni and Rashid ʿAli al-Kaylani for Axis recognition as the sole leader of the Arab cause.

To Arslan, a joint German-Italian declaration granting official independence to the Arab states was of the utmost urgency. Such a declaration would confirm the Arabs' faith in German disinterestedness, would curb Italian ambitions, and would secure Arslan's credibility. On the eve of what he and many other observers felt to be the fall of Tobruk, he explained to von Oppenheim that it was "absolutely necessary" for Germany to make a solemn proclamation to the Egyptians and to the Muslims of the world that German arms were entering Egypt only for the purpose of liberating it from the British and uniting it with the Sudan.[84] Most of the letters he wrote to the baron during the war contained similar admonitions, whether the area referred to was Syria, Iraq, or Bosnia.

Shunted aside though he was, Arslan tried hard not to let himself become a forgotten figure. In addition to maintaining his voluminous correspondence, he performed his liaison role within Switzerland, conferring with Balafrej and Fuʾad Hamzah in Geneva, with a German consular official in Basel, and with Prüfer in Bern.[85] Initiatives from other quarters also served to keep his name alive. During one of their interminable squabbles with their Axis hosts, Hajj Amin and Rashid ʿAli requested that Arslan come to Rome to act as mediator between them and Mussolini.[86] Prüfer, feeling at one point that Arslan could be useful in Berlin, attempted to persuade him to come to the Reich capital in early 1943.[87] But the Swiss restrictions compelled him to remain in that country. His own initiatives were never a significant factor during the war, and he published very little after 1941. Even his principal German contact, von Oppenheim, was a private citizen—and over eighty years old. Clearly, Arslan the person did not figure prominently in the Reich's propaganda schemes.

However, his fame could be exploited in ways beyond his control. Selections from his articles were occasionally read on Axis Arabic radio programs, and Yunis Bahri, the famous Iraqi announcer for Radio Berlin, proclaimed in a broadcast of 1941 directed at North Africa: "Algerians! Your liberation is at hand. Chancellor Hitler has given his word to Shakib Arslan."[88] No more pointed example can be cited of Arslan's diminished influence than this twisted attempt to use it. When the war ended, he was as much a product of what had been said about him as of what he had said and done himself. He was also impoverished, ill, and ignored.

For reasons which are not at all obvious, the Swiss police subjected him to intense surveillance in early 1946. Their reports revealed an aging man living apart from his wife and son in a residence hotel, passing the days in tearooms with his newspapers, seeing few visitors other than his son, and spending an inordinate amount of time frequenting his bank.[89] The latter activity seemed his most pressing one. He was hounded by creditors and was reduced to writing humiliating letters to friends and acquaintances asking for assistance. For several months, he existed in this fashion, ignored by those who once claimed him as champion or friend. Muhammad ʿAli al-Tahir, with his typical directness, lashed out at Arslan's former Arab allies who failed to use their new positions of power to assist the man whose life had been devoted to achieving the circumstances from which they now benefited.[90] Al-Tahir did what he could by notifying potential contributors of Arslan's plight and by sending him accumulated royalty payments which he personally collected from Cairo publishers.

Perhaps it was fitting that in the end Arslan was rescued from his creditors by that sector of Arab-Islamic society whose voice he had so clearly been. While snubbed by those to whom he was either an embarrassment or a relic, he found his benefactor in Amir ʿAbdullah, the son of Imam Yahya of the Yemen, who sent him the funds to pay his most pressing debts.[91] This released Arslan from his financial captivity in Europe and launched what was obviously becoming a race against time if he was to have a homecoming.

In the autumn of 1946, the Amir began his final voyage to the East. Although frail, he was well enough to enjoy what few are permitted, a nostalgic trip through the past. As though he had prearranged it, he docked once again at Alexandria, where his career as pan-Islamic journalist had begun over half a century earlier and where his hopes had so often been dashed in the interwar years. He spent there a final evening with al-Tahir and Hajj Amin al-Husayni before going on to Beirut, where he arrived quietly in late October 1946. It was only proper that his return to his homeland found it independent, the goal for which he had literally given much of his life. If he could no longer campaign for the next step, the establishment of Islamic norms, the political agitator in him might at least have derived some small satisfaction from the fact that his reputation as a threatening activist survived him for a moment. On 11 December 1946, the Swiss police deemed it safe to lift the tap on his Geneva telephone. Unknown to them, he had died two days earlier in Beirut.

CHAPTER EIGHT.
CONCLUSION

A growing number of Muhammadans, more fully acquainted with modern conditions and more in touch with the aims and ideals of the present day, still cling to the faith of their childhood and the associations that have become dear to them from the Muslim atmosphere in which they grew up. These men likewise cherish an ideal of some form of political and social organization in which self-realization may become possible for them in some system of civilization that is Muslim in character and expression. They resent the predominance of European rule and the intransigence of European ideas. —*Thomas Arnold* [1]

Have confidence in yourselves, be good Muslims, and remain united in your struggle to reclaim your rights. —*Arslan* [2]

ARSLAN BEGAN his autobiography with the disclaimer that he was unworthy of one. That was as unrepresentative of his view of himself as it was inaccurate. Whether he was always a positive force may be disputed; that he was a notorious one should not be.

His long-running performance was filled with acclaim and denunciation and embraced most of the major Middle Eastern crises of the times. Arslan's importance to these crises was not just that he lived through them, but that he endeavored to determine their outcome. He was a major Arab figure during the final two Ottoman decades, and in the aftermath of the Ottoman defeat, he carved out a special role for himself. During the interwar period, his skillful manipulation of a popular issue, his controversial political maneuverings, his ability to pose as the champion of the entire Arab-Islamic world, and his flair for publicity all contributed to create his unique reputation.

Arslan did not select political Islam from among several options; it was the only doctrine he knew. The product of an intensely sectarian region within a state organized on the basis of religious affiliation, he committed himself to the dominant orthodoxy early in his life. It never occurred to him to change. His outlook was also shaped by his tutelage at the hands of Muhammad ʿAbduh and his brief encounters with al-Afghani. Lacking ʿAbduh's temperament, learning, and security, he addressed the Islamic issues of his day in the manner of al-Afghani. He became an Islamic nationalist who saw in an aroused Islamic community a weapon with which to achieve political independence. He remained an avowed antisecularist whose preferred groupings were Muslim youth leagues and whose ideological allies were Rashid Rida and the *al-Fath* circle.

Arslan was not a precursor; nor was he an anachronism. The period of his renown coincided with Egypt's liberal experiment, with Sati' al-Husri's writings on secular Arabism, and with Atatürk's program of Westernization. It was also the period when the Egyptian *'alim*, 'Ali 'Abd al-Raziq, was dismissed from his teaching post for writing that the caliphate was not a fundamental Islamic political institution; when the YMMA, the Muslim Brotherhood, the Eastern Society, and other Islamic-oriented associations captured the loyalties of the young and the disenchanted; when *Li madha ta'akhkhar al-muslimun?* went through three editions in nine years (1930–1939); and when the campaign against the Berber *dahir* legitimized the power of Islam as a rallying force. Arslan embraced the longing to bring order to troubled times. Rejecting the new and the alien, he called for adherence to the moral commandments, the communal solidarity, and the religious spirit which had brought prosperity and security in the past. In doing so, he touched a responsive chord.

The popularity of Arslan's message was enhanced by the publicity given to him as an individual. His tendency toward self-promotion grated on those who opposed his politics, but it made him what he was. No self-effacing ideologue would have achieved what he did. He emerged from the apparent ruin of a career to entertain, and be entertained by, the reigning Arab monarchs of his time, to negotiate with high commissioners, to affect the policies of imperial administrations, and to serve as symbol and inspiration to his fellow Muslims.

He relished the role he created and used it the only way he knew. He sought publicity, partly out of vanity, partly to ensure that the world would not ignore the injustices done to the Arabs. Lacking the political apparatus of a state—or even the consistent backing of one— he made a remarkable impact. He was a nettlesome petitioner at the League of Nations, and although he was never formally recognized by that body, his contribution was possibly more useful than is generally recognized. He held his own political instincts in high esteem, and his willingness to make contacts with individuals whose ideology differed from his own increased his leverage. It also brought him severe criticism. He corresponded with liberals, allied with fascists, conspired with fundamentalists, and came as close as could be expected to making a viable pressure group out of the combination of Islamic reformists and French socialists. Flexible and intransigent at the same time, he was willing to compromise with France but not with Atatürk. Independence was his objective in dealing with Europeans, the reconstruction of a true Islamic society in confronting his fellow Muslims. His political activism, his ceaseless agitation, and his restless travels gave a public dimension to his career which was lacking in others who might have been more intellectually sophisticated or politically circumspect. In the end, it brought him disgrace; for a time it made him a *mujahid*.

For all his notoriety, Arslan's legacy has not been pronounced. His reputation was tarnished by his final Axis associations, and the potential utility of his message was overtaken by the attainment of Arab independence and by the fact that the postwar Arab Middle East seemed poised on the brink of secular nationalism. In the age of Nasser and the Baʿath, Islamic solidarity seemed socially irrelevant; at a time of land reform, educational expansion, and tentative state socialism, those whose aim had been to preserve an ordered aristocratic system were dismissed as socially insensitive.

The major criticism leveled at the interwar ideologues of Ottoman background, whether secular pan-Arabists like al-Husri or Islamic nationalists like Arslan, is that they had no formula for social change, no understanding of the needs of the masses. While they could hardly have been expected to be other than what they were, the charge is accurate and suggests another reason for Arslan's limited influence in the years immediately following his death. He was more a nostalgic cosmopolite than a social reformer, more concerned with cultural integrity than with the reasons for rural poverty. As long as the energies of the elite were concentrated on the task of achieving independence, Arslan had no notion that he ought to be concerned with the plight of the masses. He was a strategist of anti-imperialist protest, not a guide for governance. Once the reins of government passed to upwardly mobile, reform-minded army officers, men of Arslan's background and attitude lost their mystique and came to be reproached generally, as he and al-Jabiri once were specifically, for "their Ottoman atavism, their Turkish manners, and their *politique de façon hamidienne*."[3] Arslan died only six years before the Egyptian Free Officers' *coup d'état*; he was born nearly four decades before Nasser (b. 1918). The post–World War II years brought forward new generations as well as new ideologies. Arslan's influence was nontransferable. He left few disciples, but many who remembered him.

The memories were of a vibrant and determined personality who provided Arab Muslims with a singular presence at a time when people of stature were few. Messali Hajj captured the sentiment when he proclaimed: "I, a simple man, am proud to be a friend and a spiritual son of a person of such merit. I feel that the only way I can acknowledge him—and the only acknowledgment he would find acceptable—is to follow in his footsteps and to adopt his principles. . . ."[4] In responding to this tribute, Arslan stated: "I have always struggled for the Arab cause and for the liberation of my country. Struggle has its stages—no one should lament that or attempt to change it. You are young; the future belongs to you; work for your freedom, work to safeguard your dignity and your interests, but do so with calm and moderation."[5] Arslan followed the first part of his own advice; he failed to obey his dictum on moderation. It was not a characteristic suited to one who would be known as a *mujahid*.

A CHRONOLOGY
OF SHAKIB ARSLAN

1869	Born in Shuwayfat, Lebanon
1879–1888	Education in Beirut
1886	Publication of *al-Bakurah*; becomes disciple of ʿAbduh
1888	Appointed *mudir* of the district of Shuwayfat
1890–1892	Visits Egypt; resides in Istanbul
1892	Spends several weeks in Europe; meets al-Afghani in Istanbul
1892–1916	Principal residence in Lebanon
1902	Serves as *qaʾimaqam* of the Shuf for a few months
1908–1911	Serves as *qaʾimaqam* of the Shuf
1912	April–June, at the Libyan front
1914	Elected deputy from Hawran to the Ottoman parliament

1914–1916	Associated with Jamal Pasha's policies in Syria/Lebanon
1916	Marries Salima al-Khass
1917–1918	Two missions to Germany as envoy of Enver Pasha
1917	Son Ghalib born in Aley
1919–1920	Resides in Switzerland
1921–1923	Resides in Berlin
1921	June–July, trip to Moscow
	August, meeting of Syro-Palestinian Congress, Geneva
1922	May, serves as secretary of Congress of Oppressed Peoples, Genoa
	July, visits London
1923 (Dec.)–1925 (Sept.)	Resides in Mersin, Turkey
	Late 1924, spends several weeks in Europe
1925	Establishes permanent residence in Switzerland
	November, meets with de Jouvenal in Paris
1926	Becomes Hijazi citizen
	July, elected to Standing Committee of the Congress of the Caliphate
1927	January–April, trip to United States
	November, trip to Moscow
1928	Daughter Mayy born in Lausanne
1929	May–September, pilgrimage to Mecca

1930	Daughter Nazimah born in Geneva; *LNA* founded
	June–August, trip through Spain
	August, visit to Morocco
1932	January, trip through Balkans
1933	December, attends Oriental Students Congress, Rome
1934	January–February, trip through Balkans
	February, meetings with Mussolini, Rome
	April–June, Arabia peacekeeping mission
	July–August, visits Palestine
1935	April, incident of "forged letter" begins
	September, serves as president of European Islamic Congress, Geneva
1936	January–May, discussions with Messali Hajj, Geneva
1937	June–December, triumphal return to Syria
	September, attends Bludan Congress, elected second vice-president
1938	Appointed president of Arab Academy of Damascus
1939	February–July, in Egypt
	September, visits Berlin
1939–1946	Confined to Switzerland
1946	December, dies in Beirut

NOTES

A Note on Sources

1. When one of Arslan's earlier biographers visited the village of Shuway-fat and spoke with members of the Arslan family in the early 1950s, he gained the distinct impression that the several trunks containing the Amir's papers were not likely to be made available to scholars (Ahmad al-Sharabasi, *Amir al-bayan*, I, p. 12). The correspondence was later sent to the Moroccan government by Arslan's daughter, Princess Mayy (interview with Mayy Junbalat, 3 December 1974).

2. Their works are listed in the bibliography. Al-Sharabasi is the more analytical of the two, and his *Shakib Arslan: daʿiyah al-ʿurubah wa al-islam* is the best single-volume biography in Arabic. A comprehensive obituary article by E. Lévi-Provençal, "L'Emir Shakib Arslan (1869–1946)," *Cahiers de l'Orient Contemporain*, IX–X (1947), 5–19, has been the standard Western-language study. The article appears to be a condensed version of a lengthy report compiled by the Bureau Politique, Théâtre d'Opérations de l'Afrique du Nord in June 1940. Entitled *Contribution à l'étude de l'activité politique de l'Emir Chekib Arslan*, the report is located in Aix-en-Provence, Archives d'outre-mer, 29 H 35. It is cited in this book as *L'Activité politique*.

3. From G. S. P. Freeman-Grenville, *The Muslim and Christian Calendars*.

Introduction

1. Their works are listed in the bibliography and cited at appropriate points in the text.

2. As applied in this study, the term *Greater Syria* refers to the area presently included in the states of Syria, Lebanon, Jordan, and Israel.

3. See Hisham Sharabi, *Arab Intellectuals and the West: The Formative Years, 1875–1914*, p. 57.

4. For elaboration of this theme, see C. Ernest Dawn, *From Ottomanism to Arabism: Essays on the Origins of Arab Nationalism*, pp. 184–185.

5. Although the Arslans' standing was based on their leadership of a minority Muslim sect, they considered themselves part of the larger Sunni Muslim order. This issue is explored further in chapter 1.

6. It might be noted that, for all the mobility achieved by Shakib, those roots remain. His youngest daughter, Princess Mayy, was married to the late Druze leader Kamal Junbalat. Following Junbalat's assassination in 1977, he was succeeded as titular head of the Lebanese Druze community by his son—Shakib's grandson—Walid.

7. For example, Sylvia G. Haim, *Arab Nationalism: An Anthology*, and Albert Hourani, *Arabic Thought in the Liberal Age, 1798–1939*. Hourani has gracefully acknowledged in later writings that he may have underestimated Islamic influences at the expense of attention to European ones. See his *The Emergence of the Modern Middle East*, pp. xiv–xvi. A perceptive account of the impact of Hourani's work on shaping the study of modern Arabic intellectual history is Donald M. Reid, "*Arabic Thought in the Liberal Age* Twenty Years After," *International Journal of Middle East Studies*, 541–557.

8. This issue is examined by Michael C. Hudson, "Islam and Political Development," in John L. Esposito (ed.), *Islam and Development: Religion and Sociopolitical Change*, pp. 1–24.

9. See John Obert Voll, *Islam: Continuity and Change in the Modern World*, p. 156.

10. A *mujahid* is one who participates in *jihad*, struggle in the cause of the Islamic faith. In modern Islamic texts, the original meaning of *jihad* as warfare against non-Muslims has been broadened to embrace the concept of activism directed toward improving the status of the Islamic community. It was in this context that Arab publications of the 1920s and 1930s frequently referred to Arslan as the most courageous *mujahid* of the era. For a thorough discussion of definitions, see Rudolph Peters, *Islam and Colonialism: The Doctrine of Jihad in Modern History*.

1. The Formation of an Arab-Ottoman Gentleman

1. Ahmad al-Sharabasi, *Shakib Arslan: min ruwwad al-wahdah al-ʿarabiyyah*, p. 28.

2. Shakib Arslan, *Sirah dhatiyyah*, p. 84.

3. The most useful general study remains Kamal S. Salibi, *The Modern History of Lebanon*, upon which much of the information contained in this section is based. An analysis of how the various factions in the region managed to function within a generally recognized system is found in Iliya F. Harik, *Politics and Change in a Traditional Society: Lebanon, 1711–1845*.

4. A complete discussion of the formulation of the *Règlement* and the

evolution of its regime is the study by John P. Spagnolo, *France and Ottoman Lebanon, 1861–1914*, chaps. 2 and 4. The *Règlement* was revised in 1864. This summary is of the revised version which remained in effect until 1914.

5. An explanation of the interior aspects of belief and ritual is offered by the Druze scholar Sami Nasib Makaram, *The Druze Faith;* see also David Bryer, "The Origins of the Druze Religion," *Der Islam,* LII (1975), 47–84, and LIII (1976), 4–27, for a discussion of the Ismaili milieu within which the Druze doctrines began.

6. See, for example, the characterization drawn by Stephen Hemsley Longrigg, *Syria and Lebanon under French Mandate,* pp. 9, 17.

7. Philip K. Hitti, *The Origins of the Druze People and Religion,* p. 48. For a revealing account of Mustafa's ability to manipulate the policies of the *mutasarrifiyyah,* see Spagnolo, *Ottoman Lebanon,* pp. 225–237. See also Yusuf al-Hakim, *Bayrut wa lubnan fi ʿahd al-ʿuthman,* p. 45.

8. The bulk of the information on Shakib's early life has been obtained from his autobiography, *Sirah dhatiyyah.* His other biographers seem to have used the same source, so reference is made to their work only when they provide new evidence or variant interpretations of the old.

9. See the *diwan* of Nasib Arslan, which was edited and published posthumously by Shakib under the title *Rawd al-shaqiq fi al-jazl al-raqiq,* pp. 17–28. A summary of ʿAdil's career is found in his memoirs, *Dhikrayat al-Amir ʿAdil Arslan,* pp. 9–12. Little is known of the other brother, Hasan (b. 1879).

10. See George Antonius, *The Arab Awakening,* chap. 3; and A. L. Tibawi, *American Interests in Syria, 1800–1901.*

11. Tibawi, *American Interests,* pp. 77–78, 92–96, 187.

12. Arslan, *Sirah dhatiyyah,* p. 24.

13. Arslan in Muhammad Rashid Rida, *Taʾrikh al-ustadh al-imam al-shaykh Muhammad ʿAbduh,* I, p. 399.

14. The most complete study of this individual is now Nikki R. Keddie, *Sayyid Jamal ad-Din "al-Afghani": A Political Biography.*

15. Malcolm H. Kerr's statement that "So much has been written about ʿAbduh by both orientalists and Muslims that it may seem redundant to say anything more" (*Islamic Reform: The Political and Legal Theories of Muhammad ʿAbduh and Rashid Rida,* p. 103) suggests the bibliographical richness of the subject. In addition to Kerr, it may be sampled in Hourani, *Arabic Thought,* chap. 4; and Charles C. Adams, *Islam and Modernism in Egypt.*

16. Arslan in Rida, *Taʾrikh,* I, p. 400. A somewhat different version appears in al-Sharabasi, *Shakib Arslan,* p. 24.

17. Arslan in Rida, *Taʾrikh,* I, pp. 400–401.

18. Arslan, *Sirah dhatiyyah,* p. 30.

19. Ibid., p. 30; see also Arslan in Rida, *Taʾrikh,* I, pp. 402–404.

20. Shakib Arslan, *al-Bakurah,* p. 3.

21. Arslan, *Sirah dhatiyyah,* p. 32.

22. The fullest accounts of Arslan's first visit to Egypt are found in his

Shawqi aw sadaqah arbaʿin sanah, pp. 4–5; and in al-Sharabasi, *Shakib Arslan*, pp. 25–28.

23. Arslan, *Sirah dhatiyyah*, pp. 32–33.

24. Arslan has recounted it in every autobiographical work. See, in particular, Arslan, *Shawqi*, pp. 10–14. Ahmad Shawqi (1868–1932) came to be honored by the entire Arabic-speaking world as "the prince of poets" and is still regarded by many critics as the greatest of modern Arab poets. He met Arslan toward the end of his four years of legal studies in France. Upon his return to Egypt, he flourished under the reign of ʿAbbas Hilmi (1892–1914) as "a virtual poet laureate" (M. M. Badawi, *A Critical Introduction to Modern Arabic Poetry*, pp. 29–42).

25. Cited in Arslan, *Sirah dhatiyyah*, p. 33.

26. Al-Afghani's last years in Istanbul are treated in Keddie, *"al-Afghani"*, chap. 13. For Arslan's appreciation of al-Afghani's importance to Islam and passing references to their meetings, see his *Hadir al-ʿalam al-islami*, II, pp. 289–303.

27. Arslan, *Hadir al-ʿalam al-islami*, II, p. 298.

28. Ibid., p. 301. Of the impression made by al-Afghani on Arslan, one scholar has written, "He discovered in him his spiritual master and his model for the future" (Toufic Touma, *Paysans et institutions féodales chez les druses et les maronites du Liban du XVIIe siècle à 1914*, II, p. 721).

29. Al-Sharabasi, *Amir al-bayan*, I, pp. 134–135. See also Sami al-Dahhan, *al-Amir Shakib Arslan: hayathu wa atharhu*, p. 70.

30. The development of Egyptian journalism is surveyed in P. J. Vatikiotis, *The History of Egypt: From Muhammad Ali to Sadat*, chap. 9. For ʿAli Yusuf, see Abbas Kelidar, "Shaykh ʿAli Yusuf: Egyptian Journalist and Islamic Nationalist," in Marwan R. Buheiry (ed.), *Intellectual Life in the Arab East, 1890–1939*, pp. 10–20.

31. On the distinction between "vocational" and "leisure-time" intellectuals, see Sharabi, *Arab Intellectuals*, p. 4.

32. *Al-Durrah al-Yatimah* was first published in Beirut in 1897 and reissued in Cairo in 1910; *al-Mukhtar min rasaʾil Abu Ishaq al-Sabi* was published in 1898.

33. This romantic portrayal of an impossible love between a girl of the Spanish nobility and the last survivor of a distinguished Arab clan abounds in beautiful, if fanciful, descriptions of the Alhambra. Arslan's translation was published in 1898 and reissued in 1925.

34. From Arslan's introduction to *al-Durrah al-Yatimah* as cited in al-Dahhan, *Amir Shakib*, p. 211.

35. An example is his series of articles in *al-Muqtataf* entitled variously "Islam in China" and "The Future of China" in XXIV, no. 8 (1900), and XXVI, nos. 6, 7, 9, 10 (1901), which served the purpose of providing information about a little-known area, but which approached the subject through Islamic assumptions.

36. Khalil Mutran, "Preface" to Arslan's *Diwan*.

37. Marun ʿAbbud, *Ruwwad al-nahdah al-hadithah*, p. 147 (the full sketch of Shakib is on pp. 141–147). A more recent critic has found Arslan's

poetic style and subject matter so deeply conservative as to be out of tune with the changing times in which he lived (Salma K. Jayyusi, *Trends and Movements in Modern Arabic Poetry*, I, pp. 244–246).

38. The most perceptive discussion of Abdulhamid's pan-Islamic policy as it related to the Arabs is still Antonius, *Arab Awakening*, pp. 68–75. The perspective from Istanbul is superbly drawn by Niyazi Berkes, *The Development of Secularism in Turkey*, chap. 9.

39. Cited in Jamal Mohammed Ahmed, *The Intellectual Origins of Egyptian Nationalism*, pp. 60–61. The fullest discussion of Egypt's Ottoman ties is James Jankowski, "Ottomanism and Arabism in Egypt, 1860–1914," *Muslim World*, LXX (1980), esp. 226–245.

40. Arslan knew the first two well and had much contact with them throughout his life. Their position in the trends of their time is mentioned in Sharabi, *Arab Intellectuals*, pp. 24–25, 122–123; and Hourani, *Arabic Thought*, pp. 223–224. Kurd ʿAli's prewar activities are studied in Samir Seikaly, "Damascene Intellectual Life in the Opening Years of the 20th Century: Muhammad Kurd ʿAli and *al-Muqtabas*," in Buheiry (ed.), *Intellectual Life*, pp. 125–153.

41. Arslan, *Diwan al-amir Shakib Arslan*, p. 90. This is from a poem written in 1892. Other *qasidah*s to Abdulhamid appear on pp. 91–93.

42. See Spagnolo, *Ottoman Lebanon*, pp. 235–237.

43. Arslan, *Sirah dhatiyyah*, pp. 36–39. A detailed record of this affair, not always favorable to the delegation of notables, is Bisharah al-Khuri, *Haqaʾiq lubnaniyyah*, I, pp. 55–58. The matter was reconsidered by some of the notables, and they decided the *mutasarrif* was correct in his original assessment of the situation. Thus, Mount Lebanon did not, after all, send a representative to Istanbul. See Spagnolo, *Ottoman Lebanon*, pp. 250–254.

44. Arslan, *Sirah dhatiyyah*, pp. 39–40.

45. The episode is discussed in Arslan, *Sirah dhatiyyah*, pp. 79–80. More remarkable than the conception of the scheme itself is Arslan's claim that one of the contingents actually reached Derna.

46. See Edmund Burke III, "Pan-Islam and Moroccan Resistance to French Colonial Penetration, 1900–1912," *Journal of African History*, XIII (1972), 110–113.

47. *Al-Muʾayyad*, 16 November 1911.

48. Letter to Rashid Rida, 1911, cited in al-Sharabasi, *Shakib Arslan*, p. 32.

49. *Al-Muʾayyad*, 16 November 1911.

50. Ibid., 11 January 1912.

51. Ibid., 15 January 1912.

52. Jawish's career is outlined in Arthur Goldschmidt, "The Egyptian Nationalist Party, 1892–1919," in P. M. Holt (ed.), *Political and Social Change in Modern Egypt*, pp. 323–327; for his opposition to Ottoman decentralization, see the several references in Tawfiq ʿAli Burru, *al-ʿArab wa al-turk fi al-ʿahd al-dusturi al-ʿuthmani, 1908–1914*, chap. 9; Arslan mentions his high regard for Jawish and confirms their common political viewpoint in *RR*, pp. 266–268.

53. On the special force, see Philip H. Stoddard, "The Ottoman Government and the Arabs, 1911 to 1918: A Preliminary Study of the Teşkilat-i Mahsusa," esp. pp. 60–75.

54. For details of the membership and programs of these societies, see Antonius, *Arab Awakening*, pp. 108–111; and Rashid Ismail Khalidi, *British Policy towards Syria and Palestine, 1906–1914*, chaps. 4 and 5. A social and political analysis of the background to Arab discontent is given in Philip S. Khoury, *Urban Notables and Arab Nationalism*, chap. 3.

55. The statistical evidence for this is presented in C. Ernest Dawn, *From Ottomanism to Arabism*, chap. 6; for the example of a specific individual, see William L. Cleveland, *The Making of an Arab Nationalist*, pp. 38–40.

56. Arslan, *Sirah dhatiyyah*, p. 106.

57. *Al-Mu'ayyad*, 27 January 1912.

58. Arslan, "God Does Not Rectify the Work of the Corrupt Ones," *al-Ra'y al-ʿAmm*, 7 Ayyar (May) 1913.

59. Arslan, "These Are the Differences," ibid., 19 Haziran (June) 1913.

60. Arslan, *Sirah dhatiyyah*, p. 108.

61. Burru, *al-ʿArab wa al-turk*, p. 509.

62. Arslan, "The Answer Is the Answer of the Community," *al-Ra'y al-ʿAmm*, 20 Haziran (June) 1913.

63. ʿAli Riyad al-Sulh, "The New Wilayat Law and al-Amir Shakib," *al-Islah*, 30 Haziran (June) 1913; Arslan, *Sirah dhatiyyah*, p. 108.

64. Muhammad Rashid Rida, "The Islamic University and Politics," *al-Manar*, XVII (28 December 1913), 76; and "Nationalities in the Ottoman Kingdom," ibid., XVII (23 June 1914), 537–538.

65. Asʿad Daghir, *Mudhakkirati ʿala hamish al-qadiyyah al-ʿarabiyyah*, p. 69.

66. Sulayman Musa, *al-Harakah al-ʿarabiyyah: sirah al-marhalah al-ula li nahdah al-ʿarabiyyah al-hadithah, 1908–1924*, p. 67, n. 1.

2. War and Exile

1. *RR*, p. 361, n. 1.

2. Ibid., pp. 196–197.

3. Zeine N. Zeine, *The Emergence of Arab Nationalism*, p. 123.

4. Arslan, *Sirah dhatiyyah*, pp. 119–121.

5. Cf. Touma, *Paysans*, II, p. 729.

6. Arslan, *Sirah dhatiyyah*, p. 135.

7. Antonius, *Arab Awakening*, p. 151.

8. Arslan, *Sirah dhatiyyah*, pp. 140–147. Stoddard's sources corroborate Arslan's role and mention the Druze contingent he equipped and led as comprised of between 100 and 200 men ("The Teşkilat-i Mahsusa," p. 105).

9. "The Advice of Shakib Arslan to the Lebanese," *Awraq lubnaniyyah*, II (1956), 340. This is from a letter Arslan wrote to his friend Wahbah Taliʿ in 1925.

10. FO 371/7882/E2235, d'Abernon (Berlin) to the Foreign Office, 24 February 1922, transmitting "Notes of a Conversation on Oriental Affairs"

which had reached the ambassador "from a very reliable source"; and *al-Sa'ih*, 7 February 1927.

11. Touma, *Paysans*, II, p. 728; see also pp. 729–740 for a reasoned account of Arslan's actions during the war. Al-Dahhan and al-Sharabasi present brief apologia but otherwise avoid discussing this critical period in Arslan's life. See al-Dahhan, *al-Amir Shakib*, pp. 74–77; and his *Muhadarat ʿan al-amir Shakib Arslan*, pp. 14–15; and al-Sharabasi, *Amir al-bayan*, I, pp. 87–89; and *Shakib Arslan*, pp. 34–40. In this instance, al-Dahhan's treatment is preferred, although it is flawed by a tendency to oversimplify the ramifications of Arslan's activities.

12. Arslan's version of this incident is consistent in two sources, *Sirah dhatiyyah*, pp. 136–139, and "Syrian Catastrophes during the War Years," *al-Manar*, XXIII (1922), 125–126. Praise for his intercession on behalf of the patriarch is contained in the passages by Amin al-Ghurayyib in Muhammad ʿAli al-Tahir (ed.), *Dhikra al-amir Shakib Arslan*, pp. 161–162.

13. See Touma, *Paysans*, II, pp. 705–709; and ʿArif Abu Shaqra, "The Day Jamal Pasha Visited the Shuf Region," *Awraq lubnaniyyah*, I (1955), 547–549.

14. Ahmed Djemal Pasha, *Memories of a Turkish Statesman, 1913–1919*, p. 213.

15. The figure for Anatolia is Arslan's, given in *Sirah dhatiyyah*, p. 155. Antonius does not give a total figure, but one is left with the impression that he would regard 1,000 as an excessive estimate. See also al-Hakim, *Bayrut*, pp. 167–169, for a list of exiles from among the great families.

16. Jamal's reasoning for the banishments is given in his *Memories*, pp. 202–203; Arslan's account is in *Sirah dhatiyyah*, pp. 147–149; and "Syrian Catastrophes," p. 126.

17. Al-Khuri, *Haqa'iq lubnaniyyah*, II, p. 96.

18. Touma, *Paysans*, II, p. 731.

19. Arslan, *Sirah dhatiyyah*, p. 154.

20. The documents, including letters from local individuals sympathetic to French aims, had been concealed behind a false wall by the consul, Georges Picot, when hostilities began. The secret was entrusted to Picot's Maronite translator, Philippe Zalzal. When Zalzal was deported to Damascus, he exchanged his valuable information for his freedom. See Nicholas Z. Ajay, Jr., "Political Intrigue and Suppression in Lebanon during World War I," *International Journal of Middle East Studies*, V (1974), 155–157.

21. Djemal Pasha, *Memories*, p. 207.

22. For an account of these measures and the climate of fear they produced, see Ajay, "Political Intrigue," pp. 150–160; and Antonius, *Arab Awakening*, pp. 185–190.

23. Arslan, *Sirah dhatiyyah*, pp. 170–183; and "Syrian Catastrophes," pp. 129–132.

24. Ahmad Qadri, *Mudhakkirati ʿan al-thawrah al-ʿarabiyyah al-kubra*, p. 53. See also Arslan, *Rawd al-shaqiq*, pp. 22–23, for reference to the role played by the family reputation in diverting official displeasure over some articles by Shakib's older brother, Nasib.

25. See Antonius, *Arab Awakening*, pp. 203–204, 240–242.

26. His account of this is exceedingly detailed in *Sirah dhatiyyah*, pp. 225–236, and in his "Preface" to E. Rabbath, *L'Evolution politique de la Syrie sous mandat*, pp. xii–xiv. His own accusation is that the Allies, by refusing to lift the blockade even for humanitarian relief efforts, were to blame for the thousands of lives lost in Lebanon.

27. Touma, *Paysans*, II, p. 739.

28. Arslan, *Sirah dhatiyyah*, p. 157.

29. Ibid., p. 160.

30. Ibid., p. 180.

31. Ibid., pp. 175–176.

32. Antonius, *Arab Awakening*, p. 255.

33. A brief summary of the objectives and personnel of *al-Sharq* may be found in Adib Khuddur, *al-Sihafah al-suriyyah*, pp. 110–112. Arslan's description of the publication is in *Sirah dhatiyyah*, pp. 169–170.

34. On Salima, see al-Sharabasi, *Amir al-bayan*, I, pp. 125–126, who writes that she was about twenty when she married Arslan; AFS, Report of 27 February 1940, lists her date of birth as 1890.

35. See, for example, Amin al-Ghurayyib, "The Man Who Served Lebanon," in al-Tahir, *Dhikra al-amir*, pp. 161–164; and al-Tahir's own "al-amir Shakib," ibid., p. 15. A further contribution to the genre is ʿAli al-Ghayyati, "Reminiscences," a series of several parts in *Minbar al-Sharq*, the first four of which, 23 and 30 January and 6 and 13 February 1953, treat Arslan's wartime activities in Syria.

36. Al-Ghayyati, "Reminiscences," 23 January 1953.

37. These missions are described in Arslan, *Sirah dhatiyyah*, pp. 221–226, 261–262.

38. For his forceful presentation of the Ottoman Empire as a worthy partner in imperial greatness, see Emir Schekib Arslan, "Das osmanische Reich," *Süddeutsche Monatshefte* (July 1918), 235–240. Denunciations of the schemes of the Allies, assertions of Arab loyalty to the Ottoman system, and declarations of gratitude to Germany are found in his "Die Araber und die Engländer," *Der Neue Orient*, I (April–September 1917), 263–266; "Was Syrien vom Kriege erwartet," ibid., II (October 1917–March 1918), 6–9; and "Die neuen Intrigen der Entente in Syrien," ibid., II (October 1917–March 1918), 399–401.

39. Arslan, *Sirah dhatiyyah*, pp. 264–265. The concerns of these refugees were well founded. On 5 July 1919, the principal CUP leaders were sentenced to death in absentia by the sultan's government. According to the Swiss documents, Arslan was one of them. See Archives Fédérales Suisses, Ministère des Affaires Etrangères, E2001(B)1/5a/A.43.8/1918–1920, "Jungtürkische Revolutionäre Treiben in Der Schweiz," Report of the Ottoman Legation, Bern, 9 November 1919. See also Bernard Lewis, *Emergence*, pp. 240–241; and A. A. Cruickshank, "The Young Turk Challenge in Postwar Turkey," *Middle East Journal*, XXII (1968), 17.

40. Arslan, *Sirah dhatiyyah*, p. 262.

41. The names which reoccur in Arslan's discussion of his years in Berlin in *Sirah dhatiyyah*, pp. 238–239, 269, and 280, include Dr. Bahaeddin Şakir, a member of the CUP central committee and chief of the political section of the Teşkilat-i Mahsusa; Dr. Nazim, also a member of the central committee and "perhaps the most influential Unionist behind the scene"; Mehmet Cemal Azmi, the wartime governor of the sensitive province of Konya; and Badri Bey, director of the Istanbul police. Arslan and ʿAbd al-ʿAziz Jawish were the Arabs who worked most closely with this group. This information is based on the biographical sketches provided in the appendix to Feroz Ahmad, *The Young Turks: The Committee of Union and Progress in Turkish Politics 1908–1914*.

42. D. A. Rustow, "Enwer Pasha," in *The Encyclopaedia of Islam*, 2nd ed.; see also Edward Hallett Carr, *A History of Soviet Russia: The Bolshevik Revolution, 1917–1923*, III, pp. 246–247; and Şevket Süreyya Aydemir, *Enver Pasa: Makedonya'dan Ortaasya'ya*, III, 1914–1922, pp. 550–551, for evidence of Russian support of Enver and, through him, of Arslan and other CUP exiles.

43. The proceedings of the Congress and the intriguing difficulties associated with Enver's lack of proletarian and democratic credentials are examined in Carr, *History*, pp. 260–270.

44. FO 371/6473/E8652, d'Abernon (Berlin) to Curzon, 20 July 1921, Enclosure, Report by Major Breen on Russian-Turkish-Afghan Relations, 14 July 1921 (hereafter cited as Breen Report). See also Arslan, *Sirah dhatiyyah*, p. 270.

45. Arslan concluded *Sirah dhatiyyah* (pp. 236–292) with a lengthy essay entitled "The Martyr Enver Pasha and His Companions." The same essay was included in at least one of Arslan's other books, *Hadir al-ʿalam al-islami*, IV, pp. 364–395.

46. Cited in Cruickshank, "The Young Turk Challenge," p. 22, n. 10.

47. FO 371/6473/E8652, Breen Report. See also Arslan, *Sirah dhatiyyah*, p. 265.

48. *L'Activité politique*, pp. 6–7.

49. Arslan, *Rawd al-shaqiq*, p. 26.

50. Letter from Arslan to Rida, 12 May 1924, in al-Sharabasi, *Amir al-bayan*, II, p. 648.

51. Letter from Arslan to Rida, 3 July 1924 in ibid., p. 665.

52. In December 1924, the Syrian community in Berlin hosted a reception for Arslan which was attended by Streseman and von Seekt. See Lévi-Provençal, "L'Emir Shakib," p. 9; and *al-Shura*, 5 March 1925.

53. Arslan, *Rawd al-shaqiq*, p. 26.

3. Adoption of the Arab Cause

1. *RR*, p. 160.

2. MAE, Série E, Syrie-Liban 215, telegram from Shakib Arslan to President Raymond Poincaré, 6 December 1928.

3. Stephen Hemsley Longrigg, *Syria and Lebanon under French Mandate*, p. 117. Longrigg's treatment of the establishment of the Mandate in chapter 4 is detailed and balanced.

4. A. H. Hourani, *Syria and Lebanon: A Political Essay*, pp. 170–179.

5. Longrigg, *French Mandate*, p. 104. Arslan remained on a special blacklist until 1937.

6. Ibid., p. 143.

7. The declaration was co-authored by Ihsan al-Jabiri and is summarized in al-Sharabasi, *Amir al-bayan*, II, p. 499.

8. *RR*, p. 161. Arslan's Arab biographers use this statement to support their contention that he was deeply involved with the Arab cause at a time in his life when other evidence points to his continuing commitment to the Ottoman restoration. See al-Sharabasi, *Shakib Arslan*, p. 41; al-Dahhan, *al-Amir Shakib Arslan*, pp. 82–84.

9. *Al-Shura*, 27 August 1925.

10. Shakib Arslan, "The Druze, or the Tribe of Excellence in Everything," *al-Shura*, 1 October 1925.

11. Ibid.; and Shakib Arslan, "Do Not Say to Those Who Say Salam to You, 'You Are Unbelievers,'" *al-Shura*, 31 December 1925.

12. *L'Activité politique*, p. 33.

13. Al-Sharabasi, *Amir al-bayan*, I, p. 74; there is less certainty in Touma's evaluation, *Paysans*, II, pp. 751–753.

14. For a review of their relationship from 1895 to 1914, see *RR*, pp. 144–155.

15. Ibid., p. 160.

16. An account of the Congress based primarily on MAE sources is Marie-Renée Mouton, "Le Congrès syrio-palestinien de Genève (1921)," *Relations Internationales*, No. 19 (1979), 313–328.

17. An engaging account of the family is found in Robert de Beauplan, *Ou va la Syrie?*, pp. 89–100. See also Philip S. Khoury, "Factionalism among Syrian Nationalists during the French Mandate," *International Journal of Middle East Studies*, XIII (1981), 445.

18. de Beauplan, *La Syrie*, p. 89.

19. *RR*, pp. 157–158. In 1924, Kin'an was replaced on the delegation by Riyad al-Sulh, who served in Geneva for three years.

20. *LNA* (January–April 1938), 910. Al-Jabiri's full political career extended to the post–World War II years when he was deputy to the Syrian parliament and a figure of some influence in the Nationalist party.

21. See *Oriente Moderno*, II (June 1922), 14–15; ibid. (September 1922), 221–223; and Arslan, *Sirah dhatiyyah*, p. 284.

22. FO 371/7779/E8540, Graham (Rome) to the Foreign Office, 20 August 1922; FO 371/7882/E2235, d'Abernon (Berlin) to the Foreign Office, 24 February 1922; and FO 371/7852/E12650, d'Abernon to Curzon, 8 November 1922.

23. See Joyce Laverty Miller, "The Syrian Revolt of 1925," *International Journal of Middle East Studies*, VIII (October 1977), 545–563; and Longrigg, *French Mandate*, pp. 154–169.

24. *Al-Shura*, 29 October 1925. For a more detached account of the bombardment, see Longrigg, *French Mandate*, pp. 159−160.

25. Letter from Rida to Arslan, 13 Dhu al-Hijjah 1343, in *RR*, p. 339; Arslan, *Rawd al-shaqiq*, p. 26.

26. Arslan resided in Lausanne until 1930, when he moved to Geneva.

27. "Interview with al-Amir Shakib," *al-Fath*, 16 May 1929.

28. *Al-Shura*, 8 October 1925.

29. Permanent Mandates Commission (PMC), *Minutes of the Eighth Session (Extraordinary)*, Rome, 16 February−26 March 1926, pp. 157−160. As an example of the disproportionate volume of the Syro-Palestinian delegation's petitions, ten of the sixteen petitions received on Syria and Lebanon by the eleventh session of the PMC were from al-Jabiri and Arslan (PMC, *Minutes of the Eleventh Session*, Geneva, 20 June−26 July 1927).

30. *Al-Shura*, 26 November 1925. The content of these discussions is treated later in this chapter.

31. PMC, *Minutes of the Eighth Session (Extraordinary)*, p. 157.

32. Ibid., p. 168. The exaggerated probity of the Commission on the matter of representation was demonstrated when a member raised this question concerning one of Arslan's earlier petitions: "Could the commission accept a petition coming from an Arab who was a Turkish subject inhabiting a country (the city of Mersina) other than the mandated territory?" (PMC, *Minutes of the Fifth Session (Extraordinary)*, Geneva, 23 October−6 November 1924, p. 115). The circumstances which imposed such nationalist criteria on a man whose Ottoman passport was still valid need no comment.

33. PMC, *Minutes of the Eighth Session (Extraordinary): Report of the PMC to the Assembly*, pp. 200−208.

34. For an excellent discussion of this issue, see Michael H. Van Dusen, "Syria: Downfall of a Traditional Elite," in Frank Tachau (ed.), *Political Elites and Political Development in the Middle East*, pp. 115−155.

35. See Khoury, "Factionalism among Syrian Nationalists," pp. 441−469.

36. Yusuf al-Hakim, *Suriyyah wa al-ʿahd al-faysali*, p. 82.

37. His career is sketched in the preface to *Mudhakkirat al-duktur ʿAbd al-Rahman Shahbandar*, pp. 5−6; a perceptive portrait is drawn in Khoury, "Factionalism among Syrian Nationalists," pp. 445−446.

38. Letter from Arslan to Rida, 9 November 1930, in al-Sharabasi, *Amir al-bayan*, II, p. 723; and letter from Arslan to Rida, 14 May 1931, ibid., pp. 749−750.

39. Arslan's proposals were published in *al-Shura*, 11 February 1926 and 19 January 1928; they are also reproduced, from one of his petitions, in PMC, *Minutes of the Eleventh Session*, 4−14 November 1927, p. 195; de Jouvenal's comment is found in *Minutes of the Ninth Session*, p. 115. See also Elizabeth MacCallum, *The Nationalist Crusade in Syria*, pp. 174−175.

40. See Khoury, "Factionalism among Syrian Nationalists," pp. 456−459.

41. The dispute attracted front-page coverage in the Arab press and continued for nearly three years. See *Oriente Moderno*, VII (November 1927), 564−567; ibid., VIII (January 1928), 56−58. The issues are outlined in an article by Ahmad Zaki and Ihsan al-Jabiri, who joined with the Palestinian

leader, Hajj Amin al-Husayni, to act as mediators. See "The Mediators' Report on Efforts to Achieve Harmony among the Syrians," *al-Shura*, 5 January 1928. The general confusion created by Arslan's proposals to de Jouvenal is evident in Rida's response to them. See, for example, a letter from Rida to Arslan, 15 Jumada al-Akhirah 1344, in *RR*, pp. 419−424; and Rida to Arslan, 25 Jumada al-Ula 1344, in ibid., pp. 428−430.

42. *Al-Shura*, 1 October 1925.

43. *LNA* (May−June 1931), 8.

44. About thirty telegrams dated between 3 and 7 July 1927, each bearing the name of a particular chapter of Arslan supporters in the United States, are contained in a file in the Quai d'Orsay, MAE, Série E, Syrie-Liban, 399, April−December 1927.

45. A reader, "Amir Shakib Arslan and Ahmad Jamal Pasha," *al-Shura*, 20 October 1927; Muhammad Isma'il, "Ahmad Jamal Pasha and al-Amir Shakib Arslan," ibid., 17 November 1927; a reader, "An Historical Account of the Enmity of Jamal Pasha to al-Amir Shakib," ibid., 2 August 1928. These vituperative exchanges never really ceased. 'Adil later joined the fray with a stinging critique of Dr. Shahbandar's participation in the 1925 revolt, suggesting it was somewhat less than he claimed (*al-Shura*, 7 and 14 January 1931).

46. Arslan, "They Make Religion a Trap," *al-Shura*, 26 November 1925.

47. Arslan, "Preface" to E. Rabbath, *L'Evolution politique de la Syrie sous mandat*, pp. vi, xix.

48. *RR*, p. 161.

49. Al-Tahir was the publisher of *al-Shura* (1924−1931), *al-Shabab* (1936−1939), and other, shorter-lived weeklies. His life and writings are favorably reviewed in B. Nuwayhid al-Hut and Khayriyyah Qasimiyyah, "The Death of Two Great Palestinians," *Shu'un Filastiniyyah*, No. 39 (November 1974), 150−163.

50. Muhammad 'Ali al-Tahir, *Zalam al-sijn*, p. 678. This anecdotal autobiography contains numerous references to al-Tahir's friendship with Arslan.

51. Al-Khatib's orientation toward the neo-Hanbalite doctrines of Ibn Taymiyyah is mentioned in G. Kampffmeyer, "Egypt and Western Asia," in H. A. R. Gibb (ed.), *Whither Islam?*, pp. 101−154; and Henri Laoust, "Le Réformisme orthodoxe des 'salafiya' et les caractères généraux de son orientation actuelle," *Revue des Etudes Islamiques*, VI (1932), 183. His close relationship to Hassan al-Banna' and the Muslim Brotherhood is documented in Richard P. Mitchell, *The Society of the Muslim Brothers*, pp. 185, 322−323.

52. Khoury, "Factionalism among Syrian Nationalists," pp. 450, 459. Quwatli (b. 1891), who became the first president of independent Syria, greatly admired Arslan and cooperated with him in anti-French schemes.

53. PMC, *Minutes of the Ninth Session*, p. 118.

54. MAE, Série E, Syrie-Liban, 210, Report of the Commissaire Spécial at Annemasse, 15 and 27 January 1926.

55. Ibid., de Jouvenal (Beirut) to the Foreign Ministry, 23 January 1926. Ihsan al-Jabiri did meet with German officials to request weapons and a loan

for Syria. He was refused on both counts. See NA/Roll 4900, von Richt-hofen's memorandum, 22 April 1926, frames L327744−327745.

56. MAE, Série E, Syrie-Liban, 210, Hennesy (Bern) to the Foreign Minis-try, 23 February 1926.

57. *Journal des Débats*, 20 February 1926, filed in ibid.

58. Particularly Professor G. Kampffmeyer, president of the German So-ciety for Islamic Studies. Kampffmeyer publicly supported the cause of Syr-ian independence and, to the annoyance of the Auswärtiges Amt, led the Syr-ians in Berlin to believe that Germany would provide them with assistance. NA, Roll 4900, Diel's memorandum, 22 January 1926, frames L327736−327738; and ibid., von Richthofen's memorandum, 22 April 1926, frames L327744−327745. For an assessment of Arslan's literary achievement, see G. Widmer, "Übertragungen aus der neuarabischen Literatur—III: Emir Shakib Arslan," *Die Welt des Islams*, XIX (1937), 1−93, which includes a brief biographical sketch and translations from two of Arslan's works.

59. *Al-Shura*, 5 March 1925, quoting Arslan's speech of 24 January.

60. Cited in al-Sharabasi, *Amir al-bayan*, I, p. 99.

61. Dr. Bayda was the *éminence grise* of Arslan's financial life for twenty-five years. A Syrian who lived in Berlin, Bayda managed with other members of his family an Arabic record company which distributed a product known as the "Baidaphone." With offices in Beirut, Berlin, Cairo, Jaffa, and Tripoli, it seems that the company traded in other products as well. Dr. Bayda served as Arslan's banker, broker, and private moneylender. Neither the source of his title nor the orientation of his politics is known. One thing is clear—the Amir was always in his debt.

62. NA/Roll 4900, letter from Bayda to von Richthofen, 13 May 1925, frame L327728.

63. Ibid., letter from von Richthofen to Arslan, 29 September 1925, frames L327734−327735; Arslan's letter of appreciation to von Richthofen is in ibid., frames L327731−327733.

64. The funding of the Syrian exile organizations in the mid-1920s is dis-cussed in Khoury, "Factionalism among Syrian Nationalists," pp. 458−462. Voluntary contributions were substantial, but, as Khoury shows, the compe-tition for them was intense and the distribution not always regular.

65. This study relies on the detailed explanation of Arslan's financial rela-tionship with 'Abbas which appears in *RR*, pp. 658−665.

66. See Khaldun S. Husry, "King Faysal I and Arab Unity, 1930−1933," *Journal of Contemporary History*, X (1975), 328, citing a letter from Arslan to Ibn Sa'ud.

67. Letter from Arslan to Rida, 2 April 1931, in al-Sharabasi, *Amir al-bayan*, II, p. 738.

68. The person who served as Ibn Sa'ud's chief interpreter for several years wrote that the king gave "support and assistance" to Arslan and other promi-nent Arab nationalists (Mohammed Almana, *Arabia Unified: A Portrait of Ibn Saud*, p. 245).

69. MAE, Série E, Syrie-Liban, 211, Lausanne Consulate to the Foreign Ministry, 14 October 1926.

70. AFS, "Declaration de l'Emir Shakib Arslan," 16 June 1930.
71. Touma, *Paysans*, II, p. 743.

4. Advocate of Islamic Nationalism: The Arab East

1. Cited in Touma, *Paysans*, II, p. 745.
2. Shakib Arslan, "Between Pain and Grief for Ahmad Pasha Taymur," *al-Fath*, 22 May 1930.
3. Shakib Arslan, *Li madha ta'akhkhar al-muslimun?*, p. 48.
4. Charles-André Julien, *L'Afrique du Nord en marche*, p. 24.
5. Muhammad ʿAli ʿAllubah in al-Tahir, *Dhikra al-amir*, p. 22.
6. In addition to *al-Fath* and *al-Shura*, Arslan published in such Islamic-oriented Egyptian journals as *al-Manar*, *Kawkab al-Sharq*, and occasionally *Jaridah al-Ikhwan al-Muslimin*. Many of his articles were also carried in the Damascus paper *Alif-Ba* and Jerusalem's *al-Jamʿiyyah al-ʿArabiyyah*.
7. *LNA* (March 1930), 1−2. For an assessment of *LNA* with which the present author agrees, see Antoine Fleury, "Le Mouvement national arabe à Genève durant l'entre-deux-guerres," *Relations Internationales*, No. 19 (1979), 345−353.
8. Cited in *L'Activité politique*, p. 15.
9. Fo371/19983/E3334, "Italian Propaganda in the Near East" in Lampson (Cairo) to Eden, 29 May 1936.
10. The best account of the Egyptian dynasty's attitude toward the office is Elie Kedourie, "Egypt and the Caliphate," in his *The Chatham House Version*, pp. 177−212.
11. See Gary Troeller, *The Birth of Saudi Arabia: Britain and the Rise of the House of Saʿud*.
12. A useful summary of inter-Arab conflict from the perspective of peninsular politics is A. R. Kelidar, "The Arabian Peninsula in Arab and Power Politics," in Derek Hopwood (ed.), *The Arabian Peninsula, Society and Politics*, esp. pp. 145−149.
13. See Kedourie, "Egypt and the Caliphate," pp. 185−195; the deliberations of the gathering are reproduced in Achille Sékaly, "Les deux Congrès Généraux de 1926," *Revue du Monde Musulman*, LXIV, No. 2 (1926), 29−122.
14. Ibid., pp. 125−219; and H. A. R. Gibb, "The Islamic Congress at Jerusalem in December 1931," in Arnold J. Toynbee (ed.), *Survey of International Affairs, 1934*, pp. 99−100.
15. See *RR*, p. 184. Because Ibn Saʿud did not gain from the Congress what he had hoped, the committee was never called into existence and the congress idea lapsed until revived by Hajj Amin al-Husayni in 1931.
16. Sylvia G. Haim, "The Abolition of the Caliphate," concluding chapter in Thomas W. Arnold, *The Caliphate*, p. 229. See also Hourani, *Arabic Thought*, pp. 239−244; and Kerr, *Islamic Reform*, pp. 166−186.
17. Haim, "Abolition," p. 231.
18. Letter from Arslan to Rida, 12 May 1924, in al-Sharabasi, *Amir al-*

bayan, II, p. 658. Haim has translated and commented on portions of this letter in "Abolition," pp. 231−233.

19. Letter from Arslan to Rida, 12 May 1924, in al-Sharabasi, *Amir al-bayan*, II, p. 660.

20. Letter from Arslan to Rida, 3 July 1924, in ibid., p. 669.

21. Arslan, "The Hour of Unity Approaches, O Arabs," *al-Shura*, 27 August 1925.

22. Letter from Rida to Arslan, 18 April 1929, in *RR*, p. 529. Further sources for this portion of Arslan's *hajj* are Rida's account in ibid., pp. 181−187; and Arslan's letters to Rida in al-Sharabasi, *Amir al-bayan*, II, pp. 696−700. For examples of the advance publicity surrounding the trip, see *al-Shura*, 24 April and 1 May 1929; *al-Fath*, 2 May 1929.

23. *RR*, p. 183. Members of the various delegations included Arslan's old friends, Ahmad Zaki and ʿAbd al-Rahman ʿAzzam; his editors, Muhammad ʿAli al-Tahir, Muhibb al-Din al-Khatib, and Ahmad Hafiz ʿAwwad; and his fellow organizers, ʿAbd al-Hamid Saʿid, head of the Young Men's Muslim Association, and Ahmad Shafiq, president of the Eastern society. The fullest account of this occasion is *al-Fath*, 16 May 1929. See also *al-Shura*, 15 May 1929.

24. *RR*, p. 184.

25. Arslan, *al-Irtisamat al-lutf fi khatir al-hajj ila aqdas mataf*, p. 12. Diary, travel guide, and historical summary, this work constitutes one of Arslan's tributes to Ibn Saʿud. It contains a stirring preface by Rida attesting to Arslan's nobility in performing the *hajj*.

26. Ibn Saʿud's attitude toward Arslan is documented in FO 371/13740/E3707, Bond (Jiddah) to Cairo, 28 June 1929; and FO 371/13740/E5146, Bond to Cairo, 18 September 1929. Arslan's account of the offer of a position is in a letter to Rida, 27 Muharram 1348, in al-Sharabasi, *Amir al-bayan*, II, p. 705.

27. Arslan, *al-Irtisamat*, p. 10.

28. Ibid., p. 11.

29. Letter from Arslan to Rida, 3 Muharram 1348, pp. 702−703. See also Arslan, *al-Irtisamat*, p. 12; and "Attentat contre Ibn Séoud," *LNA* (March−April 1935), 225−226.

30. In "Attentat," p. 225, the Hijazi monarch is referred to as "the chevalier without fear"; and in another passage, Arslan noted with pride that Ibn Saʿud had engaged in over 200 individual battles ("La Victoire d'Ibn Séoud," *LNA* [March 1930], 31).

31. Arslan, "How the Arabs Are Strangers in Their Own Lands," *al-Fath*, 6 February 1930.

32. FO 371/13740/E5146, Bond to Cairo, 18 September 1929.

33. Arslan, *Shawqi*, p. 82. The invitation was never taken up, and Shawqi died in 1932 without ever seeing Arslan again.

34. "The Passage of Amir Shakib through Egypt," *al-Shura*, 9 October 1929.

35. Arslan, "How the Arabs Are Strangers in Their Own Lands," *al-Fath*, 6 February 1930.

36. Accounts of the convention appear in the *Detroit News*, 17 January 1927, and *Detroit Free Press*, 17 January 1927.

37. *Detroit Free Press*, 18 January 1927. Although the publisher of *al-Sa'ih*, 'Abd al-Masih Haddad, clearly held sectarian grievances against Arslan, his comments on the relentless self-promotion surrounding the Amir's American journey ring true. Representative editorials with specific and often vitriolic remarks on Arslan may be found in Haddad's column "Between the Lines" in the issues of 10 January; 7, 17, and 21 February; and 10, 17, and 21 March 1927.

38. Weekly accounts appear in *al-Shura* from 3 February through 26 May 1927.

39. FO 371/13740/E2935, Cairo to Jiddah, 28 May 1929. It was a convenient designation for all anti-imperialist activity; in its issue of 20 February 1926, the Parisian journal *Débats* claimed that Arslan headed Syrian committees which took their orders from Moscow.

40. Arslan, *Ta'rikh ghazawat al-'arab fi faransa wa suwisra wa italya wa jaza'ir al-bahr al-mutawassit*, attempts to show the breadth and the permanence of the Arab impact not only on Spain, but on other parts of Europe as well. In addition to this work, Arslan produced the three-volume *al-Hulal al-sundusiyyah fi al-akhbar wa al-athar al-andalusiyyah*. Despite the time and effort Arslan put in writing them, the works are sterile and pedantic and contribute little new knowledge about Islamic Spain. Indeed, they rely heavily on the very European historians they were written to refute.

41. The Lebanese American Amin al-Rihani claimed to have found remnants of the Arab soul in Spain, and Muhammad Kurd 'Ali saw there the germ for a contemporary renewal of Arab greatness. See Anwar Chejne, "Amin al-Rihani and al-Andalus: A Journey into History," *al-'Arabiyya*, IX (1976), 9−18.

42. Arslan, *Ta'rikh ghazawat*, pp. 5−6.

43. Letter from Arslan to Rida, 1 September 1932, in al-Sharabasi, *Amir al-bayan*, II, pp. 796−798. Arslan did his part by publishing a series of articles on Balkan Islam by Ismail Aga Dchemalovitch, identified as "our Balkan correspondent." See *LNA* (April−June 1933), 38−48; "Les Musulmans en Roumanie," ibid. (January−February 1935), 218−222; "Les Musulmans en Yougoslavie," ibid. (March−April 1935), 268−276.

44. His efforts and concerns are described in a letter to Rida, 8 Rabi' al-Thani 1352, in al-Sharabasi, *Amir al-bayan*, II, pp. 815−818.

45. The fullest account of the proceedings is given by another of the Congress's promoters, 'Ali al-Ghayati, in *La Tribune d'Orient*, 31 October 1935; Ihsan al-Jabiri's version is found in *LNA* (July−September 1935), 369−385; for charges in the Arab press that the Congress was an Italian propaganda venture, see *Oriente Moderno*, XV (October 1935), 501−504; and ibid., XV (November 1935), 563−567.

46. Article by "a delegate" in the magazine *Great Britain and the East* (26 September 1935), 396−397, filed in FO 371/18925/E5821. A Foreign Office official noted his pleasure that Arslan's sentiments were arousing some opposition.

47. For examples of the Syro-Palestinian delegation's petitions, see *LNA*, "La Palestine martyre" (September–October 1934), 1–23; and ibid. (special issue of May–August 1936), 561–574. The petitions are carefully developed and often make telling points about British administrative practices in the Palestine Mandate.

48. Each party has provided a version of the talks. Al-Jabiri, "La Visite de M. Ben Gurion à la délégation Syro-Palestinienne à Genève," *LNA* (November–December 1934), 144–146; David Ben-Gurion, *My Talks with Arab Leaders*, translated by A. Rubinstein and M. Louvish, pp. 35–40.

49. Arslan's basic position was presented in a series of articles under the general title "By Its Very Nature, Zionism Is an Outright Attack," *al-Shura*, 16 and 23 October, 6 November 1929.

50. Arslan, "Why England Insists on the Establishment of a Jewish Kingdom in the East," *al-Shabab*, 17 November 1937.

51. NA, Roll L1279, letter from Arslan to Prüfer, 3 October 1933, frames L332805–332806.

52. Al-Khatib, "The Day of al-Aqsa Mosque," *al-Fath*, 12 September 1929. Al-Khatib was as insistent on this point as any writer of the time. See his "The Jews Violate the Muslim Holy Places," ibid., 3 October 1928; "The Blood of the Heretics in Jerusalem," ibid., 29 August 1929; and "The Judaization of Palestine," ibid., 17 Jumada al-Ula 1352. A thorough analysis of the lead taken by religious-oriented Egyptian groups in presenting Palestine as part of a larger issue is James Jankowski, "Egyptian Responses to the Palestine Problem in the Interwar Period," *International Journal of Middle East Studies*, XII (1980), esp. 20–28.

53. From his appointment as mufti of Jerusalem in 1921 until the creation of the state of Israel in 1948, al-Husayni (1897–1974) was the most internationally prominent Palestinian Arab leader of his time. As head of the Arab Higher Committee and the Supreme Muslim Council in Palestine, he commanded power and prestige which he used almost as much against his local political opponents as he did against the British and the Zionists. A controversial figure, he became vilified for his association with the Nazis during World War II. The mufti used religion as a political weapon in much the same manner as Arslan, and the two men were personal friends as well as political allies. His objectives and activities are closely examined in Y. Porath, *The Emergence of the Palestinian-Arab National Movement*, I, *1918–1929*, and *The Palestinian Arab National Movement*, II, *1929–1939*.

54. Arslan, "The University of al-Aqsa Mosque," *al-Fath*, 22 Ramadan 1351.

55. Al-Jabiri, "Congrès pan-Islamique," *LNA* (November–December 1931), 1.

56. Arslan, "The University of al-Aqsa Mosque."

57. Arslan, "Be Weak, Arab Nation," *al-Shabab*, 5 October 1938. See also Arslan, "God Knows Those Who Ask Why," ibid., 7 December 1938. Shortly after the outbreak of the rebellion, Hassan al-Banna', leader of the Muslim Brotherhood, wrote in a similar vein: "Oh Brothers—your homeland does not end at the borders of Egypt, but extends to wherever a Muslim says

'There is no God but God'" (cited in Jankowski, "Egyptian Responses," p. 21).

58. Arslan, "It Is Your Palestine, O Arabs," *al-Shabab*, 4 January 1939.

59. The character of Yahya's regime is analyzed in Robert W. Stookey, *Yemen: The Politics of the Yemen Arab Republic*, pp. 185−212; and Manfred W. Wenner, *Modern Yemen: 1918−1966*.

60. The origins of Arslan's invitation are revealed in letters to him from Rida, 23 Dhu al-Hijjah 1352 and 4 Muharram 1353, in *RR*, pp. 736−739, 740−741; see also Rida, "A Delegation of Hope and Peace," reprinted in ibid., pp. 188−193. The other members of the delegation were Hashim Bey al-Atasi, leader of the Syrian National Bloc, and the Egyptian politician Muhammad ʿAli ʿAllubah.

61. Wenner, *Modern Yemen*, p. 142. For details of the negotiations between Ibn Saʿud and Yahya, see *Oriente Moderno*, XIV (May 1934), 231−247.

62. Arslan, "La Paix fraternelle entre les deux souverains arabes," *LNA* (September−October 1934), 47.

63. Letter from Rida to Arslan, 3 Rabiʿ al-Thani 1353, in *RR*, p. 742.

64. FO 371/17831/E3847 and E4384 (1934) contain the correspondence and dispatches on this matter.

65. Letter from de Martel, 3 August 1934, cited in *L'Activité politique*, p. 19. Arslan's own version of his hasty departure from Palestine is consistent with this document (see *RR*, p. 744, n. 1).

66. Letter from Arslan to Rida, 9 November 1930, in al-Sharabasi, *Amir al-bayan*, II, p. 720.

67. There are several letters to Arslan from his Lebanese agents in AFS, 1938, informing him that they are awaiting or attempting to follow his instructions on crop selection, building construction, and the like.

68. Letter from Arslan to Rida, 21 December 1930, in al-Sharabasi, *Amir al-bayan*, II, p. 733.

69. Letter from Arslan to Rida, 18 Dhu al-Hijjah 1352, in ibid., p. 820.

70. Al-Sharabasi, *Shakib Arslan*, p. 287.

71. Letter from Arslan to Rida, 10 Rabiʿ al-Thani 1354, in ibid., pp. 836−837.

72. Arslan's version is in *RR*, pp. 262−263, 272; Rida's in ibid., pp. 189−190.

73. FO 371/17831/E3847, Arslan to Wauchope, 1 March 1934.

74. MAE, Série E, Arabie-Hedjaz 36, letter from Arslan to correspondent addressed as "Ma chère et honorable dame," 21 December 1928.

75. The discussion of Syrian events which follows is based on Longrigg, *Syria and Lebanon*, chaps. 6 and 7.

76. Lévi-Provençal, "L'Emir Shakib," p. 16. This was effective; al-Jabiri wrote that, having met with the Syrian negotiators, he and Arslan would not publish anything which might cause them difficulties (al-Jabiri, "La détente," *LNA* [January−April 1936], 468).

77. Lévi-Provençal, "L'Emir Shakib," p. 16; *Oriente Moderno*, XVII (March 1937), 139−140.

78. Arslan, "Le Traité franco-syrien," *LNA* (September−November 1936),

641–648. Longrigg notes that the treaty could have been concluded between the same parties on the same lines ten years earlier (*Syria and Lebanon*, p. 222). On such delicate issues as the separation of Syria and Lebanon, the presence of French military missions, the exclusive reliance on French civilian advisers and technicians, and the effective life of the treaty (twenty-five years), the draft of 1936 mirrored Arslan's original proposals. The treaty is reproduced in Hourani, *Syria and Lebanon*, pp. 314–320.

79. Arslan, "L'Ennemi de la France que je suis?" *LNA* (January–April 1938), 797–801.

80. The letter is cited in *L'Activité politique*, p. 28. From this developed the rumor, explored in chapter 7 below, that Viénot paid Arslan 500,000 French francs for his cooperation.

81. *L'Activité politique*, p. 31. This document provides the most complete account of Arslan's arrival and conduct in Syria. Details are also found in *Oriente Moderno*, XVII (July 1937), 329–332.

82. J. Desparmet's statement that 20,000 were on hand to mark their arrival in Beirut seems excessive. However, even the most prudent estimate by French authorities that 3,000 people awaited them at Damascus municipal hall suggests an impressive occasion. See, respectively, J. Desparmet, "L'Afrique du Nord et pan-arabisme: I. L'Afrique du Nord vue de Damas," *L'Afrique Française*, LXVIII (February 1938), 57; and *L'Activité politique*, p. 32.

83. "Shakib and Ihsan in Their Homeland," *al-Shabab*, 16 June 1937. Al-Tahir did his best, covering his front page with pictures and headlines of the various ceremonies (see *al-Shabab*, 3, 9, and 23 June 1937).

84. *L'Activité politique*, p. 31.

85. Excerpts from the speech and accounts of the Christian reaction are found in ibid., pp. 33–34; and *Oriente Moderno*, XVII (July 1937), 331–332; Arslan provides an incomplete version of his remarks in "La Réelle misère des frères Tharaud," *LNA* (January–April 1938), 853–855.

86. Elie Kedourie, "The Bludan Congress on Palestine," *Middle Eastern Studies*, XVII (January 1981), 107. This article reproduces the Foreign Office reports on the Congress submitted by the capable British consul in Damascus. See also Porath, *Palestinian-Arab National Movement*, II, pp. 231–232.

87. Cited in *L'Activité politique*, p. 31.

88. Robert Montagne, "Réactions arabes contre le Sionisme. Le Congrès de Bloudane," *Entretiens sur l'Evolution des Pays de civilisation Arabe*, III (1939), 46.

89. Cited in Kedourie, "Bludan," p. 117.

90. *L'Activité politique*, p. 36.

5. Mentor to a Generation: North Africa

1. Letter from Arslan to Rida, 26 August 1930, in al-Sharabasi, *Amir al-bayan*, II, p. 714.

2. J. Desparmet, "Afrique du Nord et pan-arabisme: I. L'Afrique du Nord vue de Damas," *L'Afrique Française*, XLVIII (February 1938), 56.

3. Julien, *Afrique du Nord en marche*, p. 25.

4. The case for prewar Maghribi, and especially Moroccan, contacts with the Middle East has been convincingly made by Edmund Burke III. This section draws on his "Moroccan Resistance, Pan-Islam, and German War Strategy, 1914–1918," *Francia* (Munich), III (1975), 434–464; "Pan-Islam and Moroccan Resistance to French Colonial Penetration, 1900–1912," *Journal of African History*, XIII (1972), 97–118; and *Prelude to Protectorate in Morocco: Precolonial Protest and Resistance, 1860–1912*, esp. chaps. 6 and 9.

5. Cited in Nicola A. Ziadeh, *Origins of Nationalism in Tunisia*, p. 80.

6. Ibid., p. 86.

7. Among them were Professor Kampffmeyer, who has been mentioned in chapter 3, and Max von Oppenheim, whose relationship with Arslan is studied in chapter 7. See Burke, "German War Strategy," p. 440.

8. The evaluation is Arslan's in *Sirah dhatiyyah*, p. 269; see also Julien, *Afrique du Nord en marche*, p. 25.

9. Edmund Burke III, "Pan-Islam and North African Resistance, 1890–1918: Patterns of Response," unpublished paper.

10. John P. Halstead, *Rebirth of a Nation*, chap. 9.

11. From their early twenties, when they came under Arslan's tutelage, until the formation of the Istiqlal party in 1944, these men had continuous involvement at the center of the Moroccan nationalist movement. Like Arslan himself, they were never in one place for very long. Collecting university experience, if not always degrees, they moved back and forth from Paris to Morocco to Geneva, organizing societies, editing journals, and sometimes heading demonstrations. Al-Ouezzani (1910–1978), of a Fasi family, was a dominant force until 1937, when he split with 'Allal al-Fasi over the question of the leadership of the National party. Balafrej (b. 1907?) was also at the center of the movement from its beginning and emerged as the virtual director of the Istiqlal from his post as secretary general of the party. Naciri (b. 1904) was from Rabat and studied at al-Azhar, the Sorbonne, and in Geneva while engaging in anti-French activities, often in close collaboration with Arslan. In 1937, he founded the Parti d'Unité Marocaine in Tetouan and continued to head it until its absorption into the Istiqlal. Muhammad al-Fasi played a significant part in organizing Moroccans in Europe and became a founding member of the Istiqlal. Information on these individuals has been collated from the various references to them in Halstead, *Rebirth*, and Robert Rézette, *Les Partis politiques marocains*.

12. Roger Le Tourneau, *Evolution politique de l'Afrique du Nord musulmane, 1920–1961*, 194, 465–466; Halstead, *Rebirth*, pp. 171–172.

13. Halstead, *Rebirth*, p. 161. See also Rézette, *Partis*, p. 6.

14. Halstead, *Rebirth*, p. 132.

15. Ibid., p. 129. Halstead's treatment of Arslan's role in the Moroccan nationalist movement, largely distilled from interviews with Moroccan participants, is superior to Juliette Bessis, "Chekib Arslan et les mouvements nationalistes au Maghreb," *Revue Historique*, CCLIX (1978), 467–489.

16. Lévi-Provençal, "L'Emir Shakib," p. 12.

17. The most complete account of Arslan's visit is Muhammad Ben-nouna, "The Honorable Amir Shakib Arslan in Morocco," *al-Fath*, 24 Jumada al-Ula 1349. Lévi-Provençal, "L'Emir Shakib," pp. 11−12, also provides some details on the journey which have been incorporated into the accounts of most subsequent authors. Arslan includes selective reminiscences in his *'Urwah al-ittihad bayn ahl al-jihad*, pp. 143−146.

18. Rézette, *Partis*, p. 72, where it is also claimed that 'Abd al-Salam met Arslan in the East, an occasion which led him to become the Amir's agent in Morocco. This seems unlikely. Arslan's high opinion of Bennouna is expressed in a rich obituary tribute in *LNA* (January−February 1935), 209−210.

19. Ahmad Balafrej, "Shakib Arslan in Morocco," *al-Fath*, 17 Jumada al-Ula 1349. A few years later, Arslan told a gathering of the AEMNA in Paris that they had preserved better than the Eastern Arabs "their religion and their Arab soul" (J. Desparmet, "Afrique du Nord et pan-arabisme," p. 56).

20. Bennouna, "Arslan in Morocco." That these various accounts all appeared in the Cairo-based *al-Fath* suggests that Arslan was at least partly successful in achieving his objective of publicizing the Moroccan case in the East.

21. Ibid.

22. The best analysis of the *dahir* and its relationship to French Berber policy as a whole is Charles-Robert Ageron, "La Politique berbère du protectorat marocain de 1913 à 1934," *Revue d'Histoire Moderne et Contemporaine*, XVIII (January−March 1971), 50−90. For its impact on the emergence of Moroccan nationalism, see Halstead, *Rebirth*, pp. 68−74; Julien, *Afrique du Nord en marche*, pp. 131−135; Le Tourneau, *Evolution politique*, pp. 180−185. The decree is reproduced in Halstead, *Rebirth*, pp. 276−277.

23. Cardinal Lavigerie was the founder of the Pères Blancs, a special Catholic order associated with French policies in North Africa. It was at Lavigerie's cathedral in Carthage that the Eucharistic Congress was held, two months after the promulgation of the *dahir*. To Muslims, these acts of Christian assertiveness were viewed as provocative. See Jacques Berque, *French North Africa: The Maghrib between Two World Wars*, translated by Jean Stewart, pp. 217−224.

24. "Tribunaux berbères," *LNA* (August−September 1930), 28. Variations on this theme appear in several of Arslan's articles in *LNA*. See, for example, "Nous ne sommes pas morts" (November 1930), 1−3; "Comment on abuse l'opinion publique en France" (February 1931), 6; "Une Réponse au 'Saint' du Maroc" (May−June 1931), 5−8. He also expressed these views privately. See letters from Arslan to Rida, 26 August and 9 November 1930, in al-Sharabasi, *Amir al-bayan*, II, pp. 712−714, 721.

25. Arslan, "Tribunaux berbères," p. 27.

26. Arslan, "La Question berbère," *LNA* (November 1930), 25.

27. Arslan, "The Question of the Expulsion of the Berbers from Islam," *al-Fath*, 17 Jumada al-Ula 1349. The quotations in the remainder of the paragraph are from this article.

28. Arslan, "The Protest to France over the Berber Question," *al-Fath*, 29 Jumada al-Akhirah 1349. At this time, Arslan also called for a boycott of French goods by the Islamic community. There was some positive response from the Muslims of India, but Egyptian merchants were not attracted to the idea and it never gained momentum (see Julien, *Afrique du Nord en marche*, p. 133).

29. Arslan's assessment of the strength of the protest appears in "La Question berbère," pp. 21–30; and "Echos de la question berbère," *LNA* (February 1931), 5. Corroborative evidence is presented in Ageron, "La Politique berbère," pp. 82–84; ʿAlal al-Fasi, *The Independence Movements in Arab North Africa*, translated by Hazem Zaki Nuseibeh, pp. 124–125; Henri Laoust, "L'Evolution politique et culturelle de l'Egypte contemporaine," *Entretiens sur l'Evolution des Pays de Civilisation Arabe*, No. 3 (1937), 70; and Robert Montagne, *Révolution au maroc*, pp. 184–186. *La Nation Arabe* was regarded by the protectorate authorities as subversive and was banned in Morocco in August 1930, although copies of it continued to be smuggled into the country (Halstead, *Rebirth*, p. 127).

30. The resolution, which was sent to the League of Nations, is reproduced in *LNA* (May–June 1932), 33–34.

31. Cited in Charles-André Julien, *Le Maroc face aux imperialismes, 1415–1956*, p. 161.

32. This was a genuine victory, but, as Halstead observes, it did not lead to the abandonment of a French Berber policy which regarded the Berber territories as distinct (*Rebirth*, pp. 186–187).

33. At the meetings of the UN General Assembly in 1952 and 1953, Muslim delegates from Middle Eastern countries told one correspondent that they first became aware of a Moroccan problem through the *dahir* protest (Rom Landau, *Moroccan Drama, 1900–1955*, pp. 147–148).

34. *Evolution politique*, p. 185.

35. Arslan's objections were raised during the final phase of the Italian reconquest of Libya when, in 1930 and 1931, General Graziani adopted the techniques of counterinsurgency warfare to subdue the resistance in the Jabal al-Akhdar region of Cyrenaica. The historical record suggests that the outcry was not without foundation (see E. E. Evans-Pritchard, *The Sanusi of Cyrenaica*).

36. Letter from Arslan to Rida, 22 May 1931, in al-Sharabasi, *Amir al-bayan*, II, p. 754.

37. Arslan, "Italian Atrocities in Tripoli," *al-Fath*, 21 Dhu al-Qaʿadah 1349; and "Procédés de guerre moyenageux ressuscités par les Italiens fascistes" *LNA* (April 1931), 8; similar rhetoric appears in Arslan's other accounts of the reconquest. See, for example, another article entitled "Italian Atrocities in Tripoli," *al-Fath*, 19 Dhu al-Hijjah 1349; "Un Evénement inouï en Cyrénaïque," *LNA* (December 1930), 1–4; "L'Occupation de Koufra," *LNA* (February 1931), 13–16; and an ethnographical, historical essay in *Hadir al-ʿalam al-islami*, II, pp. 64–128.

38. Arslan, "Omar Moukhtar," *LNA* (September–October 1931), 6.

from the Association's well-known declaration is found in Merad, *Réformisme musulman*, p. 399.

70. Arslan, "Foreign Plots against Islamic Solidarity," *al-Fath*, 8 Shuwwal 1349.

71. ʿAbd al-ʿAziz al-Thaʿalibi (1875–1944), so often unfavorably contrasted with Bourguiba, was a singular personality, a man like Arslan who combined a belief in the reconstitution of an Islamic society with a willingness to campaign for its realization. Arslan's appreciation of him is in *al-Shura*, 7 January 1925. For an account of what al-Thaʿalibi's movement meant to the Tunisia of the 1920s, see L. Carl Brown, "Stages in the Process of Change," in Charles Micaud (ed.), *Tunisia: The Politics of Modernization*, pp. 38–66.

72. Brown, "Stages in the Process of Change," in Micaud, *Tunisia*, pp. 61–63.

73. Habib Bourguiba, "Un Vétéran de la lutte anti-coloniale: L'Emir Chekib Arslan," *L'Action Tunisienne*, 3 June 1937, reprinted in *Le Néo-Destour et le front populaire en France*, I, *Le Dialogue, 1936–1938*, pp. 349–362.

74. Félix Garas, *Bourguiba et la naissance d'une nation*, p. 111. This, claims the author, is true despite all that has been written to the contrary. It has been written by, among others, Julien, *Afrique du Nord en marche*, pp. 25, 64.

75. For an appraisal of the works of these "witnesses *engagés*," see Merad, *Réformisme musulman*, pp. 14–15.

76. J. Desparmet, "La Résistance à l'occident," *L'Afrique Française* (hereafter cited as *AF*), XLIII (May 1933), 265. A by no means exhaustive list of works attributing to Arslan a monumental propaganda role includes, in chronological order, Louis Ermont, "Afrique du Nord et Proche Orient," *AF*, XLIII (April 1933), 203; Louis Jovelet, "L'Evolution sociale et politique des 'pays arabes' (1930–1933)," *Revue des Etudes Islamiques*, VII (1933), 638–640; J. Desparmet, "Le Panarabisme et l'Algérie," *AF*, XLVI (June 1936), 312–317; J. Desparmet, "Afrique du Nord et pan-arabisme," pp. 56–58; Robert Montagne, "La Crise politique de l'arabisme (juin 1937–juin 1938)," *La France Méditerranéne et Africaine*, I, No. 2 (1938), 13; Louis Jalabert, "La Turbulence de l'Islam arabe," *Etudes*, 20 January 1938, 173.

77. J. Desparmet, "Les Oulémas algériens," p. 211, in which Arslan is also identified as "le chef de l'Intelligence Service oriental."

78. Louis Jalabert, "Dans le maghreb qui bouge. Part II," *Etudes*, 5 May 1938, 356.

79. Arslan, "La 'Politique musulmane' et l'Afrique du Nord," *LNA* (January–February 1935), 185.

80. *LNA* (September–December 1938), 1233–1237.

81. See Desparmet, "Afrique du Nord et pan-arabisme," p. 56. Arslan's most expansive denunciation of this charge is his "L'Ennemi de la France que je suis?" (*LNA* [January–April 1938], 797–814), and "Une Note française relative à notre politique musulman" (ibid. [May–June 1935], 341–

346). He also published a thirty-six-page pamphlet responding to the charges that he was an intransigent agitator. The publication, *Aucune Propagande au monde ne peut défigurer le portrait d'un homme*, tends to duplicate his *LNA* articles.

82. Arslan, "L'Ennemi de la France," p. 805.

83. Ibid., p. 800.

84. Ibid., p. 803.

85. Ibid., p. 804. See also his "L'Eternelle calomnie," *LNA* (January–February 1935), 171–173; "Toucher des fonds, de Berlin, de Moscou, de Rome, tout à fois c'est vraiment du miracle!" *LNA* (January–April 1936), 509–510; and *'Urwah al-ittihad*, pp. 147–152.

86. "L'Ennemi de la France," p. 814. See also "L'Oppression française en Tunisie," *LNA* (January–February 1935), 182–183.

87. Arslan, "Comment on écrit l'histoire," *LNA* (November 1930), 37.

88. Desparmet, "Afrique du Nord et pan-arabisme," p. 56.

89. Robert Montagne, *La Politique islamique de la France*, p. 10.

90. Bourguiba, "Un Vétéran," p. 351.

91. Mekki Naciri, "Shakib Arslan," *al-Fath*, 9 Rabi' al-Thani 1351; *RR*, p. 184.

6. The Integrity of Tradition

1. Fouad Ajami, "The End of Pan-Arabism," *Foreign Affairs*, LVII (1978–1979), 355.

2. Arslan, "Foreign Plots against Islamic Solidarity," *al-Fath*, 8 Shuwwal 1349.

3. *Li madha ta'akhkhar al-muslimun wa li madha taqaddam ghayruhum?*. The publishing history of the work illustrates Arslan's place as an international commentator on Islamic issues. The book is comprised of a series of essays, first published in *al-Manar*, composed to answer the queries of an Indonesian shaykh, Muhammad Bisyuni 'Umran, on the reasons for the current weakness of the Muslims. The first English translation (*Our Decline and Its Causes*, Lahore, 1944) was made from Malayalam, a language of the Indian subcontinent. When the Arabic was translated into that language, it "sent a wave of national fervor and kindled Islamic fire in the hearts of the Moplahs" (preface of the translator, M. S. Shakoor, to the 1962 reprinted edition, p. viii). The translator's cautionary note that the English edition is twice-removed from the Arabic original is well taken. It is occasionally misleading, and portions of the Arabic work have been omitted. The citations in this study are from the third Arabic edition (Cairo, 1358).

4. Of the several studies on this topic, see in particular H. A. R. Gibb, *Modern Trends in Islam*; Hourani, *Arabic Thought*, chaps. 7 and 9; Kerr, *Islamic Reform*; Henri Laoust, "Le Réformisme orthodox des 'salafiya' et les caractères généraux de son orientation actuelle," *Revue des Etudes Islamiques*, VI (1932), 175–224; Nadav Safran, *Egypt in Search of Political Community*, chap. 5; and Wilfred Cantwell Smith, *Islam in Modern History*.

5. Arslan, *Li madha*, p. 11. Unless otherwise noted, the references in this chapter are to works written by Arslan.

6. Ibid., p. 60.

7. Ibid., p. 63.

8. Ibid., p. 96.

9. Ibid., p. 104.

10. Ibid., p. 98.

11. Ibid., p. 96.

12. Ibid., pp. 18–19, 100–101.

13. "Introduction" to ʿAbd al-Qadir al-Maghribi, *al-Bayyinat fi al-din wa al-ijtimaʿ wa al-adab wa al-taʾrikh*, I, p. ṭāʾ.

14. *Li madha*, p. 105. ʿAbduh is cited in Safran, *Egypt in Search*, p. 68.

15. *Li madha*, p. 64.

16. Ibid., p. 133. Not surprisingly, Rida, who edited the volume, inserted a footnote to this statement assuring the readers that Arslan meant the awakening of Muslims in their capacity as Muslims.

17. "L'Ennemi de la France que je suis?" *LNA* (January–April 1938), 804.

18. Sura 13:11, cited in *Li madha*, p. 14.

19. "Introduction" to *al-Bayyinat*, p. wāw.

20. *Li madha*, p. 166; cf. Hourani, *Arabic Thought*, pp. 228–229; and Rudolph Peters, *Islam and Colonialism: The Doctrine of Jihad in Modern History*, chap. 4.

21. "Introduction" to *al-Bayyinat*, p. ṭāʾ; *Li madha*, p. 166.

22. "Foreign Plots against Islamic Solidarity," *al-Fath*, 8 Shuwwal 1349.

23. "Introduction" to *al-Bayyinat*, p. zāʾ.

24. Arslan designated both nationalism and Westernization as forms of apostasy. See "Regeneration Has Come to Mean the Effort to Kill the Spirit of Islam," *al-Fath*, 29 Dhu al-Qaʿadah, 1352; and "Religious Apostasy Is Synonymous with a Decline in the Birthrate," *al-Fath*, 21 November 1929. Taha Husayn (1889–1974), novelist, essayist, and educational reformer, generated a heated controversy with his 1926 publication questioning the authenticity of much of pre-Islamic Arab poetry. Haykal (1889–1956) was also a committed Westernizer and prolific author. He served as editor of the Liberal Constitutionalist party's reformist organ, *al-Siyasah*, and eventually became president of the Egyptian senate.

25. Charles D. Smith, "The 'Crisis of Orientation': The Shift of Egyptian Intellectuals to Islamic Subjects in the 1930s," *International Journal of Middle East Studies*, IV (1973), 391; see also Safran, *Egypt in Search*, chaps. 9 and 10.

26. "Hygienic Clothing and a Hygienic Headdress," *al-Shura*, 26 August 1926.

27. "Introduction" to *al-Bayyinat*, pp. yā–ya/bāʾ.

28. "The Position of Women," *al-Shura*, 23 April 1930. The article was reprinted, presumably because Arslan's stance was endorsed, in *al-Shihab*, the journal of the Association of Algerian Ulema. See Merad, *Réformisme musulman*, p. 329, n. 2.

29. *Li madha*, pp. 77–78.

30. Arslan's most persistent refutations of Taha Husayn's early works are "There Is More to Things Than Meets the Eye," in Mustafa Sadiq al-Rafiʿi (ed.), *Taht rayah al-Qurʾan: Maʿrakah bayn al-qadim wa al-jadid*, pp. 31–39; and "History Is not Based on Suppositions" in ibid., pp. 87–96. The charge of plagiarism is leveled in a letter from Arslan to Rida, 21 Rabiʿ al-Awwal 1352, in al-Sharabasi, *Amir al-bayan*, II, pp. 808–809.

31. "Arab Civilization and Philosophy," *Majallah al-zahraʾ*, III, No. 5 (1345), 289–293. Musa, an Egyptian Copt who is often called the founder of Arab socialism, shared Arslan's anti-imperialism, but held a Westernized, secularist view of society which Arslan did not appreciate.

32. "Tribunaux berbères," *LNA* (October 1930), 7. Among the secularizing reforms carried out in the years of Mustafa Kemal Atatürk's presidency (1923–1938) were the abolition of the caliphate and the *shariʿah* courts, the adoption of the Latin alphabet, the translation of the Qurʾan into Turkish, the closing of separate religious schools, and the banning of the fez. For a full discussion of these policies, see Lewis, *Emergence*; and Berkes, *Development of Secularism*.

33. "Ankara Face to Face with the Islamic Congress," *al-Fath*, 6 Ramadan 1350; "The Turks in a State of Revolution," ibid., 9 Muharram 1352; "Regeneration Has Come to Mean the Effort to Kill the Spirit of Islam."

34. "The Turks in Revolution."

35. Ibid.

36. "Ankara Face to Face."

37. In addition to the works cited in note 33, see "The Stand of the Kemalists," *al-Fath*, 18 August 1927; "A Reply to Farid Wajdi," ibid., 1 Jumada al-Akhirah 1352; and *Hadir al-ʿalam al-islami*, I, pp. 205–212; III, pp. 351–364.

38. Letter from Rida to Arslan, 8 January 1928, in *RR*, p. 507; Arslan's explanation of his actions is in ibid., p. 510, n. 1. Arslan regarded Amanullah as a disruptive modernizer in the Kemalist mode and criticized him for his imitation of Ankara's policies ("The Afghan Revolution," *al-Fath*, 24 January 1929).

39. "Despised by the State, Honored by the People," *al-Shura*, 21 March 1927.

40. "The Present Real Crisis of Islam," *al-Fath*, 17 April 1930.

41. "There Is More to Things," p. 34.

42. See *Li madha*, pp. 55–57, 87–95; "The Separation of Religion from Politics?" *al-Fath*, 9 February 1928; "Prayers in All English Churches for the Health of the King," ibid., 27 December 1928; "Do They Say That Germany Is Backward?" ibid., 28 Shuwwal 1351; "Religion and State Work Together," ibid., 6 Dhu al-Hijjah 1352; "Their 'Secular' Governments!" *al-Shura*, 28 January 1931.

43. "The Agreement of the Pope with Italy," *al-Fath*, 7 March 1929; and "The Present Real Crisis in Islam."

44. *Li madha*, p. 64; see also *al-Nahdah al-ʿarabiyyah fi al-ʿasr al-hadir*, p. 40.

45. "The Turks in Revolution."

46. *Hadir al-ʿalam al-islami*, III, p. 253.

47. "Ankara Face to Face"; "Reply to Farid Wajdi"; "The Present Real Crisis of Islam." In his obituary tribute to Atatürk, Arslan dropped much of his open hostility, but did insist that credit for the initial resistance to the Treaty of Sèvres should go to Kazim Karabekir and the Turkish ulema who roused the populace with a call to holy war. Thus, it was the men of religion who were "the principal saviors of Turkey" ("La Mort de Kémal Atatürk," *LNA* [September–December 1938], 1077–1078).

48. Safran, *Egypt in Search*, p. 152.

49. Charles D. Smith, "The Intellectual and Modernization: Definitions and Reconsiderations: The Egyptian Experience," *Comparative Studies in Society and History*, XXII (1980), 518.

50. "Ankara Face to Face."

51. "Introduction" to *al-Bayyinat*, p. ḥāʾ.

52. "The Present Real Crisis of Islam."

53. Ibid.; and "The Current Eastern Awakening," *al-Muqtataf* (February 1927), 136–137.

54. "La Revue 'Maghreb,'" *LNA* (May–June 1932), 38.

55. Cited in Kerr, *Islamic Reform*, p. 172, n. 67. Cf. Hourani, *Arabic Thought*, pp. 231–232.

56. See Merad, *Réformisme musulman*, pp. 218–219. This intelligent reformer also admired certain of Atatürk's policies and suggested that the attacks on the Turkish president were sterile and unproductive (ibid., pp. 374–376).

57. *Al-Nahdah al-ʿarabiyyah*, pp. 30–31; "Remnants of the Kings of the Maghrib," *al-Shura*, 9 April 1930; "Nouvelles du Hedjaz et Nedjd," *LNA* (May 1930), 143; "Les Réformes dans les états d'Ibn Séoud," ibid. (September–October 1931), 46.

58. "One Subject," *al-Fath*, 22 August 1929.

59. "L'Alliance des trois pays arabes independents," *LNA* (January–April 1936), 471.

60. Letter from Arslan to Rida, 17 Rabiʿ al-Thani 1350, in al-Sharabasi, *Amir al-bayan*, II, p. 789.

61. See especially the "Introduction" to al-Sharabasi, *Shakib Arslan: min ruwwad al-wahdah al-ʿarabiyyah*; and the same author's *Shakib Arslan*, pp. 77–155. The evidence al-Sharabasi uses to make his case for Arslan as Arab nationalist could also be applied to an interpretation of the Amir as pan-Islamicist. Although al-Dahhan also stresses Arslan's role as a spokesman of Arabism, he does suggest that Arslan often mixed the concepts of religion and nationalism and that he tended to present Islam as a nationality (*al-Amir Shakib Arslan*, p. 331).

62. Dr. Zaki Bey ʿAli, "The Pilgrim of the East in the West," *al-Shabab*, 24 March 1937.

63. *Al-Wahdah al-ʿarabiyyah*, p. 8. Summaries of the address may be found in J. Desparmet, "Afrique du Nord et pan-arabisme," pp. 56–57; and Enrico Nunè, "L'Idea dell'unità araba in recenti dibattiti alla stampa del

vicino oriente," *Oriente Moderno*, XVIII, No. 8 (August 1938), 403–405.

64. *Al-Wahdah al-ʿarabiyyah*, pp. 11–12.

65. "Ils prennent leurs désirs pour des réalités," *LNA* (May–August 1938), 933. For al-Husri's notion of the naturally existing Arab nation, see Cleveland, *Making of an Arab Nationalist*, pp. 116–127.

66. "Foreign Plots against Islamic Solidarity."

67. Ibid.

68. This apt phrase is the title of Nikki R. Keddie's *An Islamic Response to Imperialism: Political and Religious Writings of Sayyid Jamal ad-Din "al-Afghani"*.

69. For the context of the speech and the irritation it caused, see chapter 4, above.

70. Letter from Arslan to Rida, 3 July 1924, in al-Sharabasi, *Amir al-bayan*, II, p. 667. In the same letter (p. 666) Arslan commented that since a Greek Orthodox family like the Sursuqs had such a strong commitment to France, one could well imagine what the Catholics were like.

71. His attitude on the Assyrians is found in "Le Traité franco-syrien: est-ce un traité ou un chiffon de papier?" *LNA* (May–August 1938), 914. His complaints on the other matters were made in letters to Rida, 2 May 1929, in al-Sharabasi, *Amir al-bayan*, II, p. 700; and 17 Rabiʿ al-Thani 1350, in ibid., p. 787.

72. "Arabism, a Total Community," in al-Sharabasi, *Shakib Arslan*, pp. 161–188. The article was written in July 1940.

73. Muhammad Kurd ʿAli, *al-Mudhakkirat*, II, p. 419. A friend, not a sycophant, Kurd ʿAli also remarked on Arslan's political errors.

74. "The Question of al-Amir Shakib Arslan," *al-Shabab*, 12 May 1937.

75. Interview with Mayy Junbalat, November 1975. Cf. al-Sharabasi, *Shakib Arslan*, pp. 311–312.

76. Interview with Ihsan al-Jabiri, 5 January 1975.

77. Ben-Gurion, *My Talks with Arab Leaders*, p. 35.

78. NA, Roll 4900, Auswärtiges Amt internal memorandum, 12 December 1934, frame L327722.

79. *La Tribune d'Orient*, 9 May 1932. Arslan's summer meetings with Faysal began in Antibes in 1930 and continued regularly, usually in Bern, until a few weeks before the Iraqi monarch's death. They are chronicled in Arslan's letters to Rida, all of which are in al-Sharabasi, *Amir al-bayan*, II, p. 769 (23 July 1931); p. 785 (13 Rabiʿ al-Thani 1350); p. 812 (8 Rabiʿ al-Thani 1352).

80. Louis Jovelet, "L'Evolution sociale et politique des 'pays arabes' (1930–1933)," *Revue des Etudes Islamiques*, VII (1933), esp. 454–455, 460, 590, 627, 639.

81. Roger Le Tourneau, *L'Islam contemporain*, p. 65. The other three were Faysal, Hajj Amin al-Husayni, and ʿAbd al-Rahman ʿAzzam.

82. *Paris Soir*, 21 December 1939. Allard's article was clipped and filed in AFS, 1939.

7. Toward the Axis

1. Arslan, "Une Campagne de mensonge," *LNA* (September–October 1931), 36.

2. MPF, Report of 3 October 1939.

3. Most particularly, Lukasz Hirszowicz, *The Third Reich and the Arab East*. Subsequent works have added archival detail, but have not substantially modified Hirszowicz's interpretations. See Robert Lewis Melka, "The Axis and the Arab Middle East, 1930–1945"; M. J. Schröder, "Les Rapports des puissances de l'Axe avec le monde arabe," in *La Guerre en Méditerranée (1930–1945)*, pp. 607–626; and Francis Nicosia, "Arab Nationalism and National Socialist Germany, 1933–1939: Ideological and Strategic Incompatibility," *International Journal of Middle East Studies*, XII (1980), 351–372.

4. Hirszowicz, *The Third Reich*, p. 30; and R. L. Melka, "Nazi Germany and Palestine," *Middle Eastern Studies*, V (October 1969), 221–233. Melka shows that these activities were undertaken by the Nazi apparatus and were not part of the regular Foreign Office recommendations.

5. The most thorough examination of Italy's interwar Arab policy is Rosaria Quartararo, *Roma tra Londra e Berlino*, chap. 4.

6. The techniques and content of Italian propaganda are discussed in Quartararo, *Roma*, pp. 211–218; Mario Tedeschini Lalli, "La propaganda araba del fascismo e l'Egitto," *Storia Contemporanea*, VII (December 1976), 717–749; Callum A. MacDonald, "Radio Bari: Italian Wireless Propaganda in the Middle East and British Countermeasures 1934–1938," *Middle Eastern Studies*, XIII (May 1977), 195–207.

7. The phrase is Melka's, "The Axis," p. 249.

8. These contacts are reviewed in Hirszowicz, *Third Reich*, chaps. 2 and 3.

9. Quartararo, *Roma*, p. 214.

10. Letter from Arslan to von Oppenheim, 18 June 1942, as summarized in Fritz Grobba, *Männer und Mächte im Orient*, p. 270.

11. They were exceptional not only for the longevity of their careers, but for their direct experience of Middle Eastern affairs. Von Hentig had undertaken a T. E. Lawrence style of mission to raise the Afghan population against the British in World War I. Although deeply involved in the implementation of Third Reich Near Eastern policy as head of Political Division VII in the late 1930s and later as the officer responsible for affairs relating to Iran, Turkey, and the ex-khedive, he was one of the group of aristocratic civil servants who "despised in private the Nazi masters whom in public they served" (R. L. Melka, "Max Freiherr von Oppenheim: Sixty Years of Scholarship and Intrigue in the Middle East," *Middle Eastern Studies*, IX [January 1973], 82). Prüfer began his diplomatic career as a dragoman trainee at the Cairo embassy in 1907 and qualified as a Privatdozent in Semitic languages before transferring to Istanbul, where, during the First World War, he met Arslan. In 1942, he returned from the ambassadorship in Brazil to head the Arab section in the Auswärtiges Amt (Hirszowicz, *Third Reich*, p. 268). Von Richthofen, another prewar foreign service officer, was deputy chief of the

Middle Eastern Division during the 1920s, in which capacity he had frequent contact with Arslan. For mention of him and for an analysis of the durability of the aristocratic tradition in the German diplomatic service following World War I, see Paul Seabury, *The Wilhelmstrasse: A Study of German Diplomats under the Nazi Regime*, chap. 1.

12. AFS, "Procès-verbal d'audition," 6 October 1938. See also Arslan's vigorous defense of Wilhelm's character in "Qu'est-ce que vous voulez qu'un homme d'état français dise de Guillaume II," *LNA* (March–April 1935), 236–255.

13. This biographical sketch relies on Melka, "Von Oppenheim," pp. 81–82.

14. NA, Roll 4900, von Cramon memorandum, undated (December 1927), frame L327793.

15. Ibid., AA internal memorandum, 14 December 1927, frame L327790. Auswärtiges Amt documents consistently stress Arslan's Germanophilia and frequently refer to him as *deutschfreundlich*. See, for example, ibid., AA to Konrad Giesal, 17 February 1925, frame L327727; Baron von Richthofen to Arslan, 29 September 1925, frames L327734–327735.

16. The various exchanges among von Oppenheim, von Richthofen, and the Geneva Consulate are found in ibid., 13–16 December 1926, frames L327758–327762; and von Richthofen to Arslan, 26 April 1926, frames L327740–327742.

17. Von Oppenheim began one of his covering notes to his Auswärtiges Amt contact of the time, von Richthofen, with the words, "As agreed, I am sending you Amir Shakib Arslan's latest letter with my request for a response so that I can write to him myself" (ibid., 14 December 1928, frame L327807; and 13 December 1926, frame L327758).

18. Sultan Abdulhamid had appointed Arslan to act as the kaiser's escort in Damascus (Al-Tahir, *Dhikra al-amir*, p. 55). Arslan resurrected the kaiser's statement in 1935, claiming that because of it, the German ruler had won the enduring sympathies of the Muslim world (Arslan, "Guillaume II," pp. 252, 255). See also Bernard Vernier, *La Politique islamique d'Allemagne*, pp. 54–55.

19. NA, Roll 4900, von Richthofen's memorandum, 22 April 1926, frames L327744–327745; von Richthofen to Arslan, 26 April 1926, frames L327740–327742.

20. NA, Roll 2904, Prüfer's memorandum, 7 November 1934, frames E461986–461989.

21. Daniel Guérin, *Au Service des colonisés*, p. 20.

22. ASMAE, Italia 1942, busta 85, paraphrased translation of letter from Arslan to al-Husayni, 7 November 1942.

23. NA, Roll 726, letter from Arslan to Sulayman Agha, 2 October 1941, frames 325933–325938.

24. Arslan, "La Politique coloniale n'a rien à voir avec l'antisémitisme," *LNA* (September–December 1938), 1200–1203; "La Guerre des ondes," *LNA* (January–April 1938), 876–877; "Their Differences Please Them," *al-*

Shabab, 14 December 1938; "Muslims and Independent Muslims," *al-Shabab*, 19 May 1937.

25. Arslan, "L'Acharnement des Juifs contre le Grand Mufti de Jérusalem," *LNA* (September–December 1938), 1221.

26. Arslan, "La Question de race," *LNA* (May–August 1938), 981. Arslan was more strident in the Arab press, offering the opinion that Zionist policies in Palestine gave credence to the theory of an international Jewish conspiracy. See his "If the Arab Nation Is Weak," *al-Shabab*, 5 October 1938; and "Their Differences Please Them."

27. FO371/2460/J214, "Middle East Intelligence Center," Summary No. 9, 26 December 1939–2 January 1940, letter from Arslan to al-Tahir; FO371/24546/E41, letter from Arslan to al-Saʿid, 17 November 1939 in Newton (Bagdad) to Halifax, 27 December 1939.

28. ASMAE, Pacco 1573, Siria 1923, fascio 7174, 26 December 1922; and ASMAE, Pacco 1672, Turchia 1922, fascio 7797.

29. Evans-Pritchard, *The Sanusi*, p. 202; chapter 7 of this work provides a summary of Italian colonial practices after 1931.

30. ASMAE, Libia, busta 7, 1.1, 1933, "Campagna Islamica Antitaliana: Atteggiamento dello Scekib Arslan," Minister of Foreign Affairs to Ministers of Colonies, 23 June 1933. It is clear from the tone of surprise in this document that Arslan's article was published without the advance knowledge of the Foreign Office in Rome.

31. *Al-Jamʿiyyah al-ʿArabiyyah*, 4 April 1935, as reproduced in *Oriente Moderno*, XV (May 1935), 197.

32. *Al-Jamʿiyyah al-ʿArabiyyah*, 9 May 1935, as reproduced in *Oriente Moderno*, XV (June 1935), 252–253. Arslan claimed to have "a clear conscience" over his agreement with Mussolini, but he did continue to press the Italian government to implement additional specific reforms in Libya (*RR*, p. 746; ASMAE, AVUR, N. 105, summary of Professor Enderle's meeting with Shakib Arslan, 31 October 1935).

33. Arslan, "Le Traité franco-syrien," *LNA* (September–November 1936), 647; and Arslan, "Le Problème éthiopien," ibid. (January–April 1936), 516.

34. Arslan, "A Propos de l'Ethiopie," ibid. (September–November 1936), 680–692 (the quotation is from p. 680); other articles in *LNA* which address this question include "L'Italie en Erythrée" (September–October 1934), 48–51; "Les Musulmans d'Abyssinie" (January–February 1935), 177–178; "Le Conflit italo-éthiopien et les arabes" (May–June 1935), 307–311; "Un Article pernicieux" (September–November 1936), 653–655. Arslan wrote virtually identical articles for the Arab press—for example, in *al-Shabab*, 14 April and 19 May 1937. See also the lengthy explanatory footnotes in *RR*, pp. 760–762, 764–766, 791–792; and his comments in Bourguiba, "Un Vétéran de la lutte anti-coloniale," p. 361.

35. Letter from Rida to Arslan, 6 Safr 1354, in *RR*, p. 783.

36. Arslan, *ʿUrwah al-ittihad*, pp. 237, 241; G. W. Rendel, more astute than those among his Whitehall colleagues who saw a fascist plot behind every Palestinian demonstration, observed of Arslan: "Like many other Arab

intellectuals he probably has no love of the Italians as such—but no doubt relies on being able to prevent Italy actually replacing us and France in the Middle East if and when we are got rid of" (FO371/19983/E3334, "Italian Propaganda in the Near East," Report contained in Lampson [Cairo] to Eden, 29 May 1936; Rendel's comments attached).

37. Letter from Arslan to Rida, 12 Safr 1354, in al-Sharabasi, *Amir al-bayan*, II, p. 829.

38. Arslan, "L'Italie et le monde arabe," *LNA* (April–June 1933), 24.

39. Arslan, "Une Perfidie inouïe," p. 279.

40. Arslan, "Le Conflit italo-éthiopien et les arabes," p. 309.

41. The articles, and the hostile reaction to them, are summarized in *Oriente Moderno*, XV (May 1935), 195–198.

42. For the domestic political background to this incident, see Porath, *Palestinian Arab National Movement*, II, pp. 62–66. A full translation of the letter appears in the Esco Foundation, *Palestine: A Study of Jewish, Arab, and British Policies*, II, pp. 774–775; and *Oriente Moderno*, XV (May 1935), 199.

43. Esco Foundation, *Palestine*, II, p. 775.

44. Ibid., pp. 825–827; and letter from Arslan to Rida, 12 Safr 1354, in ibid., pp. 828–834. For Arslan's offer to come to Palestine to defend himself, see his "'Le Petit Parisien' se fait l'instrument d'une propagande sioniste mensongère," *LNA* (May–August 1938), 1053–1062; and his correspondence with High Commissioner Wauchope, FO371/18958/E4300.

45. "'Le Petit Parisien,'" p. 1056.

46. Letter from Rida to Arslan, 6 Safr 1354, in *RR*, pp. 784–785. Al-Sharabasi, too, is convinced the letter was a forgery. See his treatment of the incident in *Amir al-bayan*, I, pp. 103–106.

47. Letter from Arslan to Rida, 12 Safr 1354, in al-Sharabasi, *Amir al-bayan*, II, p. 829.

48. Letter from Rida to Arslan, 6 Safr 1354, in *RR*, p. 784.

49. Esco Foundation, *Palestine*, II, p. 774.

50. FO371/19983/E3334, "Italian Propaganda in the Near East," Report contained in Lampson (Cairo) to Eden, 29 May 1936. An earlier report asserted that the reason for the mufti's pro-Italian stand "can be attributed to Ihsan al-Jabri [sic] and Shakib Arslan" (FO371/18960/E2639, Royal Air Force Intelligence Summary, Palestine and Transjordan, March 1935).

51. One of them was identified as Muhammad 'Ali al-Tahir, who was imprisoned in September 1940 partly because of his correspondence with Arslan (FO371/19983/E3334, "Italian Propaganda in the Near East"; al-Tahir, *Zalam al-sijn*, p. 371; FO371/18908/E5638, "Italian Propaganda in Palestine," Report contained in Wauchope to M. MacDonald, 10 August 1935).

52. Melka, "The Axis," p. 347.

53. To the attacks of old enemies was added the voice of Libya betrayed. Its most persistent spokesman was Sulayman al-Baruni, whose charges that Arslan had excluded Libya from his schemes of Arab unity in order to ingratiate himself with Mussolini were refuted by the Amir with the same en-

ergy he had devoted to the forged letter episode. His defense is contained in a series of articles entitled "The Amir's Reply to al-Baruni Pasha" which ran weekly in *al-Shabab* from December 1937 through April 1938. See also Muhammad Fu'ad al-Shukri, *Milad dawlah libiya al-hadithah*, II, pp. 655–659, 955–964, for further accusations on Arslan's switch of loyalties.

54. NA, Roll K879, Prüfer memorandum, 17 June 1943, frame K221519; AFS, letter from the Union Civique de Genève, 14 January 1935.

55. AFS, Reports of 16 October 1938 and 29 January 1946; and "Procès-verbal d'audition," 6 October 1938. This seems preposterous, but Juliette Bessis, working with different documentation, claims that "irrefutable evidence" (which she does not cite) exists to prove Arslan's acceptance of considerable sums from Viénot (see her "Chekib Arslan," p. 468).

56. FO371/18960/E2639, Royal Air Force Intelligence Summary, March 1935; later in the year, it was asserted that al-Jabiri and his unnamed associates had as much as £30,000 at their disposal (FO371/18958/E5638, "Italian Propaganda in Palestine," Report from Wauchope to MacDonald, 10 August 1935). In his study of Axis propaganda, Robert L. Baker alleges that Arslan received £60,000 in subsidies from Italy (*Oil, Blood and Sand*, p. 122).

57. FO371/20786/E1488, "Italian Anti-British Activities in the Middle East," Foreign Office Memorandum, 13 March 1939. The British figures are estimates derived from indirect evidence. No less suspect is the French intelligence summary which claimed to rely on the report of "a prominent woman particularly well-informed about the Arab world," which stated that the Amir received an annual subsidy of 2,500 lire ($130) from Rome (*L'Activité politique*, p. 24). More precise information is provided by Quartararo, who has discovered an order issued in 1934 for the transfer of 15,000 lire from the Banca Commerciale Italiana to Arslan's account in Geneva (*Roma*, pp. 246 and 720, n. 201). While confirming Arslan's receipt of Italian funds, this information does not, as Quartararo seems to suggest, prove that paid Italian agents exercised a determinative role in the Palestinian revolt of 1936–1939.

58. Arslan, "La 'Politique musulmane,'" p. 185.

59. Letter from Arslan to Majdi Nassif, 13 December 1939, as translated in FO371/24640/J214, "Middle East Intelligence Center," Summary No. 9, 26 December 1939–2 January 1940.

60. Arslan, "L'Ennemi de la France," p. 804.

61. The British Foreign Office claimed that *La Nation Arabe* was indirectly subsidized by Rome in the form of subscriptions sent in by Italians residing in various Mediterranean countries (FO371/19983/E3334, "Italian Propaganda in the Near East" in Lampson [Cairo] to Eden, 29 May 1936).

62. AFS, "Procès-verbal d'audition," 6 October 1938.

63. Ibid. The Italian government noted in particular that their enemy, Ahmad al-Sharif al-Sanusi, was one of these contributors (ASMAE, Arabia, busta 11, 1933, pos. 1, Pignatti [Paris] to Minister of Foreign Affairs, 19 August 1933).

64. Letter from Arslan to Rida, 18 Dhu al-Hijjah 1352, in al-Sharabasi, *Amir al-bayan*, II, p. 821.

65. From 1939 until its defeat in 1940, France forbade the export of any money from Syria and Lebanon, thus depriving Arslan of that portion of his income derived from his family holdings (FO371/24640/J381, "Middle East Intelligence Center," Summary of Information, 10–16 January 1940). As he indicated in letters of 1939 and early 1940 to Arab correspondents, this was a terrible financial blow to him. It suggests the Lebanese income was more important than the British and French believed. The letters are reproduced in *L'Activité politique*, p. 48. Following the Allied occupation of Vichy Mandates in July 1941, Arslan's property was officially seized (*Cahiers de l'Institut d'Etudes de l'Orient Contemporain*, III [1946], 641).

66. The baron responded positively, and the transaction appears to have been completed (NA, Roll 726, von Oppenheim to Woermann, 10 April 1941, frames 326008–326009; von Oppenheim to von Hentig, 1 August 1941; Arslan to von Oppenheim, 2 September 1941, frames 325952–325960).

67. AFS, Report of 22 February 1946.

68. This includes the 1,200 Swiss francs by which his account was overdrawn for all of July, a practice which was habitual with him. His average monthly expenditure of 2,967 Swiss francs would, if constant throughout the year, produce an annual total of approximately 36,000 Swiss francs ($8,280). This figure corresponds to what Arslan would probably need to maintain his existence, but would seem to exceed his known sources of income. In 1930, he claimed that he earned, exclusive of donations to the cause, the equivalent of $5,346. Yet if the 1938 figure of $8,280 included the deposits and expenditures related to his public as well as his private responsibilities, then it is quite modest. The Swiss felt Arslan must have had another bank account through which he channeled clandestine contributions, but he asserted that he did not. His original bank statement is in AFS, attached to the Report of 16 October 1938. Conversions to United States dollars have been made from the tables in *The League of Nations Yearbook*.

69. AFS, letters from Arslan to Hani, 4 August, 30 November, and 23 December 1942. The Misr Society of Egyptian Students at the University of Geneva was founded in 1937. It was a political rather than a purely student organization with definite pro-Axis leanings.

70. NA, Roll 726, von Oppenheim to von Hentig, 30 July 1940, frames 326014–326015.

71. The German contributions are cited from Nuremberg testimony in Melka, "The Axis," p. 384. Italian figures are in ASMAE, Italia, busta 84, 1942, two undated cabinet memoranda from the Ministry of Foreign Affairs.

72. Arslan, "L'Eternelle calomnie," *LNA* (January–February 1935), 172. Even at the time he wrote this, Arslan's economic position was precarious.

73. In 1943, he was compelled to pawn several pieces of jewelry. Even after receiving 3,000 SF for this humiliating act, he still owed his Geneva bank 1,000 SF. These are small sums, but they were sufficient to cause him distress (AFS, letter from Arslan to Yussif Hayba, 17 February 1943). Hayba was another member of the Misr society.

74. AFS, letters to Arslan from Faris al-Khuri and 'Arif (last name illegible) in January and February of 1939 show strong encouragement for his can-

didacy. Once appointed, he was also given the benefit of a hefty increase in the stipend attached to the position (*Oriente Moderno*, XVIII [December 1938], 658).

75. Cf. articles by Muhammad ʿAli al-Tahir and Arslan in *al-Shabab*, 8 February 1939.

76. These activities, accompanied by several photographs, are reported in *al-Shabab*, 8 and 15 March 1939; see also *Oriente Moderno*, XIX (April 1939), 215; and *L'Activité politique*, pp. 41–43, which emphasizes the "particulièrement chaleureuse" reception Arslan got in Egypt.

77. French intelligence received information from Cairo about the occasion and reported that it had been announced on Radio Berlin and performed at a ceremony presided over by von Oppenheim (*L'Activité politique*, p. 47). According to British sources, Radio Berlin later defended Arslan from these "French accusations," an act which may have given them some credibility ("Middle East Intelligence Center," 26 December 1932–2 January 1940). Arslan also denied the whole affair, but, while none of the sources is completely reliable, it certainly could have occurred (see *ʿUrwah al-ittihad*, p. 24, and FO371/24546/E41, Arslan to Nuri al-Saʿid).

78. AFS documentation on this question is dated 6 January 1938, 3 October 1939, 27 February 1940, 17 and 30 April 1940, and 3 October 1941. This material shows that the Swiss were uneasy with Arslan's presence even before the war and that, contrary to Hirszowicz, their efforts to restrict his movements were undertaken independently of the German setbacks in late 1942 (*Third Reich*, p. 309). Rézette, *Partis*, pp. 16, 199, is incorrect in stating that Arslan spent the last stages of the war in Brazil and that he died there.

79. AFS, Report of 3 October 1939; NA, Roll 726, von Oppenheim to Arslan, 7 and 19 June 1941, frames 325972–325974; 3 December 1941, frames 325921–325923; Arslan to von Oppenheim, 2 and 10 September 1941, frames 325952–325960, 325947–325948.

80. NA, Roll 726, von Hentig to von Oppenheim, 11 October 1941, frames 325943–325945.

81. Ibid., Arslan to von Oppenheim, 2 September 1941, frames 325952–325960.

82. Ibid., Arslan to von Oppenheim, 3 October 1941, frame 325932.

83. Summaries and a translation of a few of Arslan's Tetouan publications are given in *Oriente Moderno*, XX (August 1940), 376–382; XXI (August 1941), 394; XXI (September 1941), 449. The paper *al-ʿAlam al-ʿArabi* issued a collection of articles Arslan had published between 1939 and 1941 as the previously cited *ʿUrwah al-ittihad*.

84. NA, Roll 726, Arslan to von Oppenheim, 10 April 1941, frames 325996–326003.

85. AFS, Reports of 1 April and 5 November 1940; 17 June 1943; 2 March 1944. Fuʾad Hamzah was, at this time, the Saʿudi ambassador to the Vichy government.

86. AFS, Correspondence of April 1942; Report of 20 July 1942.

87. NA, Roll K880, Prüfer to Arslan, 11 January 1943; Arslan to Prüfer, 27 January 1943.

88. Cited in Charles-Robert Ageron, "Les Maghrébins et la propagande allemande," in his *"L'Algérie algérienne" de Napoléon III à de Gaulle*, p. 192.

89. AFS, Reports of 9, 11, 14, 15, 18, 19, and 22 February 1946.

90. Al-Tahir, *Zalam al-sijn*, pp. 677–687.

91. Ibid., p. 678; and al-Tahir, *Dhikra al-amir*, p. 486.

8. Conclusion

1. Arnold, *The Caliphate*, p. 183.

2. From a speech by Shakib Arslan to the North African Muslim Students' Association, Paris, 1937, cited in *L'Activité politique*, p. 30.

3. MAE, Série E, Syrie-Liban, 213, Intelligence Report of 12 July 1927.

4. Cited in *L'Activité politique*, p. 30.

5. Cited in ibid., p. 30.

SELECT BIBLIOGRAPHY

I. Archival Sources

France
    Archives du Ministère des Affaires Etrangères, Paris. Selected files from
    Direction des Affaires Politiques et Commerciales, Série E, Syrie-
    Liban, 1922–1929.
    Archives d'Outre Mer, Aix-en-Provence. Thèâtre d'Operations de l'Afrique
    du Nord, Bureau Politique, Contribution à l'Etude de l'Activité Politique
    de l'Emir Chekib Arslan, 4 June 1940, 29 H 35.
Germany
    Records of the German Foreign Office received by the Department of State
    and held in the U.S. National Archives, Washington, D.C. Microcopy
    Number T-120, Rolls 63, 726, 4900, K868–869, K879, K880, L1279.
Great Britain
    Foreign Office Records, the Public Record Office, London. Volumes in the
    series FO 371 for the period 1921–1943.
Italy
    Archivio Storico del Ministero degli Affari Esteri, Rome. Numerous vol-
    umes, identified by country, covering the years 1921–1945.
League of Nations
    Minutes of the Permanent Mandates Commission. Sessions 1–25 (1921–
    1934).
Switzerland
    Archives Fédérales Suisses, Bern. E 4320 Arslan.

II. Published Documents

Documenti Diplomatici Italiani, Settima Serie, 1922–1935. Vol. X, Rome,
    1978.

Documents on German Foreign Policy, 1918–1945. Series D., Vol. X: *The War Years,* 1940. Washington, D.C., 1957.

III. Newspapers and Journals

Detroit Free Press, January 1927.
Detroit News, January 1927.
al-Fath, Cairo, 1926–1936.
al-Islah, Beirut, 1912–1914.
Majallah al-Zahra', Cairo, 1924–1929.
al-Manar, Cairo, 1912–1914.
Minbar al-Sharq, Cairo, January–March 1953.
al-Mu'ayyad, Cairo, 1911–1912.
al-Muqtataf, Cairo, 1900–1902.
La Nation Arabe, Geneva, 1930–1938.
Der Neue Orient, Berlin, 1917–1918.
Oriente Moderno, Rome, 1922–1942.
al-Ra'y al-'Amm, Beirut, 1913–1914.
al-Sa'ih, New York, 3 January–5 May 1927.
al-Shabab, Cairo, 1936–1939.
al-Shura, Cairo, 1924–1930.
Le Temps (Colonial), Paris, 1930–1931.
La Tribune de l'Orient, Geneva, 1922–1937.

IV. Works by Shakib Arslan consulted for this study (a complete listing of his works may be found in al-Sharabasi, *Amir al-bayan,* II)

A. Books

Aucune Propagande au monde ne peut défigurer le portrait d'un homme. Geneva, 1936.

al-Bakurah (Beginnings). Beirut, 1886.

Diwan al-amir Shakib Arslan (Collected Poems). Edited by Rashid Rida. Cairo, 1354/1935.

Hadir al-'alam al-islami (The Present World of Islam). 3rd ed. 4 vols. Beirut, 1971–1973. A translation by 'Ajjaj Nuwayhid of Lothrop Stoddard's *The New World of Islam* with commentary by Arslan. The far-ranging commentaries are lengthier than the translation, and the work became Arslan's own.

al-Hulal al-sundusiyyah fi al-akhbar wa al-athar al-andalusiyyah (The Richness of the Remnants of al-Andalus). Vol. I. Beirut, 1966. Reproduction of 1936 edition.

al-Irtisamat al-lutf fi khatir al-hajj ila aqdas mataf (Expressions of Kindness during My Pilgrimage). Cairo, 1350.

Li madha ta'akhkhar al-muslimun wa li madha taqaddam ghayruhum? (Why Are the Muslims Backward While Others Are Advanced?). 3rd ed. Cairo, 1358/1939. Translated by M. S. Shakoor as *Our Decline and Its Causes,* reprint ed., Lahore, 1962.

al-Nahdah al-ʿarabiyyah fi al-ʿasr al-hadir (The Modern Arab Awakening). Cairo, n.d. From lectures given in Damascus in 1937.

Rawd al-shaqiq fi al-jazl al-raqiq (The Simple Eloquence of a Bird in the Meadow). Damascus, 1925. The Diwan of Nasib Arslan. Edited and introduced by Shakib.

al-Sayyid Rashid Rida aw ikhaʾ arbaʿin sanah (Rashid Rida, or a Brotherhood of Forty Years). Damascus, 1356/1937.

Shawqi aw sadaqah arbaʿin sanah (Shawqi, or a Friendship of Forty Years). Cairo, 1355/1936.

Sirah dhatiyyah (The Story of My Life). Beirut, 1969.

Taʾrikh ghazawat al-ʿarab fi faransa wa suwisra wa italya wa jazaʾir al-bahr al-mutawassit (A History of the Arab Conquests in France, Switzerland, Italy, and the Mediterranean Islands). Cairo, 1352/1933.

Taʾrikh Ibn Khaldun (The Chronicle of Ibn Khaldun). Cairo, 1355/1936. With commentary by Arslan. Vol. III.

ʿUrwah al-ittihad bayn ahl al-jihad (The Bonds of Unity among the People of the Jihad). Buenos Aires, 1941.

al-Wahdah al-ʿarabiyyah (Arab Unity). Damascus, 1937.

B. Articles which do not appear in the works listed in III, above

"Kawarith suriyyah fi sanawat al-harb" (Syrian Catastrophes during the War Years). *al-Manar*, XXIII (1922), 121–134.

"Ma waraʾa al-akamah" (There Is More to Things Than Meets the Eye) and "Al-Taʾrikh la yakun bi al-iftirad wa la bi al-tahakkum" (History Is Not Based on Assumptions). *Taht rayah al-Qurʾan: al-maʿrakah bayn al-qadim wa al-jadid*. Edited by Mustafa Sadiq al-Rafiʿi. 4th ed. Cairo, 1956.

"Muqaddimah" (Introduction). ʿAbd al-Qadir al-Maghribi, *al-Bayyinat fi al-din wa al-ijtimaʿ wa al-adab wa al-taʾrikh*, Vol. I. Cairo, 1344.

"al-Nahdah al-sharqiyyah al-hadithah" (The Current Eastern Awakening). *al-Muqtataf* (February 1937), 136–143.

"Das osmanische Reich." *Süddeutsche Monatshefte* (July 1918), 235–240.

"Preface." E. Rabbath. *L'Evolution politique de la Syrie sous mandat*. Paris, 1928.

"Syrian Opposition to French Rule." *Current History and Forum* (May 1924), 239–247.

V. Unpublished Ph.D. Dissertations

Melka, Robert Lewis. "The Axis and the Arab Middle East, 1930–1945." University of Minnesota, 1966.

Stoddard, Philip H. "The Ottoman Government and the Arabs, 1911 to 1918: A Preliminary Study of the Teşkilat-i Mahsusa." Princeton, 1963.

Zagoria, Janet Dorsch. "The Rise and Fall of the Movement of Messali Hadj in Algeria, 1924–1954." Columbia University, 1974.

VI. Other Published Sources

'Abbud, Marun. *Ruwwad al-nahdah al-hadithah* (Pioneers of the Modern Awakening). Beirut, 1966.

Abu Shaqra, 'Arif. "Yawm zar Jamal Pasha mantaqah al-shufi" (The Day Jamal Pasha Visited the Shuf Region). *Awraq Lubnaniyyah*, I (1955), 547–549.

Adams, Charles C. *Islam and Modernism in Egypt*. London, 1933.

Ageron, Charles-Robert. *"L'Algérie algérienne" de Napoléon III à de Gaulle*. Paris, 1980.

———. *Histoire de l'Algerie contemporaine*. Vol. II. *De l'insurrection de 1871 au déclenchement de la guerre de liberation (1954)*. Paris, 1979.

———. "La Politique berbère du protectorat marocain de 1913 à 1934." *Revue d'Histoire Moderne et Contemporaine*, XVIII (1971), 50–90.

Ahmad, Feroz. *The Young Turks: The Committee of Union and Progress in Turkish Politics, 1908–1914*. Oxford, 1969.

Ahmed, Jamal Mohammed. *The Intellectual Origins of Egyptian Nationalism*. London, 1960.

Ajami, Fouad. "The End of Pan-Arabism." *Foreign Affairs*, LVII (1978–1979), 355–373.

Ajay, Nicholas Z., Jr. "Political Intrigue and Suppression in Lebanon during World War I." *International Journal of Middle East Studies*, V (1974), 140–160.

Almana, Mohammed. *Arabia Unified: A Portrait of Ibn Saud*. London, 1980.

Antonius, George. *The Arab Awakening*. New York, Capricorn Books, 1965.

Arnold, Thomas W. *The Caliphate*. New York, 1966. Reprint of 1924 edition with a concluding chapter by Sylvia G. Haim.

Arslan, 'Adil. *Dhikrayat al-Amir 'Adil Arslan*. Beirut, 1962.

Aydemir, Şevket Süreyya. *Enver Pasa: Makedonya'dan Ortaasya'ya*. Vol. III. *1914–1922*. Istanbul, 1972.

Badawi, M. M. *A Critical Introduction to Modern Arabic Poetry*. Cambridge, 1975.

Baker, Robert L. *Oil, Blood and Sand*. New York, 1942.

Batay, Rafa'il. "Shakib Arslan." *al-Kitab*, III (February 1947), 566–574.

Beauplan, Robert de. *Ou va la Syrie?*. Paris, 1929.

Ben-Gurion, David. *My Talks with Arab Leaders*. Translated by A. Rubinstein and M. Louvish. New York, 1973.

Berkes, Niyazi. *The Development of Secularism in Turkey*. Montreal, 1964.

Berque, Jacques. *Egypt: Imperialism and Revolution*. Translated by Jean Stewart. New York, 1972.

———. *French North Africa: The Maghrib between Two World Wars*. Translated by Jean Stewart. London, 1967.

Bessis, Juliette. "Chekib Arslan et les mouvements nationalists au Maghreb." *Revue Historique*, CCLIX (1978), 467–489.

Bourguiba, Habib. "Un Vétéran de la lutte anti-coloniale: L'Emir Chekib Arslan." *Le Néo-Destour et le front populaire en France*. Vol. I. *Le Dialogue, 1936–1938*. Tunis, 1969.

Bryer, David. "The Origins of the Druze Religion." *Der Islam*, LII (1975), 47–84; LII (1976), 4–27.

Buheiry, Marwan R. (ed.). *Intellectual Life in the Arab East, 1890–1939.* Beirut, 1981.

Burke, Edmund III. "Moroccan Resistance, Pan-Islam, and German War Strategy, 1914–1918." *Francia* (Munich), III (1975), 434–464.

———. "Pan-Islam and Moroccan Resistance to French Colonial Penetration, 1900–1912." *Journal of African History*, XIII (1972), 97–118.

———. "Pan-Islam and North African Resistance, 1890–1918: Patterns of Response." Unpublished paper.

———. *Prelude to Protectorate in Morocco: Precolonial Protest and Resistance, 1860–1912.* Chicago, 1976.

Burru, Tawfiq ʿAli. *al-ʿArab wa al-turk fi al-ʿahd al-dusturi al-ʿuthmani, 1908–1914* (Arabs and Turks during the Ottoman Constitutional Period). Cairo, 1960.

Carr, Edward Hallett. *A History of Soviet Russia: The Bolshevik Revolution, 1917–1923.* Vol. III. London, 1953.

Chejne, Anwar. "Amin al-Rihani and al-Andalus: A Journey into History." *al-ʿArabiyya*, IX (1976), 9–18.

Cleveland, William L. "Atatürk Viewed by His Arab Contemporaries: The Opinions of Satiʿ al-Husri and Shakib Arslan." *International Journal of Turkish Studies*, II (1983), 15–23.

———. *The Making of an Arab Nationalist: Ottomanism and Arabism in the Life and Thought of Satiʿ al-Husri.* Princeton, 1971.

———. "Sources of Arab Nationalism: An Overview." *Middle East Review*, XI (1979), 25–33.

Cruickshank, A. A. "The Young Turk Challenge in Postwar Turkey." *Middle East Journal*, XXII (1968), 17–28.

Daghir, Yusuf Asʿad. *Masadir al-dirasah al-adabiyyah: al-fikr al-ʿarabi al-hadith min sayr aʿlamhu* (Sources for the Study of Literature: Modern Arabic Thought through the Lives of Its Outstanding Contributors). Vol. II, Part I. *1800–1955.* Beirut, 1955.

———. *Mudhakkirati ʿala hamish al-qadiyyah al-ʿarabiyyah* (My Memoirs Concerning the Arab Question). Cairo, 1959.

al-Dahhan, Sami. *al-Amir Shakib Arslan: hayathu wa atharhu* (Arslan: His Life and Influence). Cairo, 1960.

———. *Muhadarat ʿan al-amir Shakib Arslan* (Lectures on Arslan). Cairo, 1958.

———. *Qudamaʾ wa muʿasirun* (Ancients and Moderns). Cairo, 1961.

Dawn, C. Ernest. *From Ottomanism to Arabism: Essays on the Origins of Arab Nationalism.* Urbana and Chicago, 1973.

Desparmet, J. "Afrique du Nord et pan-arabisme: I. L'Afrique du Nord vue de Damas." *L'Afrique Française*, XLVIII (February 1938), 56–58.

———. "Les Oulémas algériens et la propagande italienne (1931–1938)." *L'Afrique Française*, XLVIII (May 1938), 210–214.

———. "Le Panarabisme et l'Algérie." *L'Afrique Française*, XLVI (June 1936), 312–317.

————. "La Résistance à l'occident." *L'Afrique Française*, XLIII (May 1933), 265–269.

Djemal Pasha, Ahmed. *Memories of a Turkish Statesman, 1913–1919*. London, 1922.

The Encyclopaedia of Islam, 2nd edition. Leiden, 1954–.

Ermont, Louis. "Afrique du Nord et Proche Orient." *L'Afrique Française*, XLIII (April 1933), 197–205.

————. "Afrique du Nord et Proche Orient." *L'Afrique Française*, XLII (September 1932), 505–512.

Esco Foundation. *Palestine: A Study of Jewish, Arab, and British Policies*. Vol. II. New Haven, 1947.

Esposito, John L. (ed.). *Islam and Development: Religion and Sociopolitical Change*. Syracuse, 1980.

Evans-Pritchard, E. E. *The Sanusi of Cyrenaica*. Oxford, 1949.

al-Fasi, ʿAlal. *The Independence Movements in Arab North Africa*. Translated by Hazem Zaki Nuseibeh. New York, 1970.

Fleury, Antoine. "Le Mouvement national arabe à Genève durant l'entre-deux-guerres." *Relations Internationales*, No. 19 (1979), 329–354.

Freeman-Grenville, G. S. P. *The Muslim and Christian Calendars*. London, 1963.

Garas, Félix. *Bourguiba et la naissance d'une nation*. Paris, 1956.

Gibb, H. A. R. "The Islamic Congress at Jerusalem in December 1931." *Survey of International Affairs, 1934*. Edited by Arnold J. Toynbee. London, 1935.

————. *Modern Trends in Islam*. New York, 1972. Reprint of 1947 edition.

———— (ed.). *Whither Islam? A Survey of Modern Movements in the Moslem World*. London, 1932.

Gordon, David C. *The Passing of French Algeria*. London, 1966.

Grobba, Fritz. *Männer und Mächte im Orient*. Göttingen, 1967.

Guérin, Daniel. *Au Service des colonisés, 1930–1953*. Paris, 1954.

Haim, Sylvia G. *Arab Nationalism: An Anthology*. Berkeley and Los Angeles, 1964.

al-Hakim, Yusuf. *Bayrut wa lubnan fi ʿahd al-ʿuthman* (Beirut and Lebanon under the Ottomans). Beirut, 1964.

————. *Suriyyah wa al-ʿahd al-faysali* (Syria during the Reign of Faysal). Beirut, 1966.

Halstead, John P. *Rebirth of a Nation: The Origins and Rise of Moroccan Nationalism, 1912–1944*. Cambridge, Mass., 1967.

Harik, Iliya F. *Politics and Change in a Traditional Society: Lebanon, 1711–1845*. Princeton, 1968.

Hirszowicz, Lukasz. *The Third Reich and the Arab East*. London, 1966.

Hitti, Philip K. *The Origins of the Druze People and Religion*. New York, 1928.

Holt, P. M. (ed.). *Political and Social Change in Modern Egypt*. London, 1968.

Homet, Marcel. *L'Histoire secrète du traité Franco-Syrien*. Paris, 1938.

Hourani, Albert. *Arabic Thought in the Liberal Age, 1798–1939*. London, 1970.

———. *The Emergence of the Modern Middle East*. London, 1981.

———. *Syria and Lebanon: A Political Essay*. London, 1946.

Husry, Khaldun S. "King Faysal I and Arab Unity, 1930–1933." *Journal of Contemporary History*, X (1975), 323–340.

al-Hut, B. Nuwayhid and Khayriyyah Qasimiyyah. "Faqidan filastiniyan kabiran: ʿAbd al-Hamid Shuman and Muhammad ʿAli al-Tahir" (The Death of Two Great Palestinians: Shuman and al-Tahir). *Shuʿun Filastiniyyah*, No. 39 (November 1974), 143–163.

Jabbur, Jibraʾil. "Al-Amir Shakib Arslan bi munasabah marur sabaʿ sanawat ʿala wifathu" (Arslan on the Occasion of the Passing of Seven Years since His Death). *al-Abhath*, VII (1954), 33–38.

Jalabert, Louis. "Dans le maghreb qui bouge." *Etudes* (20 April 1938), 164–178; (5 May 1938), 342–360.

———. "La Turbulence de l'Islam arabe." *Etudes* (20 January 1938), 170–184.

Jankowski, James. "Egyptian Responses to the Palestine Problem in the Interwar Period." *International Journal of Middle East Studies*, XII (1980), 1–38.

———. "Ottomanism and Arabism in Egypt, 1860–1914." *Muslim World*, LXX (1980), 226–259.

Jayyusi, Salma K. *Trends and Movements in Modern Arabic Poetry*. Vol. I. Leiden, 1972.

Jovelet, Louis. "L'Evolution sociale et politique des 'pays arabes' (1930–1933)." *Revue des Etudes Islamiques*, VII (1933), 425–644.

Julien, Charles-André. *L'Afrique du Nord en marche: nationalismes musulmans et souveraineté française*. 3rd ed. Paris, 1972.

———. *Le Maroc face aux imperialismes, 1415–1956*. Paris, 1978.

Keddie, Nikki R. *An Islamic Response to Imperialism: Political and Religious Writings of Sayyid Jamal ad-din "al-Afghani"*. Berkeley and Los Angeles, 1968.

———. *Sayyid Jamal ad-Din "al-Afghani": A Political Biography*. Berkeley and Los Angeles, 1972.

Kedourie, Elie. "The Bludan Congress on Palestine." *Middle Eastern Studies*, XVII (January 1981), 107–125.

———. *The Chatham House Version and Other Middle-Eastern Studies*. London, 1970.

Kelidar, A. R. "The Arabian Peninsula in Arab and Power Politics." *The Arabian Peninsula, Society and Politics*. Edited by Derek Hopwood. London, 1972.

Kerr, Malcolm H. *Islamic Reform: The Political and Legal Theories of Muhammad ʿAbduh and Rashid Rida*. Berkeley and Los Angeles, 1966.

Khadduri, Majid. *Political Trends in the Arab World: The Role of Ideas and Ideals in Politics*. Baltimore, 1970.

Khalidi, Rashid Ismail. *British Policy towards Syria and Palestine, 1906–*

1914: A Study of the Antecedents of the Hussein-McMahon Correspondence, the Sykes-Picot Agreement and the Balfour Declaration. London, 1980.

Khoury, Philip S. "Factionalism among Syrian Nationalists during the French Mandate." *International Journal of Middle East Studies,* XIII (1981), 441–469.

———. *Urban Notables and Arab Nationalism: The Politics of Damascus 1860–1920.* Cambridge, 1983.

Khuddur, Adib. *al-Sihafah al-suriyyah* (The Press of Syria). Damascus, 1972.

al-Khuri, Bisharah. *Haqaʾiq lubnaniyyah* (Lebanese Realities). Vol. I. Beirut, 1960.

Kurd ʿAli, Muhammad. *al-Mudhakkirat.* 3 vols. Damascus, 1948–1949. Translated as *Memoirs* by Khalil Totah. Washington, D.C., 1954.

Lalli, Mario Tedeschini. "La propaganda araba del fascismo e l'Egitto." *Storia Contemporanea,* VII (December 1976), 717–749.

Landau, Rom. *Moroccan Drama, 1900–1955.* London, 1956.

Laoust, Henri. "L'Evolution politique et culturelle de l'Egypte contemporaine." *Entrentiens sur l'Evolution des Pays de Civilisation Arabe,* No. 3 (1937), 68–94.

———. "Le Réformisme orthodoxe des 'salafiya' et les caractères généraux de son orientation actuelle." *Revue des Etudes Islamiques,* VI (1932), 175–224.

Le Tourneau, Roger. *Evolution politique de l'Afrique du Nord musulmane, 1920–1961.* Paris, 1962.

———. *L'Islam contemporain.* 2nd printing. Paris, 1950.

Lévi-Provençal, E. "L'Emir Shakib Arslan (1869–1946)." *Cahiers de l'Orient Contemporain,* IX–X (1947), 5–19.

Lewis, Bernard. *The Emergence of Modern Turkey.* 2nd ed. London, 1968.

Longrigg, Stephen Hemsley. *Syria and Lebanon under French Mandate.* London, 1958.

MacCallum, Elizabeth. *The Nationalist Crusade in Syria.* New York, 1928.

MacDonald, Callum A. "Radio Bari: Italian Wireless Propaganda in the Middle East and British Countermeasures 1934–1938." *Middle Eastern Studies,* XIII (May 1977), 195–207.

Makaram, Sami Nasib. *The Druze Faith.* Delmar, New York, 1974.

Melka, R. L. "Max Freiherr von Oppenheim: Sixty Years of Scholarship and Intrigue in the Middle East." *Middle Eastern Studies,* IX (January 1973), 81–93.

———. "Nazi Germany and Palestine." *Middle Eastern Studies,* V (October 1969), 221–233.

Merad, Ali. *Ibn Badis, commentateur du Coran.* Paris, 1971.

———. *Le Réformisme musulman en Algérie de 1925 à 1940: essai d'histoire religieuse et sociale.* Paris and The Hague, 1967.

Micaud, Charles (ed.). *Tunisia: The Politics of Modernization.* New York, 1964.

Miller, Joyce Laverty. "The Syrian Revolt of 1925." *International Journal of Middle East Studies,* VIII (October 1977), 545–563.

Mitchell, Richard P. *The Society of the Muslim Brothers*. London, 1969.
Montagne, Robert. "La Crise politique et l'arabisme (Juin 1937–Juin 1938)." *La France Méditerranéene et Africaine*, I (1938), 7–39.
———. "La Fermentation des partis politiques en Algérie." *Politique Etrangère*, II (April 1937), 124–147.
———. *La Politique islamique de la France*. Paris, 1939.
———. "Réactions arabes contre le Sionisme. Le Congrès de Bloudane." *Entretiens sur l'Evolution des Pays de Civilisation Arabe*, III (1939), 42–61.
———. *Révolution au Maroc*. Paris, 1953.
Mouton, Marie-Renée. "Le Congrès syrio-palestinien de Genève (1921)." *Relations Internationales*, No. 19 (1979), 313–328.
Musa, Sulayman. *al-Harakah al-ʿarabiyyah: sirah al-marhalah al-ula li nahdah al-ʿarabiyyah al-hadithah, 1908–1924* (The Arab Movement: The History of the First Stage of the Modern Arab Awakening). Beirut, 1970.
Nicosia, Francis. "Arab Nationalism and National Socialist Germany, 1933–1939: Ideological and Strategic Incompatibility." *International Journal of Middle East Studies*, XII (1980), 351–372.
Peters, Rudolph. *Islam and Colonialism: The Doctrine of Jihad in Modern History*. The Hague, 1979.
Porath, Y. *The Emergence of the Palestinian-Arab National Movement, 1918–1929*. London, 1974.
———. *The Palestinian Arab National Movement: From Riots to Rebellion*. Vol. II. *1929–1939*. London, 1977.
Qadri, Ahmad. *Mudhakkirati ʿan al-thawrah al-ʿarabiyyah al-kubra*. Damascus, 1956.
Quartararo, Rosaria. *Roma tra Londra e Berlino: La politica estera fascista dal 1930 al 1940*. Rome, 1980.
Reid, Donald M. "*Arabic Thought in the Liberal Age* Twenty Years After." International Journal of Middle East Studies, XIV (1982) 541–557.
Rézette, Robert. *Les Partis politiques marocains*. Paris, 1955.
Rida, Muhammad Rashid. *Taʾrikh al-ustadh al-imam al-shaykh Muhammad ʿAbduh*. Vol. I. Cairo, 1931.
Safran, Nadav. *Egypt in Search of Political Community: An Analysis of the Intellectual and Political Evolution of Egypt, 1804–1952*. Cambridge, Mass., 1961.
Salibi, Kamal S. *The Modern History of Lebanon*. London, 1965.
Schröder, M. J. "Les Rapports des puissances de l'Axe avec le monde arabe." In *La Guerre en Méditerranée (1930–1945)*. Paris, 1971.
Seabury, Paul. *The Wilhelmstrasse: A Study of German Diplomats under the Nazi Regime*. Berkeley and Los Angeles, 1954.
Sékaly, Achille. "Les deux Congrès Généraux de 1926." *Revue du Monde Musulman*, LXIV, No. 2 (1926), 3–219.
Semidei, Manuela. "Les Socialistes français et le problème colonial entre les deux guerres (1919–1939)." *Revue Française de Science Politique*, XVIII (1968), 1115–1153.
al-Sharabasi, Ahmad. *Adab amir al-bayan* (The Literature of the Prince of Eloquence). Cairo, 1964.

————. *Amir al-bayan, Shakib Arslan*. 2 vols. Cairo, 1963.

————. *Shakib Arslan: daʿiyah al-ʿurubah wa al-islam* (Arslan, Spokesman for Arabism and Islam). Cairo, n.d. (1963).

————. *Shakib Arslan: min ruwwad al-wahdah al-ʿarabiyyah* (Arslan, One of the Pioneers of Arab Unity). Cairo, 1963.

Sharabi, Hisham. *Arab Intellectuals and the West: The Formative Years, 1875–1914*. Baltimore, 1970.

Shukri, Muhammad Fuʾad. *Milad dawlah libiya al-hadithah: wathaʾiq tahrirha wa istiqlalha* (The Birth of Modern Libya: Records of Its Freedom and Independence). Part I, Vol. II. Cairo, 1957.

Smith, Charles D. "The 'Crisis of Orientation': The Shift of Egyptian Intellectuals to Islamic Subjects in the 1930s." *International Journal of Middle East Studies*, IV (1973), 382–410.

————. "The Intellectual and Modernization: Definitions and Reconsiderations: The Egyptian Experience." *Comparative Studies in Society and History*, XXII (1980), 513–533.

Smith, Wilfred Cantwell. *Islam in Modern History*. New York, 1959.

Spagnolo, John P. *France and Ottoman Lebanon: 1861–1914*. London, 1977.

Stoddard, Lothrop. *The New World of Islam*. New York, 1922.

Stookey, Robert W. *Yemen: The Politics of the Yemen Arab Republic*. Boulder, 1978.

al-Tahir, Muhammad ʿAli. *Zalam al-sijn* (The Darkness of Prison). Cairo, 1951.

———— (ed.). *Dhikra al-amir Shakib Arslan* (In Memory of Arslan). Cairo, 1947.

Tibawi, A. L. *American Interests in Syria, 1800–1901*. Oxford, 1966.

Touma, Toufic. *Paysans et institutions féodales chez les druses et les maronites du Liban du XVIIe siècle à 1914*. Vol. 2. Beirut, 1972.

Troeller, Gary. *The Birth of Saudi Arabia: Britain and the House of Saʿud*. London, 1976.

Van Dusen, Michael H. "Syria: Downfall of a Traditional Elite." *Political Elites and Political Development in the Middle East*. Edited by Frank Tachau. New York, 1975.

Vatikiotis, P. J. *The History of Egypt: From Muhammad Ali to Sadat*. 2nd ed. London, 1980.

Vatin, Jean-Claude. *L'Algérie politique: histoire et société*. Paris, 1974.

Vernier, Bernard. *La Politique islamique d'Allemagne*. Paris, 1939.

Voll, John Obert. *Islam: Continuity and Change in the Modern World*. Boulder, 1982.

"Wasiyyah al-amir Shakib Arslan li lubnaniyyin" (The Advice of Arslan to the Lebanese). *Awraq Lubnaniyyah*, II (1956), 337–342.

Wenner, Manfred W. *Modern Yemen, 1918–1966*. Baltimore, 1967.

Widmer, G. "Übertragungen aus der neuarabischen Literatur—III: Emir Shakib Arslan." *Die Welt des Islams*, XIX (1937), 1–93.

Zeine, Zeine N. *The Emergence of Arab Nationalism*. Revised ed. Beirut, 1966.

Ziadeh, Nicola A. *Origins of Nationalism in Tunisia.* Beirut, 1962.

Zuʿaytir, Akram. "Risalah taʾrikhiyyah li al-amir Shakib Arslan hawl muha-walat faransa ikhraj al-barbar min al-islam" (A Historical Letter from Arslan Concerning the Efforts of France to Expel the Berbers from Islam). *Tihamah* (Jiddah), 16 September 1983.

VII. Interviews

Mme. Mayy Junbalat, Beirut, 3, 5, 17, 24 December 1974.

Ihsan al-Jabiri, Cairo, 5 January 1975.

President Habib Bourguiba, Carthage, 7 April 1975.

INDEX